D0948172

Max Reger

Max Reger working on his Ballett-Suite, Op. 130. Kolberg, Summer 1913.
Courtesy of the Max Reger Institute, Bonn, Federal Republic of Germany.

Max Reger

A Bio-Bibliography

William E. Grim

Donald L. Hixon, Series Adviser

Bio-Bibliographies in Music, Number 7

Greenwood Press
New York • Westport, Connecticut • London

Library of Congress Cataloging-in-Publication Data

Grim, William E.
Max Reger : a bio-bibliography.

(Bio-bibliographies in music, ISSN 0742-6968 ; no. 7)
Discography: p.
Bibliography: p.
Includes index.
1. Reger, Max, 1873-1916—Bibliography. 2. Reger, Max, 1873-1916—Discography. 3. Music—Bio-bibliography.
I. Title. II. Series.
ML134.R33G7 1988 016.78'092'4 87-25153
ISBN 0-313-25311-0 (lib. bdg. : alk. paper)

British Library Cataloguing in Publication Data is available.

Library of Congress Catalog Card Number: 87-25153
ISBN: 0-313-25311-0
ISSN: 0742-6968

First published in 1988

Greenwood Press, Inc.
88 Post Road West, Westport, Connecticut 06881

Printed in the United States of America

The paper used in this book complies with the Permanent Paper Standard issued by the National Information Standards Organization (Z39.48-1984).

10 9 8 7 6 5 4 3 2 1

This book is dedicated to the author's wife, Deborah, and to his parents, William and Rosemary Grim.

Contents

Preface

Max Reger is one of the most important composers of the period between late romanticism and modernism. His influence was readily acknowledged by such disparate composers as Schönberg, Karg-Elert, Webern, and Szymanowski. Many of his contemporaries considered Reger as a composer to be on an equal footing with Richard Strauss. Although history has not been especially kind to Reger (particularly so in English-speaking countries), it is apparent that Max Reger exerted an enormous amount of influence during his lifetime as a composer, teacher, performer, and pedagogue, and as such, is an appropriate candidate for inclusion in the Greenwood Press composer bio-bibliography series.

The present volume consists of four main sections:

(1) a brief biography;

(2) a complete list of works and performances divided into works with opus numbers and works without opus numbers. Following each title is the date of composition, its publisher(s), premiere performances, timings of movements (where applicable), and when necessary, a list of song texts or names of chorales. References to the works in the discography and bibliography sections are indicated. Included in the end matter of this volume are appendices listing Reger's compositions in chronological order and by genre;

(3) a discography of commercially-produced sound recordings. Each recorded work is preceded by the mnemonic "D" (D1, D2, etc.), and;

(4) an annotated bibliography of writings by and about Max Reger, his music, compositional style, and performances, with annotations often taking on the form of quotations extracted from the articles or books included in the bibliography. Each item in the bibliography is preceded by the mnemonic "B" (B1, B2. etc.). Translations of German sources are by the author.

A complete index of names (personal, corporate, geographical and titles) concludes the volume.

Acknowledgments

For providing special assistance, the author would like to acknowledge the following individuals: Mrs. Betty Dorney, Professor Suzanne Moulton of the University of Denver, and Drs. Susanne Popp and Susanne Shigihara of the Max-Reger-Institut, Bonn, West Germany; and the library staffs of the following institutions: Dartmouth College, The Library of Congress, Johns Hopkins University, The University of Kansas, Wichita State University, Brigham Young University, The University of Denver, The University of Colorado at Boulder, Colorado State University, Colorado College, The University of Oklahoma, The University of Texas at Austin, Kansas State University, The University of Missouri, The University of Utah, The University of Northern Colorado, and The University of North Carolina at Chapel Hill.

Max Reger

Biography

Max Reger was born in Brand, Bavaria on March 19, 1873 to Joseph and Philomena Reger. Joseph Reger was a school teacher with more than an amateur interest in music, having published a harmony textbook that was in fairly wide use in German public schools. Thus, the young Max Reger grew up in a home environment in which his musical pursuits were encouraged and fostered.

At the age of 11, Reger began systematic musical studies with Adalbert Lindner, the town organist of Weiden. Lindner introduced Reger to the compositions of the great German masters, particularly Beethoven and Bach. Reger's devotion to the music of Bach no doubt originated in his years of study with Lindner which are sensitively described in the latter's Max Reger: Ein Bild seines Jugendlebens und künstlerischen Werdens.[1] Another profound influence on Reger was a visit to the Bayreuth Festival in 1888; and from the time of his earliest student works, there is in Reger's compositional style an attempted reconciliation of baroque structural principles and the free harmonic expression of late romanticism.

Reger's career was given further impetus by his years of study with Hugo Riemann in Sondershausen. Riemann was an enthusiastic supporter of his young student and the former's theoretical writings on "functional" harmony were developed further by his student, especially in the Beiträge zur Modulationslehre of 1903.[2] Although Riemann later disagreed with some of Reger's theoretical stances and compositional tendencies, it is clear that their association was instrumental in the establishment of Reger as a composer of importance.[3]

After a period of military service (in which the composer's health broke) and recuperation at his parents' home in Weiden, Reger settled in Munich in 1901. It was during his Munich years that Reger's music first became embroiled in controversy, particularly works such as the Op. 72 Violin Sonata and the Op. 90 Sinfonietta, the latter composition engendering a famous exchange between the critic Rudolf Louis and the composer.[4]

Reger's Munich period also brought him great personal happiness. In 1902 he married Elsa von Bercken, and the couple later adopted two daughters, Lotti and Christa.

Reger accepted an appointment as professor of composition at the University of Leipzig in 1907 and his fame rapidly increased as composer, performer, conductor, and pedagogue. The composer toured many European countries as well as Russia and England during his tenure at Leipzig. In 1908 he received an honorary doctorate from the University of Jena and composed for this occasion one of his most endurable works, the monumental 100th Psalm, Op. 106. Reger's composition students included Hermann Grabner, Karl Hasse, Joseph Haas, Julia Weissberg, Hermann Unger, Fritz Lubrich, Franz von Hoesslin, Botha Sigwart, Wilhelm Bettich, Else Wormser, Othmar Schoeck, Jaromir Weinberger, Hermann Keller, and many others.

Reger's stature in the musical world was further enhanced by his appointment as the conductor of the Meiningen Court Orchestra in 1911. Reger's activity as a composer remained unabated while maintaining a rigorous schedule of performances with the Meiningen Orchestra as well as numerous appearances as a solo and chamber performer.[5]

Reger resigned his position with the Meiningen Orchestra shortly before the outbreak of World War I and settled in Jena. This final period in Reger's life brought forth a remarkable resurgence in the composer's creative output. Returning primarily to chamber music composition, the works of Reger's final years (written in what the composer termed the "free Jena style" ["freier Jenaer Stil"]) display a settled maturity and eschew much of the modulatory wandering of his earlier works.

On May 10, 1916 Reger died of heart failure after returning from a concert tour. Lauded as one of the greatest and most often performed composers of the late romantic era and successor to the mantle of Bach, Beethoven, and Brahms, Reger's music quickly fell out of favor with both the general public and aficionados of the musical avant-garde.

Compositions

One of the most frequently remarked misconceptions concerning Reger's compositional procedures is that he worked too swiftly and haphazardly. This is understandable inasmuch as Reger's output was phenomenal: 146 opus numbers and numerous works without opus numbers in a creative life of only approximately 25 years. A close examination of sketches and preliminary drafts reveals that Reger often made drastic revisions in his compositions, and that revision played an important role in the organic development of his compositions.[6]

Reger's harmonic writing is often considered to be illogical or even atonal in nature; however, nothing could be further from the truth. The overriding concern of Reger was the simultaneous exploitation of harmonic expressiveness with the extension of chordal relationships through far-flung modulations. According to Paul Pisk:

> Reger's harmony does not abandon the traditional chords and tonality, but he uses rapid changes, unusual connections and juxtaposition of far distant keys. Therefore, his harmonic idiom becomes iridescent, almost experimental with very little occasion for longer stretches of relaxation. He rarely experimented with dissonance or altered chords like Wagner who sometimes temporarily suspended tonality. Reger's wide variety of chord connections, however, disturbs occasionally the unity of key and contributes to his "modern" sound.[7]

The contrapuntal aspect of much of Reger's music is a particularly distinguishing feature. Probably no other composer of the late romantic era was as influenced as Reger by the music of J.S. Bach. Fugues, canons, and non-imitative forms of counterpoint abound in Reger's oeuvre, yet the composer was not a slavish imitator of Bachian contrapuntal practices. Although a very thick texture is in evidence in many of Reger's compositions, this thickness is, more often than not, the result of a highly developed chromatic harmonic scheme placed within a contrapuntal context. Reger's contrapuntal style, therefore, instead of being strictly imitative in nature, is often constructed in a layered manner, i.e., the joining together of several independent and disparate voices.[8]

The compositional eclecticism of Reger presents the historian of music with a real dilemma as to the stylistic categorization of the composer because Reger, at various times, exhibits the hyperextension of tonality of late romanticism, the radical and oftentimes ambivalent emotionality of expressionism, an infatuation with baroque counterpoint, and a demonstrable appreciation of classical symmetry and syntax. Part of the difficulty that many critics have had in coming to terms with Reger's music (and that of his friend and kindred spirit, Ferruccio Busoni) is its all-encompassing nature, forming, as it were, an aperçu of past and contemporary musical practices. Many observers are surprised when they first learn that Reger was the most often performed composer in the concerts of Schönberg's Society for the Private Performance of Music and that the members of the Second Viennese School greatly valued Reger's music and often utilized his compositions for pedagogical purposes. To be sure, there is an intellectual affinity between Reger's extended harmonic relationships and "12 tones which are related only to one another," and a convincing case can be made that Reger's style was a necessary evolutionary stage between late romanticism and dodecaphony, yet the attraction that Reger held for composers such as Schönberg, Webern, and Berg seems more likely to stem from a common desire to appropriate all musical means available for the fulfillment of individual expression. In this regard,

Reger's music displays a real affinity with the goals and purposes of the Expressionist movement, which was also very influential in the artistic development of Schönberg and his followers. Edward Maynard Pinkney remarks:

> The violence, the hysterical emotion of these artists [the members of the Blaue Reiter School]... seems to find an echo in the music of Max Reger. Typically the sound is dense, agitated, complex; the dynamic range goes from extremity to extremity in seconds; the harmonic texture is black; the tonality lurches from one remoteness to another. The whole musical structure seems to strain and buck; the musical engine is caned--it might explode. The organ has all the stops out and the organist may well be drunk. Drunk with the driving compulsion to express his soul, his feelings in as poignant and colossal a way as he is able. Perhaps there is a touch of madness--the sort of monomania which subordinates everything to the compulsive power of the composer's will to expression.[9]

Reger's first opus was a Violin Sonata in D Minor, appropriate enough because, unlike many composers of his day, chamber music was to be a lifetime preoccupation and D minor was to become for Reger a highly personal key and one in which are composed many of his most expressive compositions. Some of Reger's most important chamber works include the Opp. 54 and 74 String Quartets[10], the Opp. 49 and 107 Clarinet Sonatas, the Opus 146 Clarinet Quintet[11], the Op. 118 String Sextet, and the Op. 131 Suites for Solo Violin, Solo Viola, and Solo Cello.

The organ compositions of Reger constitute the most significant body of 20th-century music for organ besides the works of Olivier Messiaen and the largest corpus of organ music since the time of J.S. Bach. Reger was stimulated to the composition of organ music by his close association with the great organist and Thomaskantor Karl Straube. Some of the best known of the organ works include Opp. 27, 40, 46 Fantasy and Fugue for Organ on B-A-C-H, 52, 57, 67 Fifty Two Preludes for Organ on Protestant Chorales, 73, 92, 127, and 135b. Though Reger was a lifetime Catholic, his love and exploitation of the repertory of Protestant chorales gave him the unique distinction of being one of the most significant composers of church music of both the Catholic and Lutheran confessions.

The vocal output of Reger was also exceptionally extensive and varied in both choral compositions and solo lieder. It is in the choral works (along with his chamber compositions) that the influence of Brahms becomes manifest; conversely, it is in the lied that Reger seems closest to the musical style of Richard Strauss; indeed, both Strauss and Reger set many of the same texts.[12] Reger's lieder range from the charming Op. 76 _Schlichte Weisen_ to the setting of Hölderlin's _An die Hoffnung_,

Op. 124 for alto voice and orchestra. Many of Reger's lieder seem to be reductions for piano and voice of orchestral songs, even though they were not composed originally for voice and orchestra. There are several reasons for this: (1) Reger's expansive compositional style tended to break through the traditional limits of the lied and (2) the orchestral song was a popular format of the early 20th century and Reger often arranged the lieder of Schubert and other composers as orchestral songs for use in his concerts with the Meiningen Orchestra.[13]

Reger's orchestral music dates from his later creative years and includes such works as the Op. 90 Sinfonietta[14], the Op. 100 Hiller Variations, the Op. 108 Symphonic Prologue to a Tragedy, the Op. 120 Lustspielouvertüre, the Op. 125 Romantic Suite, the Op. 128 Böcklin Suite, and the Op. 132 Mozart Variations[15]. Probably the greatest loss resulting from Reger's early death is that the composer did not write more orchestral music. The monumental proportions of Reger's compositional style were ideally suited to the orchestra, and Reger's contrapuntal ideas became much clearer in the multiplicity of tone colors afforded by the modern orchestra. Undoubtedly influenced by Brahms, Reger utilized the variations form in many of his orchestral works, including his best known and most often performed orchestral composition, the Mozart Variations, Op. 132. Although Reger eschewed programmatic connotations (except in the Böcklin Suite, Op. 128), his abilities as an orchestrator resemble in many ways the narrative qualities attributed to the orchestral works of Richard Strauss and Claude Debussy.

Finally, Reger's piano compositions, like his vocal works, display a wide variety of endeavors. They range from such works as transcriptions of Johann Strauss waltzes and the Op. 115 Episoden to the Op. 82 Aus meinem Tagebuch and the remarkable Op. 114 Concerto in F Minor for Piano and Orchestra, the latter composition admirably recorded and championed by none other than Rudolf Serkin. In addition, Reger's piano compositions include many 2-piano and 4-hand works.

Critical Assessment and Historical Position of Reger

Reger's historical position is perhaps unique in the annals of music. A large amount of scholarship has been dedicated to his life and works, a first-rate critical edition of his compositions nears completion, a dedicated group of Reger scholars and enthusiasts carries on numerous activities under the auspices of the Max-Reger-Institut in Bonn, West Germany, and numerous composers of unquestioned stature have acknowledged Reger's seminal contribution to the development of 20th-century music, and yet, outside of Germany, Reger remains largely an unknown composer who is often the subject of denigrating comments by musicians and musicologists, many of whom have never heard a single composition by Reger. This phenomenon is somewhat curious in that with the exception of his Munich period (when he was at odds with the critics of the "New German School" such as Rudolf Louis) Reger's works were generally met with approval and critical acclaim. At the time of his death, Reger was internationally acknowledged as a master composer, and memorial concerts occurred throughout the world, even in Russia which was at war with Germany at the time.

Reger's critical descent, however, began shortly after his death. In America, negative commentary on Reger appeared in short order. In an obituary article in The New Republic, Paul Rosenfeld remarked: "It was in the dust of the library that Reger existed."[16] In fact, a Rezeptionsgeschichte of Reger's works in America cannot even be attempted because critical opposition surfaced before the compositions gained a foothold in the orchestral, ecclesiastical, and solo repertories. There are a number of possible explanations for this. (1) The difficulty of many of Reger's compositions prevented their appreciation by an unschooled general audience. Carl Dahlhaus has commented on this aspect of Reger's music in his article "Warum ist Regers Musik so schwer verständlich?"[17] According to Dahlhaus, Reger's music is difficult to understand not because its harmonic structure is complicated, but that the complex harmonies cause alterations in the other aspects of the music. In conclusion, Dahlhaus states: "Reger is a composer...who listeners in strong measure...reject." (2) Many more popular composers (such as Richard Strauss and Gustav Mahler) are usually presented as artistic antipodes of Reger. Although some partisans of Strauss did try to initiate a Reger-Strauss rivalry similar to the Brahms-Wagner rivalry of a generation earlier, the two composers remained friends and were supportive of each other's artistic efforts. (3) Reger's death in 1916 was at a time of widespread anti-Germanic feeling which greatly influenced the critical assessment and reception of all German contributions to the arts. (4) Among the musical progressives and the avant-garde composers of the 1920s and 1930s Reger was considered a backward-looking composer, and the attention of this younger generation of composers and critics was drawn to the exploits of the dodecaphonists. (5) The perception of many people is that Reger was primarily a church composer whose contrapuntal style was an atavistic parody of that of J.S. Bach. (Ironically, the critical assessment of Richard Strauss declined rapidly in his later works as he began to incorporate more counterpoint into his compositional idiom.)

Needless to say, the final chapter in the critical reception has yet to be written. Time has not been especially favorable to the posthumous reputation of Reger in the non-German speaking countries of the world, and particularly in America where his works have yet to gain even a modicum of acceptance. With the current critical reappraisal of composers of the romantic period from Berlioz and Liszt to Reinecke and Schreker, it is hoped that the long-awaited "canonization" of Reger, a composer capable of the most profound expression and subtle musicality, will finally occur. This is in reality the least that should be expected for a composer whose works paved the way for such further musical developments as expressionism, dodecaphony, and neoclassicism.

---

[1] Adalbert Lindner, Max Reger: Ein Bild seines Jugendlebens und künstlerischen Werdens (Stuttgart: Engelhorn, 1922).

[2] Max Reger, Beiträge zur Modulationslehre (Leipzig: C.F. Kahnt, 1903).

[3] Less clear, however, is the degree to which Reger's compositional style is indebted to Riemann's theoretical writings. For differing viewpoints on this matter see Hermann Grabner, Regers Harmonik, 2nd ed. (Wiesbaden: Breitkopf & Härtel, 1961) and Gerd Sievers, Die Grundlagen Hugo Riemanns bei Max Reger (Wiesbaden: Breitkopf & Härtel, 1967).

[4] Reprinted in Nicolas Slonimsky, Lexicon of Musical Invective: Critical Assaults on Composers Since Beethoven's Time, 2nd ed. (Seattle: University of Washington Press, 1965), p. 139.

[5] For more details of Reger as performer and conductor see Ottmar and Ingeborg Schreiber's excellent three-volume study, Max Reger in seinen Konzerten (Bonn: Dümmler Verlag, 1981).

[6] This is particularly evident in a comparison of first drafts and final versions in a performance setting. One remarkable instance of this was a consecutive performance of the first draft of movements 1 and 2 of Op. 139 and its final version performed by Ulf Hoelscher and Benedikt Koehlen on Friday, May 23, 1986 in Bonn-Bad Godesberg as part of a Symposium on the 70th anniversary of Reger's death held under the aegis of the Max-Reger-Institut.

[7] Paul A. Pisk, "Max Reger: An Appreciation" Diapason 64:6 (1973): 14.

[8] The best example of this layered approach to counterpoint is found in the Schule des Triospiels, in which Reger and Karl Straube added a third voice to the 2-Part Inventions of J.S. Bach.

[9] Edward Maynard Pinkney, "Reger--Expressionist, Karg-Elert--Impressionist" Musical Opinion (1973): 255.

[10] For more information see Rainer Wilke, Brahms. Reger. Schönberg. Streichquartette: motivisch-thematische Prozesse und formale Gestalt (Hamburg: Verlag der Musikalienhandlung, 1980).

[11] For more information see Roland Häfner, Max Reger Klarinettenquintett op. 146 (Munich: Wilhelm Fink Verlag, 1982).

[12] For more information see Barbara A. Peterson, Ton und Wort: The Lieder of Richard Strauss (Ann Arbor: UMI Research Press, 1980).

[13] Indeed, Reger (along with Busoni) was one of the foremost and most prolific arrangers of other composers' music. These arrangements are for a wide variety of performing media. See especially Johannes Lorenzon, Max Reger als Bearbeiter Bachs (Wiesbaden: Breitkopf & Härtel, 1982) Volume II of Schriftenreihe des Max-Reger-Instituts.

[14] For more information see Hugo Leichtentritt, Sinfonietta von Max Reger (Leipzig: Breitkopf & Härtel, 1908) and Eugen Schmitz, Max Regers Sinfonietta (Munich: Georg Müller, 1905).

[15] For more information see Helmut Wirth, Max Reger: Variationen und Fuge über ein Thema von Mozart op. 132 (Munich: Institut für Film und Bild in Wissenschaft und Unterricht, 1962).

[16] Paul Rosenfeld, "An Erudite Composer" The New Republic 9:106 (1916): 47.

[17] Carl Dahlhaus, "Warum ist Regers Musik so schwer verständlich?" Neue Zeitschrift für Musik 134 (1973): 134

Works and Performances

"See" references identify related citations in other sections of this volume. Items preceded by "B," e.g., B100, may be found in the bibliography section; those preceded by "D," e.g., D111, identify citations in the discography section.

Works with Opus Numbers

Op. 1 Sonata in D Minor for Violin and Piano
(1890; Augener, Schott; 28 min.)
Premiere: Wiesbaden, November 21, 1891
Gustav Cords and Max Reger
See: B957

Op. 2 Trio in B Minor for Piano, Violin, and Viola
(1891; Augener, Schott; 22 min.)
Premiere: Berlin, February 4, 1894
Max Reger, Waldemar Mayer, and Adalbert Gülzow
See: D128, B901

Op. 3 Sonata in D Major for Violin and Piano
(1891; Augener, Schott; 23 min.)
Premiere: Wiesbaden, April 4, 1892
Gustav Cords and Max Reger
See: B957

Op. 4 Six Songs for Medium Voice and Piano
Gebet; Widmung; Winterahnung; Im April; Der zerrissnee Grabkranz; Bitte
(1890-1; Augener, Schott)
Premiere: August 8, 1892
Elisabeth Riemann and Max Reger
See: B76

Op. 5 Sonata in F Minor for Cello and Piano
(1892; Augener, Schott; 24 min.)

Premiere: October 17, 1893
Oskar Brückner and Max Reger
See: D126, D149, B957

Op. 6 Three Choruses for Soprano, Alto, Tenor, and Bass with Piano Accompaniment
Trost; Zur Nacht; Abendlied
(1892; Augener, Schott; 12 min.)
Premiere: No. 1 February 2, 1907
Barmer Lehrergesangverein, Rich. Senff, conducting
Premiere: Nos. 2 & 3 Berlin, November 22, 1911
John Petersen, conducting

Op. 7 Three Organ Pieces
(1892; Augener, Schott; 24 min.)
See: B555

Op. 8 Five Songs for High Voice and Piano
Waldlied; Tränen im Auge; Der Kornblumenstrauss; Scherz; Bauernregel
(1892; Augener, Schott)
See: B1640

Op. 9 Waltz-Caprices for Piano, 4 Hands
(1892; Augener, Schott)
Premiere: Wiesbaden, August 3, 1893
Hans Schmidt and Max Reger
See: D142

Op. 10 German Dances for Piano, 4 Hands
(1893; Augener, Schott)
See: D141

Op. 11 Seven Waltzes for Piano (2 Hands)
(1893; Augener, Schott)

Op. 12 Five Songs for One Voice (and Piano)
Friedhofsgang; Das arme Vögelein; Wennich's nur wüsst; Gruss; Um dich
(1893; Augener, Schott)
See: B76, B1640

Op. 13 Lose Blätter for Piano
(1894; Augener, Schott)
See: B76, B595

Op. 14 Five Duets for Soprano and Alto with Piano Accompaniment
See: B1889

Op. 14b Ich stehe hoch über'm See for Bass Voice and Piano
(1894; Augener, Schott)

See: B483

Op. 15 — *Ten Songs for Medium Voice (and Piano)*
Glück; Das Blatt im Buche; Nelken; Traum; Das Mädchen spricht; Scheiden; Der Schelm; Leichtsinniger Rat; Verlassen hab ich mein Lieb; Trost
(1894; Augener, Schott)
See: B76, B310

Op. 16 — *Suite for Organ in E Minor*
(1894-5; Augener, Schott)
Premiere: Berlin, March 4, 1897 Karl Straube
See: B555

Op. 17 — *Aus der Jugendzeit for Piano (2 Hands)*
(1895; Augener, Schott)
See: B76, B99, B595

Op. 18 — *Improvisations for Piano (2 Hands)*
(1896; Augener, Schott)
See: B595

Op. 19 — *Two Sacred Songs for Medium Voice with Organ Accompaniment*
(1898; Joseph Aibl Verlag, Universal Edition)
See: B923

Op. 20 — *Five Humoresques for Piano (2 Hands)*
(1898; Joseph Aibl Verlag, Universal Edition)
See: D150, D191, B380, B1330, B1643

Op. 21 — *Hymne an den Gesang for Male Choir with Orchestral Accompaniment*
(1898; Joseph Aibl Verlag, Universal Edition; 8 min.)
Premiere: Weiden, November 19, 1898
Max Reger conducting
See: B1439, B1618

Op. 22 — *Six Waltzes for Piano (4 Hands)*
(1898; Joseph Aibl Verlag, Universal Edition)
Premiere: Weiden, January 1, 1899
Adalbert Lindner and Max Reger
See: D141, D159, B1330

Op. 23 — *Four Songs for Voice with Piano Accompaniment*
Das Kleinste Lied; Pythia; Das sterbende Kind; Vom Küssen
(1898; Joseph Aibl Verlag, Universal Edition)
See: B923, B1330

Op. 24 — *Six Morceaux for Piano*
(1898: Robert Forberg, J. Rieter-Biedermann)

See: B76, B1337

Op. 25 Aquarellen for Piano (2 Hands)
(1897-8; Augener, Schott)

Op. 26 Seven Fantasy-Pieces for Piano
(1898; Robert Forberg, J. Rieter-Biedermann)

Op. 27 Fantasy for Organ on the Chorale "Ein' feste Burg ist unser Gott"
(1898; Robert Forberg, J. Rieter-Biedermann; 12 min.)
Premiere: Wesel, September 13, 1898
Karl Straube
See: D107, D138, D166, D169, D182, D183, B23, B362, B555, B1327, B1342, B1420, B1605, B1677, B1730, B1764

Op. 28 Second Sonata in G Minor for Cello and Piano
(1898; Joseph Aibl Verlag, Universal Edition; 17 min.)
See: D126, D149, B93, B957, B1330, B1355, B1543

Op. 29 Fantasy and Fugue in C Minor for Organ
(1898; Robert Forberg, J. Rieter-Biedermann; 11 min.)
Premiere: Willibroddom zu Wesel, March 8, 1899
Karl Straube
See: D135, D139, B555, B1327, B1730, B1764

Op. 30 Fantasy for Organ on the Chorale "Freu' dich sehr, o meine Seele!"
(1898; Joseph Aibl Verlag, Universal Edition; 20 min.)
Premiere: Wesel, September 13, 1898
Karl Straube
See: D107, D139, B23, B76, B555, B838, B1331, B1420, B1764

Op. 31 Six Poems of Anna Ritter for Medium Voice with Piano Accompaniment
Allein; Ich glaub', lieber Schatz; Unbegehrt; Und hab' so grosse Sehnsucht doch; Mein Traum; Schlimme Geschichte
(1898; Joseph Aibl Verlag, Universal Edition)
See: B1330

Op. 32 Seven Character Pieces for Piano (2 Hands)
(1899; Joseph Aibl Verlag, Universal Edition)
See: B1330

Op. 33 First Sonata in F# Minor for Organ
(1899; Joseph Aibl Verlag, Universal Edition; 19 min.)

Premiere: Essen, June 14, 1899
Karl Straube
See: D139, B23, B1012, B1331, B1536, B1558, B1677

Op. 34 Five Picturesque Pieces for Piano (4 Hands)
(1899; Joseph Aibl Verlag, Universal Edition)
Premiere: Munich, October 22, 1904
Schmid-Lindner and Max Reger
See: D133, D159, B1329

Op. 35 Six Songs for Medium Voice with Piano Accompaniment
Dein Auge; Der Himmel hat eine Träne geweint; Traum durch die Dämmerung; Flieder; Du liebes Auge; Wenn lichter Mondenschein
(1899; Joseph Aibl Verlag, Universal Edition)
See: B853, B1331

Op. 36 Bunte Blätter for Piano (2 Hands)
(1899; Joseph Aibl Verlag, Universal Edition)
See; B99, B380, B595, B1643

Op. 37 Five Songs for Medium Voice with Piano Accompaniment
Helle Nacht; Volkslied; Glückes genug; Frauenhaar; Nachtliche Pfade
(1899; Joseph Aibl Verlag, Universal Edition)
See: B1331

Op. 38 Seven Male Choruses
Mit Schwung; Frühlingsruf; Über die Berge; Wie ist doch die Erde so schön; Frohsinn; Abendreihn; Hell ins Fenster
(1899; Joseph Aibl Verlag, Universal Edition)
Premiere: No. 2 Zwickauer Lehrergesangverein, March 9, 1900 R.E. Vollhardt, conducting
See: B1329, B1439

Op. 39 Three Six-Voice Choruses for 1 Soprano, 2 Altos, 1 Tenor, and 2 Basses
Schweigen; Abendlied; Frühlingsblick
(1899; Joseph Aibl Verlag, Universal Edition)
See: B1319, B1328, B1469

Op. 40 Two Fantasies on the Chorales: "Wie schön leucht't uns der Morgenstern" and "Straf' mich nicht in deinem Zorn"
(1899; Joseph Aibl Verlag, Universal Edition; 23 min.)
Premiere: No. 1 Wesel, Summer 1900 Karl Straube
No. 2 Brünn, May 24, 1900 Otto Burkert
See: D4, D17. D107, D112, D138, D182, D183, B76, B102, B1328, B1420, B1729

Op. 41 — Third Sonata in A Major for Violin and Piano
(1899; Joseph Aibl Verlag, Universal Edition)
Premiere: Munich, December 11, 1900
Joseph Hösl and Max Reger
See: B901, B957, B1320, B1328, B1349, B1352

Op. 42 — Four Sonatas for Violin Alone
(1900; Joseph Verlag, Universal Edition; 13 min., 8 min., 7 min., 14 min.)
Premiere: No. 1 Berlin, March 2, 1904 Jul. Ruthström
No. 2 Berlin, Nov. 16, 1905 Issay Barmas
No. 4 Berlin, Feb. 24, 1904 Ossip Schnirlin
See: D147, B23, B221, B667, B957, B1320, B1328, B1349, B1391, B1852

Op. 43 — Eight Songs for Voice with Piano Accompaniment
Zwischen zwei Nächten; Müde; Meinem Kinde; Abschied; Wiegenlied; Die Betrogene spricht; Mein Herz; Sag es nicht
(1900; Joseph Aibl Verlag, Universal Edition)
See: B910, B1328, B1790

Op. 44 — Ten Small Recital Pieces for Piano in Use in Teaching
(1900; Joseph Aibl Verlag, Universal Edition)
See: B1328, B1643, B1701

Op. 45 — Six Intermezzi for Piano (2 Hands)
(1900; Joseph Aibl Verlag, Universal Edition)
See: D191, B380, B1396, B1765

Op. 46 — Fantasy and Fugue for Organ on B-A-C-H
(1900: Joseph Aibl Verlag; Universal Edition; 20 min.)
Premiere: Wesel, Summer 1900
Karl Straube
See: D11, D104, D130, D138, D171, D172, D189, D192, B247, B362, B380, B476, B555, B746, B965, B1202, B1318, B1319, B1342, B1388, B1420, B1471, B1496, B1542, B1545, B1578, B1627, B1677, B1765

Op. 47 — Six Trios for Organ
(1900; Joseph Aibl Verlag, Universal Edition)
See: B30, B1319, B1429, B1765

Op. 48 — Seven Songs for Medium Voice with Piano Accompaniment
Hütet euch; Leise Lieder; Im Arm der Liebe; Ach, Liebster, in Gedanken; Junge Ehe; Am Dorfsee; Unvergessen
(1900; Joseph Aibl Verlag, Universal Edition)
See: B483, B1765

Op. 49 — Two Sonatas (Ab Major and F# Minor) for Clarinet and

Piano
(1900: Joseph Aibl Verlag, Universal Edition; 25 min., 28 min.)
Premiere: No. 1 Munich, April 18, 1902
Karl Wagner and Max Reger
No. 2 Munich, April 29, 1904
Anton Walch and Max Reger
See: D35, D84, D117, D137, D162, B483, B745, B957, B1583, B1592, B1713, B1760. B1777, B1780, B1843, B1887

Op. 50 Two Romances (G Major and D Major) for Violin and Small Orchestra
(string quintet, 2 fl, 2 ob, 2 cl, 2 bsn, 2 horns, timpani)
(1900; Joseph Aibl Verlag, Universal Edition; 8 min., 9 min.)
Premiere: No. 1 Munich, May 1, 1902
Wilh. Sieben and Oscar Wappenschmidt, (piano reduc.)
See: D152, B1349, B1592, B1598, B1822

Op. 51 Twelve Songs for Voice with Piano Accompaniment
Der Mond glüht; Mägdleins Frage; Träume, träume, du mein süsses Leben! Wiegenlied; Geheimnis; Mädchenlied; Schmied Schmerz; Nachtgang; Gleich einer versunkenen Melodie; Frühlingsregen; Verlorne Liebe; Frühlingsmorgen; Weisse Tauben
(1900; Joseph Aibl Verlag, Universal Edition)
See: B476, B483

Op. 52 Three Fantasies for Organ on the Chorales: "Alle Menschen müssen sterben"; "Wachet auf, ruft uns die Stimme"; "Halleluja! Gott zu loben, bleibe meine Seelenfreud
(1900; Joseph Aibl Verlag, Universal Edition; 17 min., 16 min., 17 min.)
Premiere: No. 1 Wesel, Summer 1901 Karl Straube
No. 2 Berlin, May 12, 1901 Karl Straube
No. 3 Munich, Nov. 9, 1901 Karl Straube
See: D1, D14, D17, D90, D107, D138, D139, D174, D179, D180, D183, B23, B102, B307, B483, B1045, B1202, B1420, B1542, B1733, B1741, B1748, B1845

Op. 53 Silhouetten: Seven Pieces for Piano (2 Hands)
(1900; Joseph Aibl Verlag, Universal Edition)
See: D150, D191, B319, B595, B1592, B1700, B1847

Op. 54 Two String Quartets (G Minor and A Major)
(1900-1; Joseph Aibl Verlag, Universal Edition; 25 min., 23 min.)
Premiere: No. 1 Triest, Feb. 26, 1910 Triestiner Quartet

No. 2 Munich, April 28, 1904 Hösl Quartet
See: D78, D79, D127, D198, B91, B894, B957, B965, B1239, B1349, B1569, B1843, B1853, B1872

Op. 55 Fifteen Songs for Voice with Piano Accompaniment
Hymnus des Hasses; Traum; Der tapfere Schneider; Rosen; Der Narr; Verklärung; Sterne; Zwei Gänse--Die Capitolio; Ein Paar; Wären wir zwei kleine Vögel; Viola d'amour; Nachtsegen; Gute Nacht; Allen Welten abgewandt; Der Alte
(1900-1; Joseph Aibl Verlag, Universal Edition, Louis Gregh, Breitkopf & Härtel)
See: B483

Op. 56 Five Preludes and Fugues for Organ
(1904; Joseph Aibl Verlag, Universal Edition, Breitkopf & Härtel)
See: D14, D32, D40, D71, B30

Op. 57 Symphonic Fantasy and Fugue for Organ
(1901; Joseph Aibl Verlag, Universal Edition; 19 min.)
Premiere: Berlin, Feb. 20, 1902 Karl Straube
See: D21, D138, B23, B190, B483, B555, B600, B965, B1202, B1420, B1593, B1733, B1753, B1845

Op. 58 Six Burlesques for Piano (4 Hands)
1901; Bartholf Senff, Simrock, Peters)
See: D133, B1394, B1682, B1846, B1881

Op. 59 Twelve Pieces for Organ
(1901; Peters)
Premiere: No. 2 Zwickau, Oct. 31, 1901 Paul Gerhardt
Nos. 7 & 9 Munich, Nov. 9, 1901
Karl Straube
See: D4, D11, D22, D28, D32, D71, D104, D107, D115, D138, D156, D166, D172, D178, D182, B30, B362, B555, B1420, B1547, B1590, B1592, B1679, B1733

Op. 60 Second Sonata (D Minor) for Organ
(1901; F.E.C. Leuckart, Universal Edition; 23 Min.)
Premiere: Merseberg, May 11, 1902 Hermann Dettmer
See: D139, D140, D167, D189, B23, B145, B555, B1012, B1420, B1558, B1579, B1728

Op. 61 Easy Practical Compositions for Use in Church
1. 8 "Tantum ergo"'s for Mixed Choir a cappella
2. 4 "Tantum ergo"'s for Soprano & Alto with organ
3. 4 "Tantum ergo"'s for Mixed Choir with organ
4. 8 Marian Songs for Mixed Choir a cappella
5. 4 Marian Songs for Soprano & Alto with organ
6. 4 Marian Songs for Mixed Choir with organ

7. 6 Mourning Songs for Mixed Choir a cappella
(1901; Kistner & Siegel)
See: B188, B1500, B1565, B1682, B1818

Op. 62 Sixteen Songs for Voice with Piano Accompaniment
Wehe; Waldseligkeit; Ruhe; Mensch und Natur; Wir Zwei; Reinheit; Vor dem Sterben; Gebet; Strampelchen; Die Nixe; Fromm; Totensprache; Begegnung; Ich schwebe; Pflügerin Sorge; Anmutiger Vertrag;
(1901; Joseph Aibl Verlag, Universal Edition)
See: B483, B1614, B1772

Op. 63 Monologe: Twelve Pieces for Organ
(1901-2; F.E.C. Leuckart, Universal Edition)
See: D40, D138, D170, D172, B1322, B1420, B1589, B1625, B1682, B1766, B1768, B1819

Op. 64 Quintet in C Minor for Piano, 2 Violins, Viola, and Cello
(1901; Peters, Eulenberg; 40 min.)
Premiere: Munich, May 1, 1903
Max Reger and the Hösl Quartet
See: D127, B112, B595, B901, B910, B1367, B1493, B1777, B1833

Op. 65 Twelve Pieces for Organ
(1902; Peters)
See: D10, D16, D21, D32, D71, D119, D166, B23, B307, B362, B555, B1547, B1590, B1682, B1819

Op. 66 Twelve Songs for Medium Voice and Piano
Sehnsucht; Freundlich Vision; Aus der Ferne in der Nacht; Du bist mir gut!; Maienblüten; Die Primeln; Die Liebe; An dich; Erlöst; Morgen; Jetzt und immer; Kindergeschichte
See: B910, B1474, B1494, B1500

Op. 67 Fifty Two Preludes for Organ on Protestant Chorales
1. Allein Gott in der Höh sei Ehr!
2. Alles ist on Gottes Segen
3. Aus tiefer Not schrei ich zu dir
4. Aus meines Herzens Grunde
5. Christus, der ist mein Leben
6. Ein feste Burg ist unser Gott
7. Dir, dir Jehovah will ich singen!
8. Erschienen ist der herrlich Tag
9. Herr Jesu Christ, dich zu uns wend
10. Es ist das Heil uns kommen her
11. Freu' dich sehr, o meine Seele
12. Gott des Himmels und der Erden
13. Herr, wie du willst, so schick's mit mir
14. Herzlich tut mich verlagen

15. Jauchz, Erd, und Himmel, juble!
16. Ich dank dir, lieber Herre
17. Ich will dich lieben, meine Stärke
18. Jerusalem, du hochgebaute Stadt
19. Jesu Leiden, Pein und Tod
20. Jesu, meine Zuversicht
21. Jesu, meine Freud
22. Komm, o komm, du Geist des Lebens
23. Lobt Gott, ihr Christen alle gleich
24. Lobe den Herren, den mächtigen König der Ehren
25. Mach's mit mir, Gott, nach deiner Güt
26. Meinem Jesum lass ich nicht
27. Nun danket alle Gott
28. Nun freut euch, lieben Christen
29. Nun komm, der Heiden Heiland
30. O Gott, du frommer Gott
31. O Jesu Christ, meins Lebens Licht
32. O Lamm Gottes, unschuldig
33. O Welt, ich muss dich lassen
34. Schmücke dich, o liebe Seele
35. Seelenbräutigam
36. Sollt ich meinem Gott nicht singen
37. Straf mich nicht in deinem Zorn
38. Valet will ich dir geben
39. Vater unser im Himmelreich
40. Vom Himmel hoch, da komm ich her
41. Wachet auf, ruft uns die Stimme
42. Von Gott will ich nicht lassen
43. Warum sollt ich mich denn grämen
44. Was Gott tut, das ist wohlgetan
45. Wer nur den lieben Gott lässt walten
46. Wer nur den lieben Gott lässt walten
47. Werde munter mein Gemüte
48. Wer weiss, wie nahe mir mein Ende
49. Wie schön leuchtet der Morgenstern
50. Wie wohl ist mir, o Freund
51. Jesus ist kommen
52. O wie selig

(1902; Lauterbach & Kuhn, Bote & Bock)
See: D32, D71, D139, D140, D155, D168, D171, D172, B23, B135, B261, B824, B840, B1325, B1420, B1459, B1590, B1629, B1668

Op. 68 Six Songs for Medium Voice and Piano
Eine Seele; Unterwegs; Märchenland; Engelwacht; Nachtseele; An die Geliebte
(1902; Lauterbach & Kuhn, Bote & Bock, Universal Edition)
See: B1494, B1500, B1614

Op. 69 Ten Pieces for Organ
(1903; Lauterbach & Kuhn, Bote & Bock, Universal

Edition)
Premiere: Berlin, March 4, 1904 Walter Fischer
See: D32, D71, B30, B1462, B1777, B1819

Op. 70 Seventeen Songs for High Voice and Piano
Präludium; Der König bei der Krönung; Ritter rät dem Knappen dies; Die bunten Kühe; Gruss; Elternstolz; Meine Seele; Die Verschmähte; Sehnsucht; Hoffnungstrost; Gegen Abend; Dein Bild; Mein und Dein; Der Bote; Tränen; Des Durstes Erklärung; Sommernacht
(1902-3; Lauterbach & Kuhn, Bote & Bach, Universal Edition)
See: B1466

Op. 71 Gesang der Verklärten for Five-Voice Choir (2 Sopranos, Alto, Tenor, & Bass) and Large Orchestra
(1903; Kistner & Siegel; 19 min.)
Premiere; Aachen, January 18, 1906
Eberhard Schwickerath conducting the Städt. Gesangverein of Aachen
See: B76, B673, B901, B1507, B1615, B1773, B1774, B1787

Op. 72 Fourth Sonata in C Major for Violin and Piano
(1903; Lauterbach & Kuhn, Bote & Bock, Universal Edition; 32 min.)
Premiere: Munich, November 5, 1903
Richard Rettich and Max Reger
See: D148, B23, B112, B192, B398, B957, B1010, B1145, B1190, B1247, B1360, B1371, B1398, B1422, B1450, B1512, B1584, B1598, B1608, B1737, B1760, B1777, B1780, B1822

Op. 73 Variations and Fugue on an Original Theme for Organ
(1903; Lauterbach & Kuhn, Bote & Bock, Universal Edition; 31 min.)
Premiere: Berlin, March 1, 1905 Walter Fischer
See: D22, D115, D135, D138, D174, D192, B23, B189, B294, B398, B514, B601, B910, B1388, B1420, B1461, B1506, B1542, B1777

Op. 74 Third String Quartet in D Minor
(1903-4; Lauterbach & Kuhn, Bote & Bock, Universal Edition; 58 min.)
Premiere: Frankfurt, December 30, 1904
Hugo Heermann, Arthur Rebner, Fritz Bassermann, Hugo Becker
See: D80, D153, D198, B23, B192, B362, B398, B894, B901, B910, B957, B1197, B1221, B1239, B1297, B1351, B1356, B1455, B1483, B1512, B1677, B1719, B1756,

B1761, B1775, B1872

Op. 75 <u>Eighteen Songs for High Voice and Piano</u>
Merkspruch; Mondnacht; Der Knabe an die Mutter; Dämmer; Böses Weib; Ihr, ihr Herrlichen!; Schlimm für die Männer; Wäsche im Winde; All' mein Gedanken, mein Herz und mein Sinn; Schwäbische Treue; Aeolsharfe; Hat gesagt--bleibt's nicht dabei; Das Ringlein; Schlafliedchen; Darum; Das Fenster klang im Winde; Du brachtest mir deiner Seele Trank; Einsamkeit (1903; Lauterbach & Kuhn, Bote & Bock, Universal Edition)
<u>See</u>: B1211, B1463, B1513, B1842

Op. 76 <u>Schlichte Weisen for Voice and Piano</u>
Book I:
1. Du meines Herzens Krönelein
2. Daz iuwer min engel walte!
3. Waldeinsamkeit
4. Wenn die Linde blüht
5. Herzenstausch
6. Beim Schneewetter
7. Schlect' Wetter
8. Einen Brief soll ich schreiben
9. Am Brünnele
10. Warte nur!
11. Mei Bua
12. Mit Rosen bestreut
13. Der verliebte Jäger
14. Mein Schätzelein
15. Maiennacht

Book II:
16. Glück
17. Wenn alle Welt so einig wär
18. In einem Rosengärtelein
19. Hans und Grete
20. Es blüht ein Blümlein rosenrot
21. Minnelied
22. Des Kindes Gebet
23. Zweisprach
24. Abgeguckt
25. Friede
26. Der Schwur
27. Kindeslächeln
28. Die Mutter spricht
29. Schmeichelkätzchen
30. Vorbeimarsch

Book III:
31. Gottes Segen
32. Von der Liebe
33. Das Wölklein
34. Reiterlied

35. Mittag
36. Schelmenliedchen

Book IV:

37. Heimat
38. Das Mägdlein und der Spatz
39. Abendlied
40. Wunsch
41. An den Frühlingsregen
42. Der Postillion
43. Brunnensang

Book V:

44. Klein Marie
45. Lutschemäulchen
46. Soldatenlied
47. Schlaf' ein
48. Zwei Mäuschen
49. Ein Tänzchen
50. Knecht Ruprecht
51. Die fünf Hühnerchen

Book VI:

52. Mariä Wiegenlied
53. Das Brüderchen
54. Das Schwesterchen
55. Furchthäuschen
56. Der Igel
57. Die Bienen
58. Mausefangen
59. Zum Schlafen
60. Der König aus dem Morgenland

(1903-4; Lauterbach & Kuhn, Bote & Bock, Universal Edition)
See: D92, D93, B23, B380, B936, B1053, B1241, B1340, B1460, B1463, B1585, B1744, B1747, B1790, B1832, B1844

Op. 77a Serenade in D Major for Flute, Violin, and Viola
(1904; Lauterbach & Kuhn, Bote & Bock, Paynes, Eulenburg, Universal Edition; 17 min.)
Premiere: Munich, December 14, 1904
Schellhorn, Felix Berber, and L. Vollnhals
See: D26, D116, D125, D197, B23, B345, B356, B362, B896, B957, B1006, B1373, B1437, B1463, B1471, B1526, B1598, B1658, B1677, B1777

Op. 77b Trio in A Major for Violin, Viola, and Cello
(1904; Lauterbach & Kuhn, Bote & Bock, Universal Edition, Paynes, Eulenburg; 19 min.)
Premiere: Munich, November 29, 1904
Members of the Münchener Quartetts
See: D8, D39, D85, D97, D185, D197, B345, B356, B957, B1006, B1241, B1351, B1373, B1463, B1512, B1569, B1761, B1777, B1864

Op. 78 Third Sonata in F Major for Cello and Piano
(1904; Lauterbach & Kuhn, Bote & Bock, Universal Edition; 26 min.)
Premiere: Munich, December 14, 1904
Carl Ebner and Max Reger
See: D126, D149, B957, B1362, B1463, B1721, B1777, B1781

Op. 79a Compositions for Piano
(1901-3; Hermann Beyer & Söhne)
See: D22, B1241

Op. 79b Compositions for Organ (Chorale Preludes)
(1901-3; Hermann Beyer & Söhne)
See: D107, D138, D155, B824

Op. 79c Compositions for Voice with Piano Accompaniment
Abend; Um Mitternacht blühen die Blumen; Volkslied; Friede; Auf mondbeschienenen Wegen; Die Glocke des Glücks; Erinnerung; Züge
See: B1241

Op. 79d Compositions for Violin with Piano Accompaniment
(1902-4; Hermann Beyer & Söhne)
See: D38, D151

Op. 79e Compositions for Cello with Piano Accompaniment
(1904; Hermann Beyer & Söhne)
See: D154

Op. 79f Compositions for Mixed Choir (Chorales)
Jesu, meines Lebens Leben; Auferstanden; Auf Christi Himmelfahrt allein; Zum Erntedankfest "Nun preiset alle"; Such, wer da will; Ach, Gott verlass mich nicht!; Ich weiss, mein Gott; Ich hab in Gottes Herz und Sinn; Jesu, grosser Wunderstern; Jesus soll die Losung sein; Trauungsgesang: O selig Haus; Herr, deine letzten Worte; Auferstanden; Gib dich zufrieden
(1900-1; Hermann Beyer & Söhne)

Op. 79g Compositions for Three-Voice Female (or Boys) Choir
Lobt Gott, ihr Christen, allzugleich; Dankssaget dem Vater; Nun lasst uns gehn
(1900; Hermann Beyer & Söhne)

Op. 80 Twelve Pieces for Organ
(1904; Peters; 4 min., 3 1/2 min., 4 1/2 min., 3 min., 4 min., 4 min., 4 min., 3 min., 2 min., 4 min., 3 min., 3 min.)
See: D11, D16, D32, D40, D71, D88, D115, D119, D189, B30, B555, B1420, B1547

Op. 81 Variations and Fugue on a Theme of Johann Sebastian Bach for Piano (2 Hands)
(1904; Lauterbach & Kuhn, Bote & Bock, Universal Edition; 35 min.)
Premiere: Munich, December 14, 1904
August Schmid-Lindner
See: D6, D105, D150, B359, B380, B398, B901, B965, B1005, B1035, B1042, B1298, B1392, B1421, B1445, B1463, B1512, B1513, B1577, B1603, B1610, B1636, B1685, B1756, B1777, B1781, B1790

Op. 82 Aus meinem Tagebuch for Piano (2 Hands)
Volume I: (1904; Lauterbach & Kuhn, Bote & Bock, Universal Edition; 32 min.)
Volume II: (1906; Lauterbach & Kuhn, Bote & Bock, Universal Edition; 30 min.)
Volume III: (1911; Bote & Bock, Universal Edition; 20 min.)
Volume IV: (1912; Bote & Bock, Universal Edition; 18 min.)
See: D143, D190, B291, B331, B356, B476, B896, B910, B935, B1163, B1176, B1241, B1373, B1463, B1496, B1513, B1514, B1544, B1769, B1838, B1849

Op. 83 Ten Songs for Male Choir
An das Meer; Lieblich hat sich gesellet; Abendständchen; Husarendurchmarsch; Hochsommernacht; Eine gantz neu Schelmweys; Minnelied; Freude soll in deinen Werken sein!; Abschied; Requiem
(1904; Lauterbach & Kuhn, Bote & Bock)
Premiere: Leipzig, February 20, 1905
Paul Klengel conducting the Leipzig "Arion"
See: B1596, B1790

Op. 84 Fifth Sonata in F# Minor for Violin and Piano
(1905; Lauterbach & Kuhn, Bote & Bock, Universal Edition; 23 min.)
Premiere: Berlin, March 7, 1905
Henri Marteau and Max Reger
See: D144, B1145, B1350, B1574, B1577, B1603, B1615, B1693, B1746, B1781, B1865

Op. 85 Four Preludes and Fugues for Organ
(1904; Peters; 5 1/2 min., 6 min., 7 1/2 min., 8 min.)
See: D25, D32, D40, D49, D63, D71, B30, B555, B1420

Op. 86 Variations and Fugue on a Theme of Beethoven for Piano (4 Hands) [Also arranged by the composer for orchestra]
(1904; Lauterbach & Kuhn, Bote & Bock, Universal Edition; 30 min.)

Premiere: Munich, October 22, 1904
August Schmid-Lindner and Max Reger
See: D29, D122, D160, B23, B901, B965, B1042, B1209, B1298, B1309, B1392, B1421, B1422, B1443, B1463, B1472, B1513, B1526, B1537, B1538, B1547, B1603, B1610, B1615, B1666, B1671, B1715, B1719, B1756, B1760, B1761, B1777, B1780, B1790

Op. 87 Two Compositions for Violin with Piano Accompaniment
(1905; Otto Forberg; 2 min., 11 min.)
See: B896

Op. 88 Four Songs for Medium Voice with Piano Accompaniment
Notturno; Stelldichein; Flötenspielerin; Spatz und Spätzin
(1905; Simrock, Peters; 3 min., 1 1/2 min., 3 min., 2 min.)
See: B1585

Op. 89 Four Sonatinas for Piano (2 Hands)
(1905-8; Lauterbach & Kuhn, Bote & Bock, Universal Edition; 14 min., 12 min., 12 min., 12 1/2 min.)
See: D67, D72, B291, B356, B380, B1241, B1657, B1658, B1659, B1832, B1844

Op. 90 Sinfonietta in A Major for Orchestra
(1904-5; Lauterbach & Kuhn, Bore & Bock, Universal Edition; 42 min.)
Premiere: Essen, October 8, 1905
Felix Mottl conducting
See: D108, B147, B192, B194, B341, B381, B634, B901, B972, B1209, B1218, B1310, B1311, B1388, B1386, B1404, B1444, B1468, B1510, B1526, B1567, B1579, B1615, B1645, B1689, B1696, B1715, B1726, B1867

Op. 91 Seven Sonatas for Violin Alone
(1905; Lauterbach & Kuhn, Bote & Bock, Universal Edition; 10 min., 9 min., 9 1/2 min., 12 min., 10 min., 9 1/2 min., 21 min.)
See: D82, D145, B589, B957, B1453

Op. 92 Suite for Organ in G Minor
(1905; Otto Forberg; 25 min.)
See: D130

Op. 93 Suite im alten Stil in F Major for Violin and Piano
(1906; Lauterbach & Kuhn, Bote & Bock, Universal Edition; 19 min.)
Premiere: Berlin, April 7, 1906
Ossip Schnirlin and Max Reger
See: D38, D151, B957, B972, B1360, B1370, B1437, B1453, B1456, B1543, B1559, B1577, B1608, B1716,

B1785

Op. 94 <u>Six Pieces for Piano (4 Hands)</u>
(1906; Peters; 8 min., 6 min., 7 1/2 min., 2 1/2 min., 5 min., 7 min.)
Premiere: Berlin, December 8, 1906
Paul Goldschmidt and Max Reger
<u>See</u>: D 133, D159, B1602

Op. 95 <u>Serenade in G Major for Orchestra</u>
(1906; Lauterbach & Kuhn, Bote & Bock, Universal Edition; 40 min.)
Premiere: Cologne, October 23, 1906
Fritz Steinbach conducting
<u>See</u>: B901, B972, B1004, B1209, B1217, B1454, B1475, B1511, B1527, B1680, B1716, B1882

Op. 96 <u>Introduction, Passacaglia and Fugue in B Minor for Two Pianos (4 Hands)</u>
(1906; Lauterbach & Kuhn, Bote & Bock, Universal Edition; 25 min.)
Premiere: Cologne, November 12, 1906
Henriette Schelle and Max Reger
<u>See</u>: D109, D122, B189, B965, B968, B1390, B1413, B1437, B1443, B1515, B1533, B1544, B1554, B1716, B1746, B1786, B1825

Op. 97 <u>Four Songs for Voice and Piano</u>
Das Dorf; Leise, leise weht ihr Lüfte; Ein Drängen; Der bescheidene Schäfer
(1906; Lauterbach & Kuhn, Bote & Bock, Universal Edition; 1 3/4 min., 1 3/4 min., 2 min., 1 1/4 min.)
<u>See</u>: B1144, B1324, B1486

Op. 98 <u>Five Songs for Medium or Low Voice with Piano Accompaniment</u>
Aus den Himmelsaugen; Der gute Rat; Sonntag; Es schläft ein stiller Garten; Sommernacht
(1906; Simrock, Peters; 1 1/2 min., 1 1/4 min., 2 1/4 min., 1 1/2 min.)

Op. 99 <u>Six Preludes and Fugues for Piano (2 Hands)</u>
(1906-7; Lauterbach & Kuhn, Bote & Bock, Universal Edition; 6 1/2 min., 4 min., 4 min., 7 min., 3 1/2 min., 6 min.)
<u>See</u>: B380, B1324, B1656

Op. 100 <u>Variations and Fugue in E Major on a Theme of J.A. Hiller for Orchestra</u>
(1907; Lauterbach & Kuhn, Bote & Bock, Universal Edition; 40 min.)
Premiere: Cologne, October 15, 1907

Fritz Steinbach conducting
See: D74, D95, D157, D193, D195, B76, B114, B278, B380, B901, B965, B968, B972, B1010, B1209, B1219, B1344, B1347, B1389, B1395, B1405, B1409, B1423, B1427, B1472, B1476, B1499, B1501, B1523, B1547, B1551, B1559, B1561, B1578, B1606, B1616, B1641, B1671, B1679, B1686, B1690, B1745, B1782, B1784, B1792, B1798, B1801, B1860, B1869, B1870, B1874

Op. 101 Concerto in A Major for Violin with Orchestral or Piano Accompaniment
(1907-8; Peters; 55 min.)
Premiere: Leipzig, October 15, 1908
Henri Marteau with the Gewandhaus Orchestra, Arthur Nikisch conducting
See: D30, B76, B360, B693, B834, B901, B929, B952, B987, B1346, B1354, B1357, B1408, B1412, B1518, B1783, B1791

Op. 102 Trio in E Minor for Violin, Cello and Piano
(1907-8; Lauterbach & Kuhn, Bote & Bock, Universal Edition; 40 min.)
Premiere: Leipzig, March 22, 1908
Edgar Wollgandt, Julius Klengel, and Max Reger
See: D123, B93, B586, B1353, B1360, B1543, B1608, B1740, B1802, B1878

Op. 103a Six Recital Pieces for Violin and Piano
(1908; Lauterbach & Kuhn, Bote & Bock, Universal Edition; 27 min.)
Premiere: Prague, November 7, 1908
Henri Marteau and Max Reger
See: D110, D144, B244, B356, B896, B957, B1352, B1744, B1746, B1784, B1802, B1850

Op. 103b Two Small Sonatas (D Minor & A Major) for Violin and Piano
(1909; Bote & Bock, Universal Edition; 30 min., 19 min.)
See: D134, D148, B356, B957, B1241, B1372

Op. 103c Twelve Small Pieces after Specific Songs (from Op. 76)
(Bote & Bock, Universal Edition; 1 3/4 min., 1 min., 1 min., 1 1/4 min., 1 1/4 min., 2 min., 1 1/2 min., 3/4 min., 1 min., 1 min., 1 1/2 min., 1 1/4 min.)
See: D151, B56, B957

Op. 104 Six Songs for Voice with Piano Accompaniment
Neue Fülle; Warnung; Mutter, tote Mutter; Lied eines Mädchens; Der Sausewind; Mädchenlied
(1907; Otto Forberg, Friedrich Hofmeister; 1 3/4

min., 1 1/2 min., 3 min., 1 1/4 min., 2 min., 3 min.)
See: B1144

Op. 105 Two Sacred Songs for Medium Voice with Organ, Harmonium, or Piano Accompaniment
Ich sehe dich in tausend Bildern; Meine Seele ist still zu Gott
Premiere: Dortmund, May 5, 1910
Fischer-Maretzki and Max Reger
See: B1477, B1590

Op. 106 The 100th Psalm for Mixed Choir, Orchestra, and Organ
(1908-9; Peters, Eulenburg, Wiener Philharmonischer Verlag; 30 min.)
Premiere (of the complete work): Chemnitz, February 23, 1910 St. Lukas Church Choir conducted by Reger
See: D186, B217, B345, B382, B489, B512, B832, B901, B902, B939, B996, B1010, B1207, B1209, B1257, B1326, B1385, B1410, B1413, B1429, B1430, B1442, B1506, B1507, B1530, B1537, B1546, B1578, B1605, B1627, B1634, B1641, B1661, B1665, B1667, B1697, B1712, B1717, B1758, B1759, B1803, B1830

Op. 107 Third Sonata in Bb Major for Clarinet and Piano
(1908-9; Bote & Bock, Universal Edition; 25 min.)
Premiere: Darmstadt, June 9, 1909
Julius Winkler and Max Reger
See: D117, D118, D124, D161, D165, D196, B93, B345, B745, B957, B1356, B1366, B1384, B1419, B1542, B1568, B1569, B1671, B1693, B1740, B1767, B1795, B1825

Op. 108 Symphonic Prologue to a Tragedy in A Minor for Large Orchestra
(1908; Peters; 35 min.)
Premiere: Cologne, March 9, 1909
Fritz Steinbach conducting
See: D188, B76, B145, B345, B362, B507, B801, B901, B916, B931, B972, B976, B1209, B1229, B1441, B1448, B1529, B1666, B1677, B1740, B1756, B1788, B1802, B1823

Op. 109 Fourth String Quartet in Eb Major
(1909; Bote & Bock, Universal Edition, Paynes, Eulenburg; 29 min.)
Premiere: Frankfurt, September 30, 1909
Frankfurter String Quartet
See: D39, D78, D154, D198, B892, B894, B901, B957, B965, B1221, B1239, B1355, B1395, B1451, B1501, B1547, B1569, B1671, B1688, B1740, B1753, B1756, B1785

Op. 110 Sacred Songs for Five-Voice Mixed Choir a cappella

Mein Odem ist schwach; Ach, Herr, strafe mich nicht; O Tod, wie bitter bist du
(1909-12; Bote & Bock; 12 min., 15 min., 8 min.)
Premiere No. 1: Leipzig, Nov. 13, 1909 Thomas Church Choir, Kurt Kranz conducting
Premiere No. 2: Aachen, Dec. 11, 1913 Fritz Busch conducting
Premiere No. 3: Chemnitz, Nov. 10, 1912 Lukas Church Choir, Georg Stolz conducting
See: D7, D13, D89, D99, D120, D136, B76, B961, B1507, B1534, B1755

Op. 111a Three Duets for Soprano and Alto with Piano Accompaniment
Waldesstille; Frühlingsfeier; Abendgang
(1909; Bote & Bock, Universal Edition; 2 min., 2 1/2 min., 3 1/4 min.)
Premiere No. 3: Dresden, October 21, 1908
Sannavan Rhyn, Martha Ruben and Max Reger
See: B1612, B1702

Op. 111b Three Songs for Four-Voice Female Choir a cappella
Im Himmelreich ein Haus steht; Abendgang im Lenz; Er ist's
(1909; Bote & Bock; 1 1/2 min., 1 3/4 min., 2 min.)

Op. 112 Die Nonnen for Mixed Choir and Large Orchestra
(1909; Bote & Bock, Universal Edition, Boston Music Company; 30 min.)
Premiere: Dortmund, May 8, 1910 Dortmunder Musikverein and Philharmonic Orchestra, Julius Janssen conducting
See: B1653, B1671, B1756, B1804

Op. 113 Quartet in D Minor for Violin, Viola, Cello and Piano
(1910; Bote & Bock, Paynes, Eulenburg; 32 min.)
Premiere: Zurich, May 30, 1910 Max Reger, Willem de Boer, Joseph Ebner, and Engelbert Röntgen
See: D100, B1257, B1358, B1372, B1385, B1604, B1688, B1708, B1791, B1796

Op. 114 Concerto in F Minor for Piano and Orchestra
(1910; Bote & Bock; 48 min.)
Premiere: Leipzig, December 15, 1910 Frieda Kwast-Hodapp with the Gewandhaus Orchestra, Arthur Nikisch conducting
See: D19, D87, D91, D98, D106, D113, B76, B424, B901, B972, B1409, B1430, B1478, B1496, B1501, B1516, B1518, B1636, B1675, B1727, B1762, B1789, B1807, B1824

Op. 115 Episoden: Piano Pieces for Adults and Children

(1910; Bote & Bock, Universal Edition; 20 min.)
Premiere: Berlin, November 30, 1910 Max Reger
See: D152, B380, B1569, B1744

Op. 116 Fourth Sonata in A Minor for Cello and Piano
(1910; Peters; 28 min.)
Premiere: Hamburg, January 18, 1911
Jakob Sakom and James Kwast
See: D33, D126, D149, B145, B1338, B1551, B1578, B1607, B1711

Op. 117 Preludes and Fugues, Chaconnes, etc. for Violin Alone
(1909-12; Bote & Bock, Universal Edition, Boston Music Company; 5 1/2 min., 6 min., 6 min., 12 min., 5 1/2 min., 8 min., 6 min., 6 min.)
Premiere No. 3: Berlin, November 30, 1910
Alexander Schmuller
Premiere No. 4: Berlin, October 7, 1910
Gustav Havemann
See: D38, B957, B968, B1577, B1753, B1770, B1839, B1873

Op. 118 Sextet in F Major for 2 Violins, 2 Violas & 2 Cellos
(1910; Bote & Bock; Universal Edition, Paynes, Eulenburg; 34 min.)
Premiere: Leipzig, March 12, 1911 Edgar Wollgandt, Carl Wolschke, Carl Hermann, Friedrich Heintzsch, Julius Klengel, and Emil Robert-Hansen
See: D129, B345, B380, B901, B1359, B1542, B1709

Op. 119 Die Weihe der Nacht for Alto Solo, Male Chorus and Orchestra
(1911; Bote & Bock; 16 min.)
Premiere: Berlin, October 12, 1911 Gertrude Fischer-Maretzki with the Berlin Philharmonic Orchestra, Leonid Kreutzer conducting
See: B76, B362, B1677

Op. 120 Eine Lustspielouvertüre for Orchestra
(1911; Bote & Bock, Eulenburg; 9 min.)
Premiere: Boston, October 6, 1911
Max Fiedler conducting
See: D114, B360, B1209, B1449, B1531, B1547, B1606, B1745, B1805, B1828

Op. 121 Fifth String Quartet in F# Minor
(1911; Peters, Eulenburg; 38 min.)
Premiere: Dresden, October 10, 1911
Böhmische String Quartet
See: D79, D198, B345, B892, B894, B957, B982, B1221, B1329, B1359, B1479, B1569, B1710, B1812, B1872

Op. 122 Eighth Sonata in E Minor for Violin and Piano
(1911; Bote & Bock, Universal Edition; 37 min.)
Premiere: Duisburg, October 3, 1911
Ernst Schmidt and Max Reger
See: B892, B1369, B1436, B1578, B1630, B1664, B1711, B1825, B1840, B1859, B1873

Op. 123 Konzert im alten Stil for Orchestra
(1912; Bote & Bock, Universal Edition, Eulenburg, 21 min.)
Premiere: Frankfurt, October 4, 1912
Willem Mengelberg conducting
See: D108, B362, B896, B901, B972, B1209, B1406, B1481, B1501, B1537, B1538, B1671, B1677, B1682, B1707

Op. 124 An die Hoffnung for Alto (or Mezzo Soprano) with Orchestral or Piano Accompaniment
(1912; Peters; 10 min.)
Premiere: Eisenach, October 12, 1912 Anna Erler-Schnaudt with the Meiningen Hofkapelle Orchestra, Max Reger conducting
See: D102, B76, B901, B1205, B1361, B1428, B1501, B1579, B1620, B1670, B1725, B1743, B1850, B1877

Op. 125 Eine romantische Suite for Large Orchestra
(1912; Bote & Bock, Universal Edition, Eulenburg; 29 min.)
Premiere: Dresden, October 11, 1912
Ernst von Schuh conducting
See: D173, B76, B145, B360, B787, B901, B972, B1209, B1361, B1480, B1532, B1537, B1578, B1678, B1757, B1808, B1826, B1877

Op. 126 Römischer Triumphgesang for Male Chorus and Orchestra
(1912; Bote & Bock, Universal Edition; 12 1/2 min.)
Premiere: Jena, June 6, 1913 Fritz Stein conducting
See: B362, B923, B1622, B1836

Op. 127 Introduction, Passacaglia and Fugue in E Minor for Organ
(1913; Bote & Bock, Universal Edition; 30 min.)
Premiere: Breslau, September 24, 1913 Karl Straube
See: D139, D176, B189, B608, B901, B968, B1420, B1457, B1647, B1668, B1673, B1683, B1697, B1698, B1735

Op. 128 Four Tone Poems for Large Orchestra after Arnold Böcklin (Böcklin Suite)
(1913; Bote & Bock, Universal Edition, Eulenburg; 26 min.)
Premiere: Essen, October 12, 1913

Max Reger conducting
See: D28, D103, B76, B145, B362, B901, B902, B972, B1003, B1407, B1501, B1562, B1576, B1620, B1654, B1677, B1682, B1693, B1718, B1725, B1811, B1876

Op. 129 Nine Pieces for Organ
(1913; Bote & Bock, Universal Edition; 1 3/4 min., 5 min., 2 min., 1 1/2 min., 2 1/2 min., 3 min., 3 min., 1 3/4 min., 3 min.)
See: D40, D139, D177, B555, B1735

Op. 130 Eine Ballettsuite in D Major for Orchestra
(1913; Peters; 20 min.)
Premiere: Breslau, October 30, 1913
Ernst Wendel conducting
See: D108, D157, D195, B518, B896, B972, B1412, B1470, B1472, B1482, B1547, B1555, B1576, B1577, B1591, B1886

Op. 131a Preludes and Fugues for Violin Alone
(1914; Simrock, Peters; 6 min., 6 min., 4 1/2 min., 3 1/2 min., 5 1/2 min., 6 1/2 min.)
See: D146, B221, B763, B1376

Op. 131b Three Duos in the Old Style for Two Violins
(1914; Simrock, Peters; 5 1/2 min., 4 1/4 min., 4 3/4 min.)
See: D197, B221, B763, B965, B1376

Op. 131c Three Suites for Cello Alone
(1915; Simrock, Peters; 9 3/4 min., 16 min., 18 min.)
See: D38, D76, D132, D158, B221, B1542

Op. 131d Three Suites for Viola Alone
(1915; Simrock, Peters; 11 min., 10 1/2 min., 8 min.)
See: D9, D38, D83, D128, D184, B221, B1547, B1569

Op. 132 Variations and Fugue for Orchestra on a Theme of Mozart
(1914; Simrock, Peters; 35 min.)
Premiere: Wiesbaden, January 1, 1915
Max Reger conducting
See: D75, D101, D173, D195, B76, B323, B362, B460, B476, B609, B901, B931, B935, B965, B968, B1209, B1240, B1412, B1428, B1490, B1496, B1501, B1537, B1654, B1677, B1799, B1806, B1812, B1827, B1850, B1861

Op. 132a Variations and Fugue for Two Pianos on a Theme of W.A. Mozart
(1914; Simrock, Peters; 27 min.)
Premiere: Weimar, September 20, 1915

Hermann Keller and Max Reger
See: D121

Op. 133 — Quartet in A Minor for Violin, Viola, Cello & Piano
(1914; Simrock, Eulenburg, Universal Edition, Peters; 30 min.)
Premiere: Leipzig, February 7, 1915 Edgar Wollgandt, Carl Hermann, Julius Klengel, and Max Reger
See: B76, B333, B1471, B1569, B1752, B1855

Op. 134 — Variations and Fugue on a Theme of G.P. Telemann for Piano (2 Hands)
(1914; Simrock, Peters; 35 min.)
Premiere: Berlin, March 10, 1915
Frieda Kwast-Hodapp
See: D121, D164, B284, B904, B968, B1035, B1042, B1547, B1848

Op. 135a — Thirty Small Chorale Preludes for Organ
1. Ach bleib mit deiner Gnade
2. Allein Gott der Höh sei Ehr
3. Alles ist an Gottes Segen
4. Aus tiefer Not schrei ich zu dir
5. Ein' feste Burg ist unser Gott
6. Eins ist Not; ach Herr, dies Eine
7. Es ist das Heil uns kommen her
8. Es ist gewisslich an der Zeit
9. Freu' dich sehr, o meine Seele
10. Grosser Gott, wir loben dich
11. Herr Jesu Christ, dich zu uns wend
12. Jerusalem, du hochgebaute Stadt
13. Jesus, meine Zuversicht
14. Liebster Jesu, wir sind hier
15. Lobe den Herren, den mächtigen König der Ehren
16. Macht hoch die Tür
17. Meinem Jesum lass' ich nicht
18. Nun danket alle Gott
19. O dass ich tausend Zungen hätte
20. O Gott, du frommer Gott
21. O Haupt voll Blut und Wunden
22. O Welt, ich muss dich lassen
23. Valet will ich dir geben
24. Von Himmel hoch, da komm ich her
25. Wachet auf, ruft uns die Stimme
26. Was Gott tut, das ist wohlgetan
27. Was mein Gott will
28. Wer nur den lieben Gott lässt walten
29. Wie schön leucht't uns der Morgenstern
30. Wunderbarer König

(1914; Simrock, Peters)
See: D131, B99, B1668

Op. 135b **Fantasy and Fugue in D Minor for Organ**
(1916; Simrock, Alfred Lengnick & Co., Ltd., Max Eschig & Co., Peters; 15 min.)
Premiere: Hannover, June 11, 1916 Hermann Dettmer
See: D11, D104, D138, B307, B602, B961, B965, B1420

Op. 136 **Hymnus der Liebe for Baritone (or Alto) with Orchestral Accompaniment**
(1914; Simrock, Peters; 12 min.)
Premiere: Jena, June 1918 at the 2nd Reger Festival
See: D102, B76, B1569

Op. 137 **Twelve Sacred Songs for Voice with Piano, Harmonium or Organ Accompaniment**
Bitte um einem seligen Tod; Dein Wille, Herr, geschehe!; Uns ist geboren ein Kindelein; Am Abend; O Herre Gott, nimm du von mir; Christ, deines Geistes Süssigkeit; Grablied; Morgengesang; Lass dich nur nichts nicht dauern; Christkindleins Wiegenlied Klage vor Gottes Leiden; O Jesu Christ, wir warten dein
(1914; Peters)
Premiere Nos. 1, 3, 7 ,9: Hildburghausen, Sept. 20, 1914 Elisabeth Angelroth and Max Reger
Premiere Nos. 2, 4, 11, 12: Meiningen, Nov. 6, 1914 Friedl Hollstein and Max Reger
See: D18, B1590, B1851

Op. 138 **Eight Sacred Songs for Mixed Choir**
Der mensch lebt und bestehet nur eine kleine Zeit; Morgenstern; Nachtlied; Unser lieben Frauen Traum; Kreuzfahrerlied; Das Agnus Dei; Schlachtgesang; Wir glauben an einem Gott
(1914; Simrock, Peters; 2 min., 1 3/4 min., 2 1/2 min., 2 min., 1 3/4 min., 2 min., 1 3/4 min.)
See: D12, D13, D15, D99, D194, B832, B901, B1697

Op. 139 **Ninth Sonata in C Minor for Violin and Piano**
(1914-5; Simrock, Peters; 36 min.)
Premiere: Dortmund, October 6, 1915
Ewald Becker and Max Reger
See: D33, D134, B544, B667, B1198, B1542, B1851

Op. 140 **Eine vaterländische Ouvertüre in F Major for Large Orchestra**
(1914; Simrock, Peters; 14 min.)
Premiere: Wiesbaden, January 8, 1915
Max Reger conducting
See: B513, B901, B1225, B1428, B1434, B1547, B1581, B1800, B1827

Op. 141a **Serenade in G Major for Flute, Violin, and Viola**

(1915; Peters, Payne, Eulenburg; 14 1/2 min.)
See: D26, D110, D116, D124, D165, D197, B1006, B1199, B1707

Op. 141b String Trio in D Minor for Violin, Viola, and Cello
(1915; Peters, Payne, Eulenburg; 19 min.)
Premiere: Munich, Nov, 30, 1915 Hösl Quartet
See: D8, D125, D197, B901, B965, B982, B1006

Op. 142 Five New Children's Songs for High Voice and Piano
Wiegenlied; Schwalbenmütterlein; Maria am Rosenstrauch; Klein Evelinde; Bitte
(1915; Simrock, Peters)

Op. 143 Träume am Kamin: Twelve Small Piano Pieces
(1915; Simrock, Peters; 2-3 min. each)
See: D105, B1163

Op. 144 Two Songs for Mixed Choir and Orchestra
Der Einsiedler; Requiem (Hebbel)
(1915; Simrock, Peters; 12 min., 18 min.)
Premiere: Heidelberg, July 16, 1916
Philipp Wolfrum conducting
See: D194, B76, B657, B901, B1230, B1395, B1501, B1525, B1537, B1569, B1705

Op. 145a Requiem (unfinished)
See: D187, B657, B727, B1885

Op. 145 Seven Organ Pieces
(1915-6; H. Oppenheimer, Breitkopf & Härtel; 12 min., 8 min., 7 min., 7 1/2 min., 3 min., 5 min., 7 min.)
See: D50, D155, D181, D182, D192, B657, B1315, B1342, B1590

Op. 146 Quintet in A Major for Clarinet and String Quartet
(1915-6; Simrock, Peters, Eulenburg)
Premiere: Stuttgart, November 6, 1916
Wendling Quartet
See: D2, D31, D36, D81, D96, D197, B266, B333, B345, B657, B745, B896, B901, B1010, B1190, B1210, B1395, B1471, B1472, B1501, B1722, B1753

(Op. 147) Andante and Rondo for Violin and Small Orchestra
(incomplete work)
See: B76, B262, B657, B694

Op. 1913 Sylvester-Canonen
(1913; from the Programbook of the Meiningen Music Days 1913)

Op. 17523 Ewig Dein!: Salon Piece for Piano

(1907; appeared in Die Musik 7:1 (1907)
See: B315

Works without Opus Numbers

No. 1 Liebestraum for String Orchestra (Lyrisches Andante)
(1898; P.J. Tonger; 3 min.)
See: D152, B1508

No. 2 Scherzino for String Orchestra and Horn
(1899; Breitkopf & Härtel; 2 min.)
See: D3, B1723

No. 3 Jugendquartett in D Minor for String Quartet
(1888; Breitkopf & Härtel; 24 min.)
See: D154, B281

No. 4 Quintet (Posthumous) for String Quartet and Piano
(1897-8; Schott, Eulenburg; 33 min.)
See: B6, B280, B1365, B1758

No. 5 Muzio Clementi Op. 36: Six Sonatinas for Piano with Additional Violin Part
(1895; Augener, Schott, Max Escher)

No. 6 Romanze in G Major for Piano and Violin
(1902; Carl Grüninger, Breitkopf; 1 1/2 min.)
See: B1368

No. 7 Petite Caprice in G Minor for Violin and Piano
(1902; Otto Junne, E. Hoffmann; 1 min.)

No. 8 Allegro in A Major for Two Violins
(1914; Tischer & Jagenberg; 5 min.)
See: D197, B244

No. 9 Prelude and Fugue in A Minor for Violin Alone
(1902; Otto Junne, E. Hoffmann; 5 1/2 min.)

No. 10 Präludium in E Minor for Violin Alone
(1915; Simrock, Peters; 2 min.)

No. 11 Caprice for Cello and Piano in A Minor
(1901; Otto Junne, E. Hoffmann; 1 1/2 min.)
See: D154

No. 12 Allegretto grazioso in A Major for Flute and Piano
(1902; Otto Junne, E. Hoffmann; 2 min.)

No. 13 Albumblatt in Eb Major and Tarantella in G Major for Clarinet and Piano
(1902; E. Hoffmann, Otto Junne; 4 min.)
See: D154, D196

No. 14 Canons for Piano in All the Major and Minor Keys
(1894-5; Augener, Schott)

No. 15 Six Piano Pieces ("Grüsse an die Jugend")
(1898; Breitkopf & Härtel; 20 min.)

No. 16 Miniature Gavotte for Piano
(1898)

No. 17 Four Piano Pieces
(1901-6; E. Hoffmann, O. Junne; 7 min.)

No. 18 An die schönen blauen Donau: Improvisation for Piano (2 Hands) on a Waltz of Johann Strauss
(1898; Peters; 7 1/2 min.)
See: D68, B1374

No. 19 Albumblatt for Piano
(1899)

No. 20 Blätter und Blüten: Twelve Piano Pieces
(1900-2; Paul Zschocher, Breitkopf & Härtel; 20 min.)
See: B1375, B1601, B1613

No. 21 Five Special Studies for Piano (after Chopin)
(1899; Joseph Aibl, Universal Edition; 11 min.)
See: B1396, B1643, B1776

No. 22 Four Special Studies for the Left Hand Alone for Piano
(1901; Joseph Aibl, Universal Edition; 9 min.)
See: D68

No. 23 In der Nacht for Piano
(1902; Fritz Schuberth; 4 min.)
See: B1619

No. 24 Perpetuum mobile in C# Minor for Piano (2 Hands)
(1905; C.F. Kahnt; 1 min.)
See: D68

No. 25 Scherzo in F# Minor for Piano (2 Hands)
(1906; C.F. Kahnt; 2 1/4 min.)
See: D68

No. 26 Caprice in F# Minor for Piano
(1906; Bard, Marquardt, Kistner & Siegel; 40 sec.)

See: D68

No. 27 Fughette on a German Song
(1916; Deutsche Verlagstalt)

No. 28 Introduction and Passacaglia in D Minor for Organ
(1899; Breitkopf & Härtel; 6 min.)
See: D111, D163

No. 29 Organ Prelude in C Minor
(1900; 1 min.)

No. 30 Variations and Fugue on the English National Anthem for Organ
(1901; Joseph Aibl, Universal Edition; 7 1/2 min.)

No. 31 Prelude and Fugue in D Minor for Organ
(1902; E. Hoffmann, Otto Junne; 5 1/2 min.)

No. 32 Postlude in D Minor
(1903; 2 min.)

No. 33 Schule des Triospiels: J.S. Bach's Two-Part Inventions arranged for Organ by Max Reger and Karl Straube
(1903; Lauterbach & Kuhn, Bote & Bock, Universal Edition)
See: B845,B1464

No. 34 Romanze in A Minor for Harmonium
(1904; M.I. Schramm, Carl Simon, Peters; 3 min.)

No. 35 Prelude and Fugue in G# Minor for Organ
(1906; Otto Junne; 5 1/2 min.)
See: D63

No. 36 Prelude and Fugue in F# Minor
(1912; Bote & Bock; 4 1/2 min.)
See: D63

No. 37 "O Traurigkeit, o Herzelied" for Organ
(1893; Allgemeine Musik-Zeitung 22:6 (1894)

No. 38 "Komm, süsser Tod" for Organ
(1894; Augener, Schott)
See: B1473

No. 39 "Wer weiss, wie nahe mir mein Ende" for Organ
(1900; Monatsschrift für Gottesdienst und kirchliche Kunst 5:11 (1900): 344.)

No. 40 "Christ ist erstanden von dem Tod" for Organ

(1901; Monatsschrift für Gottesdienst und kirchliche Kunst 6:4 (1901): 144.)

No. 41 "Mit Fried und Freud ich fahr dahin" for Organ
(1902; Monatsschrift für Gottesdienst und kirchliche Kunst 7:2 (1902): 69.)

No. 42 "O wie selig ihr doch, ihr Frommen" for Organ
(1902; Monatsschrift für Gottesdienst und kirchliche Kunst 7:11 (1902): 351.)

No. 43 "Jesus ist kommen, Grund ewiger Freude" for Organ
(1902; Monatsschrift für Gottesdienst und kirchliche Kunst 8:1 (1903): 37.)

No. 44 "O Haupt voll Blut und Wunden" for Organ
(1904; Breitkopf & Härtel)
See: B1345, B1395, B1463, B1736, B1829

No. 45 "Es kommt ein Schiff geladen" for Organ
(1905; Monatsschrift für Gottesdienst und kirchliche Kunst 10:11 (1905): 347.

No. 46 "Wie schön leucht't uns der Morgenstern" for Organ
(1909; E. Crusius)

No. 47 Chorale Cantatas for the Major Festivals of the Protestant Church Year
(1903-5; Lauterbach & Kuhn, Bote & Bock, Associated Music Publishers, Peters)
See: B1524, B1814, B1829

No. 48 Weihegesang for Alto Solo, Mixed Choir and Wind Orchestra
(1908; Bote & Bock; 10 min.)

No. 49 Totenfeier (unfinished Requiem) in D Minor for Four Solo Voices, Four-Voice Mixed Choir, Organ and Orchestra
(1914; Breitkopf & Härtel; 22 min.)

No. 50 Tantum ergo Sacramentum for Five-Voice Mixed Choir
(1895; Breitkopf & Härtel; 2 min.)

No. 51 Gloriabuntur for Four-Voice Choir a cappella
(1898)

No. 52 "Maria Himmelsfreud!" for Four-Voice Choir a cappella
(1899 or 1900)

No. 53 Palm Sunday Morning for Five-Voice Mixed Choir a cappella

(1902; Joseph Aibl, Universal Edition; 5 1/2 min.)
See: D194

No. 54 Easter Motet: "Lasset uns den Herren preisen" for Five-Voice Mixed Choir
(1911; Breitkopf & Härtel)
See: D194

No. 55 Abschiedslied for Four-Voice Mixed Choir a cappella
(1914; 3 min.)

No. 56 Two Sacred Songs for Medium Voice and Organ
Wenn in bangen trüben Stunden; Heimweh
(1900; Joseph Aibl, Universal Edition, Breitkopf & Härtel; 3 1/2 min., 4 min.)

No. 57 "Befiehl dem Herrn deine Wege" for Soprano and Alto with Organ Accompaniment
(1902; E. Hoffmann, Otto Junne)

No. 58 "Wohl denen" for Medium Voice with Organ Accompaniment
(1903; Lauterbach & Kuhn, Bote & Bock; 3 min.)

No. 59 "Ehre sei Gott der Höhe" for Voice with Piano, Harmonium or Organ Accompaniment
(1905; Breitkopf & Härtel; 7 1/2 min.)

No. 60 "Es soll mein Gebet dich tragen" for Medium Voice and Piano
(1893-4; Bote & Bock)

No. 61 "Am Meer!" for Voice with Piano Accompaniment
(1894; Breitkopf & Härtel)

No. 62 "In verschwiegener Nacht" for Voice with Piano Accompaniment
(1898; Constantin Wild, Breitkopf & Härtel)

No. 63 "Wiegenlied" for Medium Voice with Piano Accompaniment
(1898; G. Taubald, Bote & Bock)

No. 64 Two Songs for Voice with Piano Accompaniment
Der Tod, das ist die kühle Nacht, Letzte Bitte
(1899; Edition Steingräber)

No. 65 "Liebeslieder" for Voice and Piano
(1900-2; Paul Zschocher, Breitkopf)

No. 66 "Tragt, blaue Träume" for Medium Voice and Piano
(1901; E. Hoffmann, Otto Junne)

No. 67 "Ostern" for Medium Voice and Piano
(1902; E. Hoffmann, Otto Junne)

No. 68 "Nun kommt die Nacht gegangen" for Medium Voice and Piano
(1903; Lauterbach & Kuhn, Bote & Bock)

No. 69 "Der Maien ist gestorben" for Voice with Piano Accompaniment
(1906; Vobach, Kistner & Siegel)

No. 70 "Abendfrieden" for Medium Voice and Piano
(1906; C.F. Kahnt)

No. 71 "Der Dieb" for Voice and Piano
(1906; Vobach)

No. 72 "In der Frühe" for Voice and Piano
(1908; Robert Forberg, Peters)

No. 73 "An Zeppelin" for Voice and Piano
(1909; Bote & Bock)
See: B1612, B1652

No. 74 Wiegenlied for Voice with Piano Accompaniment
(1909; Peters)

No. 75 Three Songs after Poems of Elsa von Asenijeff for Voice and Piano
Klage; An eine Mutter; Am selliedchen
(1912; Bote & Bock)

No. 76 Dies irae (2nd movement of incomplete Requiem Op. 145a for Solo Voices, Four-Voice Mixed Choir, Organ and Orchestra
Shigihara, Reger-Bibliographie, p. 94
See: D187, B1742, B1885

No. 77 Early Songs
Shigihara, Reger-Bibliographie, p. 94

No. 78 Pantalon, Original Fourth Movement of Op. 130
Shigihara, Reger-Bibliographie, p. 94
B518

No. 79 Prelude and Fugue in G Minor for Piano
Shigihara, Reger-Bibliographie, p. 94

No. 80 Twenty Responsories for Four-Voice Mixed Choir a cappella
Shigihara, Reger-Bibliographie, p. 94
See: D194, B452, B453

No. 81 Serenade Movement for Winds
Shigihara, Reger-Bibliographie, p. 94

No. 82 Vater unser for Twelve-Voice Choir a cappella
Shigihara, Reger-Bibliographie, p. 94
See: B443, B832, B1778

Publishers

Associated Music Publishers, Inc.
24 E. 22 St.
New York, NY 10010
[agent for Bote & Bock, Breitkopf & Härtel,
F.E.C. Leuckart, Tischer & Jagenberg]

Augener, Ltd.
Acton Lane
London, W4, England

Boston Music Co.
116 Boylston St.
Boston, Mass. 02116

Edition Peters
C.F. Peters Corp.
373 Park Ave, S.
New York, NY 10016
[agent for Eulenberg, Forberg, Kahnt]

Edition Steingraber
100 Seeburgstrasse
Leipzig, E. Germany

European American Music Distributors Corp.
P.O. Box 850
Valley Forge, PA 19482
[agent for Schott and Universal Edition]

Otto Junne
3 Egelstrasse
Leipzig, E. Germany

Kistner & Siegel
Dörrienstrasse 13
Leipzig, E. Germany

H. Oppenheimer
Bäckerstrasse 58
Hameln, W. Germany

Bartholf Senff
Leipzig, E. Germany

Carl Simon
Steglitzer Strasse 35
Berlin, W. Germany

Simrock
Taubchenweg 20
Leipzig, E. Germany

Discography (D1-D198)

This list includes all commercially-produced discs, whether or not currently available. The list is arranged alphabetically by record company and includes serial numbers, titles, solo performers, performing ensembles, and conductors. Titles of a specific nature are given in the original language; generic titles are given in English (e.g., sonata, concerto, etc.). Specific titles conform to the works list in the New Grove Dictionary of Music and Musicians.

D1 Angel 35687: Fantasia on the Chorale "Hallelujah! Gott zu loben", Op. 52/3; Fernando Germani, organ

D2 Angel RL-32130: Quintet in A for Clarinet and Strings; Gervase de Peyer, clarinet with the Melos Ensemble

D3 ARA 8084/9084: Scherzino for Horn and Strings; Munich Philharmonic Orchestra, Marinus Voorberg conducting

D4 Argo ZRG 5420: Organ Mass, Op. 59: Toccata and Fugue, Nos. 5 & 6; Chorale Fantasia, Op. 40, No. 2; Simon Preston, organ

D5 Arp-Schnitger-Records ASR 00021-00025: Reger Organ Works; Heinz Wunderlich, organ [The beginning of a complete set of recordings of Reger's organ works]

D6 ArtDir 20: Variations and Fugue on a Theme of J.S. Bach, Op. 81; Gunnar Johansen, piano

D7 Bärenreiter BM 30 L 1309: Geistliche Gesänge, Op. 110; N.C.R.V. Vocal Ensemble of Hilversum, Marinus Voorberg conducting

D8 BASF KBB 21642: String Trios, Opp. 77b and 141b; New String Trio

D9 BIS 81: Suite No. 1 in G Minor, Op. 131d for viola unaccompanied; Zahari Tchavdarov, viola

D10 BIS 193: Prelude in d for Organ Op. 65; Anders Bondeman, organ

D11 BIS 242: Ave Maria, Op. 80/5; Benedictus, Op. 59/9; Fantasia & Fugue on B-A-C-H, Op. 46; Fantasia & Fugue in d, Op. 135b; Lionel Rogg, organ

D12 Calig 30420: Acht geistliche Gesänge, Op. 138; Der Palestrina-Singkreis

D13 Camerata CM 17004: 2 Motets from Op. 138; Motet, Op. 110/3; Choir of the South German Rundfunks, Hermann Joseph Dahmen conducting

D14 Cantate 642 228: Wachet auf! ruft uns die Stimme, Op. 52/2; Prelude in E Major, Op. 56/1; Hans Klotz, organ

D15 Cantate 643 213: 5 Motets from Op. 138; Bremer Domchor, Hans Heintze conducting

D16 Cantate CAN 1128K: Toccata and Fugue in E, Op. 65/ 11 & 12; Toccata and Fugue in A Minor. Op. 80/11 & 12; Friedrich Högner, organ

D17 Cantate T 72 704 K: Chorale Cantatas and Sacred Lieder from Op. 137; Lisa Schwarzeller, soprano; Gustav Banze, tenor; Choir of the Evangelische Kirchenmusikschule, Werner Bieske conducting

D18 Cantate T 72 706 K: Hallelujah, Gott zu loben, Op. 52/3; Wie schön leucht't uns der Morgenstern, Op. 40/1; Richard Voge, organ

D19 CBS S 72402: Concerto for Piano & Orchestra in F Minor, Op. 114; Rudolf Serkin, piano with the Philadelphia Orchestra, Eugene Ormandy conducting

D20 Christophorus SCGLP 75879/80: see Musical Heritage Society MHS 1360/1361

D21 Christophorus SCGLP 75905: Symphonic Fantasia & Fugue, Op. 57; Canzone from Op. 65; Werner Jacob, organ

D22 Christophorus SCGLX 75928: Introduction, Variations & Fugue on an Original Theme in F# Minor, Op. 73; Organ Mass, Op. 59; Chorale Preludes, Op. 79; Werner Jacob, organ

D23 Christophorus SCGLX 75942: see Musical Heritage Society MHS 1563/66

D24 Christophorus SCK 70332: see Musical Heritage Society MHS 1567/70

D25 Christophorus SCLGL 73733: Prelude & Fugue in F Major, Op. 85/3; Hans Jakob Haller, organ

D26 Claves D-8104: Serenades in D & G for Flute, Violin & Viola, Opp. 77a, 141a; Peter-Lukas Graf, flute; Rainer Moog, viola; Sandor Vègh, violin

D27 Claves D-8502: Lyrisches Andante for String Orch.; Neuss Chamber Orchestra, Johannes Goritzki conducting

D28 Colosseum MST 511: 4 Tondichtungen nach Arnold Böcklin, Op. 128; 3 Pieces from Op. 59; Nürnberg Symphony Orchestra, Erich Kloss conducting; Rudolf Zartner, organ

D29 Colosseum MST 512: Variations & Fugue on a Theme of Beethoven; Nürnberg Symphony Orchestra, Erich Kloss conducting (1915 orchestral version)

D30 Colosseum MST 514: Concerto in A for Violin & Orch., Op. 101; Yuuko Shiokawa, Nürnberg Symphony Orchestra, Erich Kloss conducting

D31 Colosseum SMC 80 904: Clarinet Quintet in A Major, Op. 146; Heinrich Geuser, clarinet; Heutling Quartet

D32 Columbia C 80 666: Prelude in F Major, Op. 85/3; Romanze in A Minor, Op. 80/8; Moment musicale in D Major, Op. 69/4; Melodia in B Major, Op. 59/11; Fugue in G Major, Op. 56/3; 3 Chorale Preludes from Op. 67/20, 52, 33; Canzone in Eb Major, Op. 65/9; Benedictus, Op. 59/9; 3 Chorale Preludes from Op. 67/45, 50, 23; Max Reger, organ [from the series "Unvergänglich--unvergessen", Set 123]

D33 Columbia M 32221: Sonata in C Minor, Op. 139; Sonata in A Minor, Op. 116; Pina Camirelli, violin; Mischa Schneider, cello; Rudolf and Peter Serkin, piano

D34 CRA 777MPS: Lyrisches Andante for String Orchestra; Grosses Orchestra, Willi Stech conducting

D35 Crystal 334: Sonata No. 2 in F# Minor for Clarinet & Piano, Op. 49/2; John Russo, clarinet; Lydia Walton Ignacio, piano

D36 Da Camera 92702: Clarinet Quintet in A Major, Op. 146; Rudolf Gall, clarinet; The Keller Quartet

D37 Da Camera 92703: see Musical Heritage Society MHS 1867

D38 Da Camera 92704: Suite in the Old Style for Violin & Piano in F Major, Op. 93; 3 Pieces, Op. 79d; Prelude and Fugue for Solo Violin, Op. 117/7; Suite for Solo Violin in G Minor, Op. 131d/1; Suite for Solo Cello in G Major, Op. 131c/1; The Keller Quartet

D39 Da Camera 92705: String Quartet No. 4 in Eb Major, Op. 109; String Trio in A Minor, Op. 77b; The Keller Quartet

D40 Da Camera 92706: Max Reger: Orgelwerke I: Opp. 63/8; 56/3; 80/7; 129/1, 2, 4, 7; 85/3; Heinz Lohmann, organ

D41 Da Camera SM 92710: see Musical Heritage Society MHS 1329

D42 Da Camera SM 92724: see Musical Heritage Society MHS 1378

D43 Da Camera 92808: see Musical Heritage Society MHS 1402

D44 Da Camera 93108: see Musical Heritage Society MHS 1268

D45 Da Camera 93109: see Musical Heritage Society MHS 1292

D46 Da Camera 93212: see Musical Heritage Society MHS 1510 [Max Reger: Orgelwerke II]

D47 Da Camera 93221: see Musical Heritage Society MHS 1463 [Max Reger: Orgelwerke III]

D48 Da Camera 93222: see Musical Heritage Society MHS 1464 [Max Reger: Orgelwerke IV]

D49 Da Camera 93228: Max Reger: Orgelwerke V: Op. 85 & Preludes and Fugues in F# Minor & G# Minor; Heinz Lohmann, organ

D50 Da Camera 93239: Max Reger: Orgelwerke VI: Op. 145; Heinz Lohmann, organ

D51 Da Camera 93708: see Musical Heritage Society MHS 1465

D52 Da Camera SM 93807: see Musical Heritage Society MHS 1389

D53 Da Camera MRK 19731: Kammermusik I; Keller Quartet; Pfeifer Quartet; Hoppstock Trio; Ernst Wallfisch, viola; Lory Wallfisch, Peter Schmalfuss, Werner Genuit, pianos

D54 Da Camera MRK 19732: Kammermusik II; Philipp Nägele & Sandor Karolyi, violins; Richard Laugs, piano; Elisabeth Schwarz, piano

D55 Da Camera MRK 19733: Kammermusik III; Tel Aviv Quartet; Keller Quartet; Pfeifer Quartet; Quatuor Elysèen; Karolyi Trio; Keller Trio; Pina Camirelli & Philipp Nägele, violins

D56 Da Camera MRK 19734: Klavierwerke I; Aloys and Alfons Kontarsky, K.H. and M. Schlüter, Hugo Steurer, and Richard Laugs, pianos

D57 Da Camera MRK 19735: Klavierwerke II; Richard Laugs and Wilfried Kassebaum, piano

D58 Da Camera MRK 19736: Orgelwerke I; Heinz Lohmann, organ

D59 Da Camera MRK 19737: Orgelwerke II; Heinz Lohmann, organ

D60 Da Camera Magna 92712: see Musical Heritage Society MHS 1321

D61 Da Camera Magna 92713: see Musical Heritage Society MHS 1353

D62 Da Camera Magna 92724: see Musical Heritage Society MHS 1378

D63 Da Camera Magna 93228: 4 Preludes & Fugues, Op. 85; Preludes & Fugues (F# Minor & G# Minor), No Op.; Heinz Lohmann, organ

D64 Da Camera Magna 93807: see Musical Heritage Society MHS 1389

D65 Da Camera Magna 92904: see Musical Heritage Society MHS 1521

D66 Da Camera Magna 93122: see Musical Heritage Society MHS 1487

D67 Da Camera Magna 931123: 4 Sonatinas, Op. 89; Wilfried Kassebaum, piano

D68 Da Camera Magna SM 93131: "An die schönen blauen Donau"; Etude Brillante in C Minor; Caprice Fantastique in F# Minor; Four Special Studies for the Left Hand Alone; Improvisation in C Minor; Perpetuum mobile in C Major; Scherzo in F# Minor; Perpetuum mobile in C# Minor; Hans-Dieter Bauer, piano

D69 Da Camera Magna 93309: see Musical Heritage Society MHS 1500

D70 Da Camera Magna 93311: see Musical Heritage Society MHS 1667

D71 Da Capo C 053 28925: Max Reger Plays His Own Organ Works; Opp. 56/3; 59/9 & 11; 65/9; 67, 20, 23, 33, 45, 50, & 52; 69/4; 80/6; 85/3; Max Reger, Welte player-organ

D72 Danacord DACO-225: Sonata in E Minor for Piano, Op. 89/1; Niels Viggo Bentzon, piano

D73 Deutsche Grammophon LPEM 19090: 8 Lieder; Walther Ludwig, tenor; Walter Bohle, piano

D74 Deutsche Grammophon 18074 LPM: Variations & Fugue on a Theme of J.A.Hiller, Op. 100; Berlin Philharmonic Orchestra, Paul van Kempen conducting

D75 Deutsche Grammophon 18375 LPM: Variations & Fugue on a Theme of Mozart, Op. 132; Berlin Philharmonic Orchestra, Karl Böhm conducting

D76 Deutsche Grammophon 138890: Suite No. 3 for Solo Cello in A Minor, Op. 131c/3; Anja Thauer, cello

D77 Deutsche Grammophon 139127: 21 Lieder; Dietrich Fischer-Dieskau, baritone; Günther Weissenborn, piano

D78 Deutsche Grammophon 139438: String Quartet No. 2 in A Major, Op. 54/2; String Quartet No. 4 in Eb Major, Op. 109; Drolc Quartet

D79 Deutsche Grammophon 2530081: String Quartet No. 1 in G Major, Op. 54/1; String Quartet in F# Minor, Op. 121; Drolc Quartet

D80 Deutsche Grammophon 2530179: String Quartet No. 3 in D Minor. Op. 74; Drolc Quartet

D81 Deutsche Grammophon 2530 303: Quartet for Clarinet & Strings, Op. 146; Karl Leister, clarinet; Drolc Quartet

D82 Dover Publ. HCR-ST-7016: 3 Sonatas for Solo Violin, Op. 91/1, 3, 7; Hyman Bress, violin

D83 Dynamic 4000: Suites (3) for Viola Unaccompanied, Op. 131d; L. A. [=Luigi Alberto] Bianchi, viola

D84 Educational Music Service (Roncorp, Inc.) EMS-026: Clarinet Sonata in Ab Major, Op. 49/1; John Mohler, clarinet [cassette only]

D85 Electrola 1 C 053-28000: String Trio in A Minor, Op. 77b; Philharmonic Soloists of Berlin

D86 Electrola 1 C 053-28925: Max Reger spielt eigene Werke auf der Welte-Orgel [see Da Capo C 053 28925]

D87 Electrola 1 C 053-28929: Op. 114; Erik Thenbergh, piano; Südwestfunk-Orchester, Hans Rosbaud conducting

D88 Electrola C 063-28508: Toccata & Fugue in A Minor, Op. 80/11 & 12; Walther R. Schuster, organ

D89 Electrola C 153-29916/19: 3 Motets, Op. 110/1-3; Rundfunk Choir of Stockholm, Eric Ericson conducting

D90 Electrola E 60749: Halleluja, Gott zu loben, Op. 52/3; Fernando Germani, organ

D91 Electrola E 80439: Concerto for Piano & Orchestra in F Minor, Op. 114; Erik Thenbergh, piano; Südwestfunk-Orchester of Baden-Baden, Hans Rosbaud conducting

D92 Electrola SHZE 281: Op. 76/52 "Maria Wiegenlied"; Irmgard Seefried, soprano; Wolfgang Schneiderhan, violin; Orchestra of the Bavarian State Opera, Robert Heger conducting

D93 Electrola SMC 80376: Schlichte Weisen, Op. 76/3 "Waldeinsamkeit"; Christa Ludwig, mezzo-soprano; Gerald Moore, piano

D94 Electrola SMC 80976: Der Brief (lied); Christa Ludwig, mezzo-soprano; Gerald Moore, piano

D95 Electrola STE 91334: Variations & Fugue on a Theme of J.A. Hiller, Op. 100; Gewandhaus Orchestra, Franz Konwitschny conducting

D96 EMI SMC 80904: Clarinet Quintet, Op. 146; Heinrich Geuser, clarinet; Heutling Quartet

D97 EMI Odeon C053-28000: String Trio, Op. 77b; Philharmonische Soloisten Berlin [see Electrola 1 C 053-28000]

D98 EMI Odeon C053-28929: see Electrola E 80439

D99 EMI Odeon C063-29081: Geistliche Gesänge, Op. 138; Motets, Op. 110/2 & 3; Stockholm Radio Chorus, Eric Ericson conducting

D100 EMI Odeon C063-29097: String Quartet No. 5; Heutling Quartet

D101 Eurodisc 80 276 LK: Variations and Fugue on a Theme of Mozart, Op. 132; Sächsische Staatskapelle of Dresden, Heinz Bongartz conducting

D102 Eurodisc 80 548 KK: An die Hoffnung (Hölderlin), Op. 124; Hymnus der Liebe (Jacobowski). Op. 136; Annelies Burmeister, alto; Rundfunk Sinfonieorchester Leipzig, Heinz Bongartz conducting

D103 Eurodisc 85 125 KK: 4 Tondichtungen nach Arnold Böcklin, Op. 128; Walter Harwich, violin; Dresden Philharmonic Orchestra, Heinz Bongartz conducting

D104 Eurodisc 86 310 KK: Opp. 46, 135b. 58; Ivan Sokol, organ

D105 Eurodisc 86 474 KK: Variations and Fugue on a Theme of J.S. Bach, Op. 81; Träume am Kamin, Op. 143/1, 3, 4, 7, & 10; Dieter Zechlin, piano

D106 Eurodisc 86 475 KK: Concerto, Op. 114; Amadeus Webersinke, piano; Dresden Philharmonic Orchestra, Gunther Herbig conducting

D107 Eurodisc 86 489 XLK: Chorale Fantasias: Opp. 27, 30, 40/1 & 2; 52/1-3; 59/12; and 79b/1, 4, 6, & 9; Wilhelm Krumbach, organ

D108 Eurodisc 86 535 XEK: Sinfonietta in A Major, Op. 90; Konzert im alten Stil in F, Op. 123; Eine Ballett-suite, Op. 130; Günter Siering, Karl Suske, Heinz Schunk, violins; Dresden Philharmonic Orchestra, Heinz Bongartz conducting; Staatskapelle Berlin, Otmar Suitner conducting

D109 Garnet G 40 125: Introduction, Passacaglia and Fugue in B Minor. Op. 96; Max Martin Stein & Hansjörg von Löw, piano

D110 Gasparo 224: Serenade in G for Flute, Violin, & Viola, Op. 141a; Suite in A Minor for Flute & Piano, Op. 103a; Robert Willoughby, flute; Marilyn McDonald, violin; John Tartaglia, violin; Wilbur Price, piano

D111 Gothic 38210: Introduction & Passacaglia in D Minor for Organ; Donald Sutherland, organ

D112 Gothic 118316: Chorale Fantasia: "Wie schön leucht uns der Morgenstern", Op. 40/1; Douglas Major, organ

D113 Leonarda 113: Concerto in F Minor for Piano; Steven Mayer, piano; Hague Philharmonic Orchestra, Ernest Bour conducting

D114 LOU 734: Eine Lustspielouvertüre, Op. 120; Louisville Orchestra, Jorge Mester conducting

D115 Lyrichord LLST 7121: Introduction, Variations and Fugue, Op. 73; Toccata and Fugue in A Minor, Op. 80b; Organ Mass, Op. 59: Benedictus and Melodia, Nos. 9 & 11; Robert Noehren, organ

D116 Lyrichord LLST 7217: Serenades, Opp. 77a and 141a; John Wion, flute; Stanley Ritchie, violin; Laurance Fader, viola

D117 Mark Educational Recordings MMF 3366: Sonatas, Op. 49/1 and Op. 107; Herbert Tichman, clarinet; Ruth Tichman, piano

D118 Marlboro 12: Sonata No. 3 in Bb for Clarinet & Piano, Op. 107; David Singer, clarinet; Rudolf Serkin, piano

D119 MPS 2020765-1: Opp. 65:II/7 & 8; 80:II/8; Konrad Philipp Schuba, organ

D120 MPS CRO 833: 3 Motets, Op. 110; Junge Kantorei Darmstadt, Joachim Martini conducting

D121 Musical Heritage Society MHS 1268: Variations and Fugue on a Theme of Telemann, Op. 134; Variations and Fugue on a Theme of Mozart, Op. 132a; Alfons & Aloys Kontarsky, Hugo Steurer, piano

D122 Musical Heritage Society MHS 1292: Variations and Fugue on a Theme of Beethoven, Op. 86; Introduction, Passacaglia, and Fugue in B Minor, Op. 96; Alfons & Aloys Kontarsky, piano

D123 Musical Heritage Society MHS 1321: Trio in E Minor, Op. 102; Sandor Karolyi, violin; Uwe Zipperling, cello; Werner Hoppstock, piano

D124 Musical Heritage Society MHS 1329: Serenade, Op. 141a; Allegretto grazioso for flute & piano; Clarinet Sonata in Bb Major, Op. 107; Werner Richter, flute; Sandor Karolyi, violin; Hans Eurich, viola; Wendelin Gärtner, clarinet; Richard Laugs, piano

D125 Musical Heritage Society MHS 1353: Serenade Op. 77a; String Trio, Op. 141b; Werner Richter, flute; Sandor Karolyi, violin; Hans Eurich, viola; Uwe Zipperling, cello

D126 Musical Heritage Society MHS 1360/1: Sonatas in F Minor, Op. 5; G Minor, Op. 28; F Major, Op. 78; A Minor, Op. 116; Ludwig Hoelscher, cello; Karl Heinz Lautner, piano

D127 Musical Heritage Society MHS 1378: Piano Quartet in C Minor, Op. 64; String Quartet No. 2 in A Major, Op. 54/2; Peter Schmalfuss, piano; Pfeiffer Quartet

D128 Musical Heritage Society MHS 1389: Trio in B Minor, Op. 2; Three Suites for Solo Viola, Op. 131d; Philipp Nägele, violin; Ernst Wallfisch, viola; Lory Wallfisch, piano

D129 Musical Heritage Society MHS 1402: String Sextet in F Major, Op. 118; Wührer String Sextet

D130 Musical Heritage Society MHS 1463: Fantasia and Fugue on B-A-C-H, Op. 46; Introduction and Passacaglia in D Minor; Suite in G Minor, Op. 92; Heinz Lohmann, organ

D131 Musical Heritage Society MHS 1464: Thirty Chorale Preludes, Op. 135a; Heinz Lohmann, organ

D132 Musical Heritage Society MHS 1465: Three Suites, Op. 131c; Zoltan Racz, cello

D133 Musical Heritage Society MHS 1487: Pièces pittoresques, Op. 34; Six Burlesques, Op. 58; Six Pieces, Op. 94; Karl-Heinz & Michael Schlüter, piano

D134 Musical Heritage Society MHS 1500: Little Sonata in D Minor, Op. 103b/1; Sonata, Op. 139; Stanley Weiner, violin; Giselle de Moulin, piano

D135 Musical Heritage Society MHS 1510: Variations and Fugue, Op. 73; Fantasia and Fugue, Op. 29; Heinz

Lohmann, piano

D136 Musical Heritage Society MHS 1519: 3 Motets, Op. 110; N.C.V.R. Vocal Ensemble, Marinus Voorberg conducting

D137 Musical Heritage Society MHS 1521: Sonatas in Ab, Op. 49/1 & F Minor, Op. 49/2; Dieter Klöcker, clarinet; Werner Genuit, piano

D138 Musical Heritage Society MHS 1563/66: Selected Organ Works, Vol. I: Opp/ 27; 40/1 & 2; 52/2; 46; 57; 59/7-9; 63/5, 6, & 9; 73; 79b/4-6; & 135b; Werner Jacob, organ

D139 Musical Heritage Society MHS 1567/70: Selected Organ Works, Vol. II: Opp. 29; 30; 52/1 & 3; 33/2; 60; 67/3 & 5; 127; & 129/1, 6, & 2; Werner Jacob, organ

D140 Musical Heritage Society MHS 1604/7: Introduction to the Organ: Second Organ Sonata in D Minor, Op. 60; "O Gott, du frommer Gott", Op. 67; Heinz Wunderlich, organ

D141 Musical Heritage Society MHS 1618: Twenty German Dances, Op. 10a; Six Waltzes, Op. 22; Karl-Heinz & Michael Schlüter, piano

D142 Musical Heritage Society MHS 1619: Waltz-Caprices, Op. 9; Karl-Heinz & Michael Schlüter, piano

D143 Musical Heritage Society MHS 1620/22: Aus meinem Tagebuch, Op. 82; Richard Laugs, piano

D144 Musical Heritage Society MHS 1667: Sonata in F# Minor, Op. 84; Suite in A Minor, Op. 103a; Stanley Weiner, violin; Giselle de Moulin, piano

D145 Musical Heritage Society MHS 1697 & 1741: Seven Sonatas, Op. 91; Philipp Nägele, violin

D146 Musical Heritage Society MHS 1698: Preludes and Fugues, Op. 131a; Sandor Karolyi, violin

D147 Musical Heritage Society MHS 1719: Four Sonatas, Op. 42; Stanley Weiner, violin

D148 Musical Heritage Society MHS 1726: Sonatas in C Major, Op. 72; & A Major, Op. 103b/2; Sandor Karolyi, violin; Suzanne Godefroid, piano

D149 Musical Heritage Society MHS 1752 & 1765: Sonatas, Opp. 5, 28, 78, & 116; Gerhard Mantel, cello; Erika

Frieser, piano

D150 Musical Heritage Society MHS 1867: Variations & Fugue on a Theme of J.S. Bach, Op. 81; Humoresques, Op. 20; Silhouettes, Op. 53; Richard Laugs, piano

D151 Musical Heritage Society MHS 3996: Suite im alten Stil in F Major; Songs arranged for Violin & Piano, Op. 103c; Pieces for Violin & Piano, Op. 79; Elisabeth Schwarz, piano; Richard Laugs, piano; Philipp Nägele, violin

D152 Musical Heritage Society MHS 4136: Scherzino; Romance in G Major, Op. 50; Lyrical Andante; Episodes, Op. 115; Romanze in D Major; Richard Laugs, piano; Heidelberg Chamber Orchestra, Richard Laugs conducting

D153 Musical Heritage Society MHS 4186: String Quartet in D Minor, Op. 74; Zagreber String Quartet

D154 Musical Heritage Society MHS 4287: String Quartet in Eb Major, Op. 109; String Quartet in D Minor, No Op.; Albumblatt & Tarantella; Caprice, Op. 79/1; Kleine Romanze, Op. 79/2; Caprice in A Minor, No Op.; Keller Quartet; Lux Brahn, clarinet; Philippe Muller, cello; Richard Laugs, piano

D155 Musical Heritage Society MHS 831932L[3 LPs]: Organ Works of Reger, Vol. III: Opp. 145; 67/1, 3, 5, 7, 12, 15, 19, 20, 21, 23, 32, 33, 35, 36, 37, 39, 45, 49, 50, & 52; Op. 79b; 52/3; Heinz Lohmann, organ

D156 Opus 9111 0806: Toccata and Fugue in D Minor, Op. 59/ 5 & 6; Ferdinand Klinda, organ

D157 Orfeo S-090841A: Eine Ballettsuite, Op. 130; Variations and Fugue on a Theme of J.A. Hiller, Op. 100; Bavarian Radio Symphony, Colin Davis conducting

D158 Orion 7287: 3 Suites for Cello Solo, Op. 131; Terry King, cello

D159 Orion ORS 73130: Piéces pittoresques, Op. 34; Six Waltzes, Op. 22; Six Pieces, Op. 94; Sharon Gunderson & Jo Ann Smith, piano

D160 Orion 77281: Variations & Fugue on a Theme of Beethoven, Op. 86; Evelinde Trenkner & Vladimir Pleshakov, pianos

D161 Orion 78294: Sonata No. 3 in Bb for Clarinet & Piano,

Op. 107; John Russo, clarinet; Lydia Walton Ignacio, piano

D162 Orion 80367: Sonata No. 1 in Ab for Clarinet & Piano, Op. 49/1; John Russo, clarinet; Lydia Walton Ignacio, piano

D163 Orion 82424: Introduction & Passacaglia in D Minor for Organ; Roger Thomas, organ

D164 Orion OC-679: Variations & Fugue on a Theme of Telemann, Op. 134; Evelinde Trenkner, piano

D165 Oryx 1823: Sonata in G Major, Op. 141a; Allegretto grazioso; Sonata in Bb Major, Op. 107; Richard Laugs Quintet

D166 Pelca PSR 40510: Ein feste Burg ist unser Gott, Op. 27; Pieces from Opp. 59 and 65; Herbert Manfred Hoffmann, organ

D167 Pelca PSR 40521: Sonata in D Minor, Op. 60; Heinz Wunderlich, organ

D168 Pelca PSR 40526: Responsories & Chorale Preludes from Op. 67; Frankfurter Kantatenkreis; Herbert Manfred Hoffmann, organ and conductor

D169 Pelca PSR 40536: Ein feste Burg ist unser Gott, Op. 27; Hanns Ander-Donath, organ

D170 Philips 238 703 AY: Introduction & Passacaglia in F Minor, Op. 63; Martin Günther Förstemann, organ

D171 Philips 838 700 AY: Fantasy & Fugue on B-A-C-H, Op. 46; 2 Chorale Preludes, Op. 67; Martin Günther Förstemann, organ

D172 Philips 838 705 AY: Fantasy & Fugue on B-A-C-H, Op. 46; 2 Chorale Preludes, Op. 67; Toccata & Fugue in D, Op. 59; Introduction & Passacaglia in F Minor, Op. 63; Martin Günther Förstemann, organ

D173 Philips A 00 486 L: Variations & Fugue on a Theme of Mozart, Op. 132; Eine romntische Suite, Op. 125; Philharmonic Orchestra of the Hague, Willem van Otterloo conducting

D174 Preiser SPR 3286: Variations & Fugue on an Original Theme, Op. 73; Fantasy on the Chorale "Wachet auf", Op. 52/2; Martin Haselböck, organ

D175 Preiser SPR 3355: Songs by Max Reger, Rudi Stephan, Johannes Brahms; Robert Hall, baritone; Konrad Richter, piano

D176 Psallite PET 43/070 267: Introduction, Passacaglia & Fugue in E Minor, Op. 127; Jakob Noll, organ

D177 Psallite PET 64/150 868: Op. 129/8 & 9; Ludwig Doerr, organ

D178 Psallite PET 71/110 968: Organ Mass, Op. 59/7-12; Wolfgang Oehms, organ

D179 Psallite PET 96/291 069: Alle Menschen müssen sterben, Op. 52/1; Otfried Miller, organ

D180 Psallite PET 100/270 770: Wachet auf! ruft uns die Stimme, Op. 52/2; Paul Damjakob, organ

D181 Psallite PSA 31/171 166: Dankpsalm. Op. 145/2; Erich Ackermann, organ

D182 Psallite 101/280 770 F: Opp. 40/1; 145/3; 27; 59/ 5 & 6; George Markey, organ

D183 Quadriga 1028: Ein feste Burg ist unser Gott, Op. 27; Choral Fantasy, Op. 27; Wachet auf! ruft uns die Stimme, Op. 52/2; Wie schön leucht't uns der Morgenstern, Op. 40/1; Rosalinde Haas, organ

D184 RCA LSC 2974-B: Suites for Solo Viola, Op. 131d/1 & 3; Walter Trampler, viola

D185 RCA Victor LM-6092: History of Music in Sound Vol. X: Modern Music (1890-1950): Larghetto from String Trio in A Minor, Op. 77b

D186 SABA SB 15 134: 100th Psalm, Op. 106; Choir of the Lehrergesangverein; Nuremberg Symphony; Werner Jacob, organ; Wolfram Röhrig conducting

D187 Schwann AMS 35 27: Latin Requiem, Op. 145a; Dies irae; Y. Kawahara, M. Höffgen, H.-D. Bader, N. Hillebrand, soloists; Choir & Symphony Orchestra of the NDR, Roland Bader conducting

D188 Schwann VMS 1605: Symphonischer Prolog zu einer Tragödie, Op. 108; Radio Symphony Orchestra of Berlin, Gerd Albrecht conducting

D189 Supraphon SUA 10 491: Fantasy & Fugue on B-A-C-H, Op. 46; Sonata in D Minor, Op. 60; Intermezzo in D Major,

Op. 80/10; Jiri Reinberger & Dagmar Lèdlova, organs

D190 Teldec WE 28 004 B: Aus meinem Tagebuch, Op. 82/3 & 5; Max Reger, piano

D191 Telefunken HT 38: Opp. 20/5; 45/3; 53/2; Max Reger, piano [Recorded in 1905; from the series "Berühmte Komponisten spielen eigene Werke"]

D192 Telefunken SAT 22519: Introduction, Variations and Fugue, Op. 73; Fantasia and Fugue on B-A-C-H, Op. 46; Seven Pieces, Op. 145: Funeral Ode, No. 1; Richard Haas, organ

D193 Telefunken SLT 43064 B: Variations & Fugue on a Theme of J.A. Hiller, Op. 100; State Philharmonic Orchestra of Hamburg, Joseph Keilberth conducting

D194 Telefunken SLT 43114 B: Der Einsiedler, Op. 144a; Geistliche Gesänge, Op. 138/3, 5, & 8; Twenty Responsories, Nos. 1, 5, & 8; Palmsonntagmorgen, Ostermotette; Requiem, Op. 144b; Max van Egmond, baritone; Junge Kantorei; Berlin Symphony Orchestra, Joachim Martini conducting

D195 Telefunken TK 11520/1-2: Variations & Fugue on a Theme of J.A. Hiller, Op. 100; Variations & Fugue on a Theme of Mozart, Op. 132; Eine Ballettsuite, Op. 130; Hamburg Philharmonic State Orchestra, Joseph Keilberth conducting; Bamberg Symphony Orchestra, Keilberth conducting

D196 Tudor 73041: Clarinet Sonata in Bb Major, Op. 107; Albumblatt & Tarantella; Eduard Brunner, clarinet; Gerhard Oppitz, piano

D197 VOX SVBX 586: The Complete Chamber Music, Vol. I: Opp. 77a; 141a; 131b/1-3; 77b; 141b; 146; & Allegro for Two Violins in A Major; Aurèle Nicolet, flute; Susanne Lautenbacher & George Egger, violins; Ulrich Koch, Viola; String Trio Bel Arte; Bel Arte Ensemble

D198 VOX SVBX 587: The Complete Chamber Music, Vol. II: Opp. 54; 74; 109; 121; The Reger Quartet

Bibliography (B1-B1894)

Abbreviations for Journals

AMZ	Allgemeine Musik-Zeitung
K	Der Kirchenmusiker
M	Die Musik
ME	Der Merkur
MG	Musik und Gesellschaft
MGKK	Monatsschrift für Gottesdienst und kirchliche Kunst
MK	Musik und Kirche
MMR	Monthly Musical Record
MO	Musical Opinion
MS	Musica Sacra
MT	Musical Times
MU	Musica
MW	Musikalisches Wochenblatt
NMZ	Neue Musikzeitung
NZFM	Neue Zeitschrift für Musik
[N]ZFM	Zeitschrift für Musik (continuation of NZFM)
RMI	Rivista Musicale Italiana
SMW	Signale für die Musikalische Welt
SMZ	Schweizerische Musikzeitung

Articles

B1 No Author. "No Title." M 15 (1923): 835ff.
On the Vienna Max-Reger-Gesellschaft.

B2 No Author. "Biographie von Max Reger." NMZ (1900).

B3 No Author. "Contemporary Chronicle: The Case of Max Reger." MO 76 (1953): 539-541.

B4 No Author. "Elsa Reger." MU 5 (1951): 380.

B5 No Author. "Erinnerung an Karl Straube." Der Musikhandel 24:2 (1973): 57.

B6 No Author. "Erinnerung an Max Reger." Zeitschrift für Instrumentenbau 52 (1932): 366.
Concerns the Piano Quintet, Opus Posthumous.

B7 No Author. "Liste Sämtlicher mit opus-Zahlen erschienenen Werke Max Regers, mit Angabe ihrer Verleger." SMW 74 (1916): 456-460.

B8 No Author. "Max Reger." MGKK 5:8 (1900).

B9 No Author. "Max Reger." ME 7:11-12 (1916).

B10 No Author. "Max Reger." Die Musik-Woche 42 (1901).

B11 No Author. "Max Reger als vocaal componist." Symphonia 19 (1936): 75ff.

B12 No Author. "Max Reger und die Orgel." Dur und Moll 2:2 (1923): 1-2.

B13 No Author. "Max-Reger-Archiv." Börsenblatt für den deutschen Buchhandel 140 (1973): 252.

B14 No Author. "Max Regers Beisetzung." AMZ 43:20 (1916).

B15 No Author. "Musikalische Zeitfragen: Draesekes Mahnruf und sein Echo." NMZ 28:5 (1907): 98-101.

B16 No Author. "Reger-Sondermarke." MG 23 (1973): 152.

B17 No Author. "Reger's Brief but Prolific Life." Clavier 12:4 (1973): 10.

B18 No Author. "Regers Ernennung zum Professor." SMW (1907): 1187.

B19 No Author. "Über das Hinscheiden Max Regers." AMZ 43:21 (1916).

B20 No Author. "Was fangen wir mit Reger an? Gedanken zu seinem 80. Geburtstag am 19. März 1953." Der evangelische Kirchenmusiker 30 (1953).

B21 Ahrens [sic, Arens], Hanns. "Stefan Zweig und die Musik." NMZ 125 (1964): 244-249.
Discusses the major composers who have set Zweig's poetry to music, including Reger of whom the poet remarked, "The most unexpected surprise of all was that

Max Reger, next to Richard Strauss then the greatest living composer, asked me for permission to set six poems from my book Silberne Saiten [Silver Strings]."

B22 Ahrens, Joseph. "Der Weg zur neuen Orgelmusik." Zeitschrift für Kirchenmusik 70:3/4 (1950): 67-69.

B23 A.J.J. "Max Reger." MT (1905): 326-327.
Brief biographical sketch. Works mentioned include Opp. 86, 57, 77, 67, 33, 60, 73, 27, 30, 52, 42, 76, 74, and details of the controversy surrounding Op. 72 are given. "There are the enthusiastic admirers [of Reger] on the one hand, and the unbelieving detractors on the other; the prophets of their hero's great future, and the augurs of ill-omen who foresee the early collapse of the Reger 'boom.'" [p. 326.]

B24 Alf, Julius. "Regers Mozart-Sehnsucht." MU 27 (1973): 346-349.
Details Reger's reverence for Mozart and his music. Also describes Reger's historical position vis-à-vis the major composers of the 20th century.

B25 Allinger, Helen. "Max Reger." Music (AGO) 7 (1973); 48-55.

B26 Altmann, Wilhelm. "Reger als Kritiker und Selbstbeurteiler." AMZ 63 (1936): 319-321, 335ff.

B27 Anders, Erich. "Max Reger in memoriam." NZFM 90:6 (1923).

B28 Antcliffe, Herbert. "The Early Compositions of Reger." MMR 42 (1911): 495.

B29 Anton, Max F. "Der lineare Reger." M 23 (1931): 277ff.

B30 Athearn, Robert A. "Small Reger for Small Organs: A Personal Selection, With Suggestions for Coping." The American Organist 18:9 (1984): 28-31.
A practical guide to the performance of Opp. 47, 56, 59, 65, 69, 80, & 85 is offered.

B31 Auler, Wolfgang. "Korrektur der Musikgeschichte im Lehrplan? Zu Helmut Walchas Aufsatz 'Regers Orgelschaffen Kritisch betrachtet.'" MK 22 (1952): 56-57.
A reply to Helmut Walcha's article in MK 22 (1952): 2-14.

B32 Bacon, A. "The Choral Preludes of Max Reger." Diapason 53:2 (1961): 30ff; 53:12 (1961): 40ff.

B33 Bagier, Guido. "Drei Bruckner-Dirigenten: Reger,

Abendroth, Busch." Musikalische Rundschau 1 (1914): 5.

B34 -----. "Max Reger und die Orgel." M 15:5 (1923).

B35 -----. "Sorge um Reger." M 23 (1931): 274-275.
A short essay on modern common thinking about Reger and his work.

B36 Bagster, G. "Max Reger's Organ and Piano Music." Musical Standard (1899): 427.

B37 Bannard, Joshua. "Max Reger." Musical Standard 37 (1912): 962.

B38 Baresel, Alfred. "Reger in Leipzig." Neue Musik-Zeitschrift 2 (1948): 80ff.

B39 Barker, John Wesley. "Reger's Organ Music." MT 108 (1967): 939-940; 1142-1143; 109 (1968): 170-173. [first appeared in Miscellanea Musicologica: Adelaide Studies in Musicology 1 (1966): 56-73.
This is an excellent discussion of the harmonic and contrapuntal techniques employed by Reger in his organ works. Some attention is given to performance problems encountered in these works. Hugo Riemann's influence on Reger's contrapuntal procedures is discussed.

B40 Barmas, Issay. "Max Reger." The Strad (1938): 541-543.

B41 Bartels, Wolfgang von. "Max Reger und wir." M 23:4 (1931).

B42 Baser. Friedrich. "Max Reger will Heidelberger Kapellmeister werden." M 23 (1931): 267-271.
An account of Reger's desire to become the kapellmeister of Heidelberg.

B43 Batka, Richard. "Max Reger als Liederkomponist." Deutsche Gesangkunst 2:13/14 (1902): 146-148.

B44 Beckmann, Gustav. "Erinnerung an Max Reger." AMZ 55:23 (1928).

B45 -----. "Max Reger." MGKK 21:7/8 (1916).

B46 -----. "Max Reger als Orgelkomponist." M 4 (1904/05): 263-271.
Very favorable review of Reger's works for the organ. In the conclusion Beckmann states that Bach's organ compositions constitute the "Old Testament" of the genre, whereas, Reger's organ works are the "New

Testament."

B47 -----. "Max Reger über Orgel, Orgelkomposition und--spiel." NMZ 44:14 (1925).

B48 Beer, Kurt. "Max Reger und die evangelische Kirchenmusik." Der evangelische Kirchenmusiker No. 160: 944ff.

B49 Beringer, Karl. "Organistisches." NMZ 37:20 (1916).

B50 Bird, Arthur. "Mahler, Reger, Pfitzner & Co." Music 11:1 (1906).

B51 Birkby, Arthur. "Let's Look at the Organ Works." Clavier 12:4 (1973): 8-9.
Birkby presents a balanced assessment of Reger's contribution to organ literature and compares Reger's position in music history to that of Salvador Dali in art history.

B52 Blankenburg, Walter. "Abschliessendes Wort des Schriftleiters." MK 22 (1952): 110ff.

B53 B.L.L. "Das originelle Schaufenster." Börsenblatt für den deutschen Buchhandel 140 (1973): 486.

B54 Bolt, Karl Fritz. "Max Reger und der Männerchor." Die Tonkunst 42 (1938): 190ff.

B55 Bopp, A. "Max Reger." MS 64 (1933): 248-250.

B56 Bornefeld, Helmut. "Walchas Reger-Verdikt kritisch betrachtet." MK 22 (1952): 49-52.

B57 Böttcher, Lukas. "Bach, Reger und das Barock: Aphoristische Betrachtungen." NZFM 107 (1940): 137-138.
A discussion of Reger's use of baroque forms and compositional procedures in view of organic developmental theory. Reger's neo-baroqueisms find general approbation from Böttcher: "Reger's true greatness arises from his reliance on his honesty."

B58 Brand, Erna. "Aus Max Regers Kindheit und Jugendzeit." Das innere Reich 4 (1937): 1056-1077.
On Reger's youth. Also gives backgroung information on his parents.

B59 -----. "Der Meister und sein Lehrer: Ein Rückblick und Aufblick zu Max Regers 70. Geburtstag am 19 März 1943." [N]ZFM 110 (1943): 104-108.
Concerns Reger and his first teacher Adalbert Lindner. Includes a photograph of Reger at 28 years of age and

Lindner at 41.

B60 -----. "Weiden, die Max Reger-Stadt." [N]ZFM 106 (1939): 755-757.
Interesting article about Reger's life and career while living in Weiden (1882-1886 and 1898-1901). In Weiden Reger studied with Adalbert Lindner and composed his Opp. 20 through 64.

B61 Brand, W. Paul-Manfred. "Max Reger en Belgique." La Vie Musicale Belge 12 (1973): 1-3.

B62 Braun, Peter. "Max Reger--Musiker des 20. Jahrhunderts." Musik im Unterricht 57 (1966): 217-221.

B63 -----. "Max Reger--Musiker des 20. Jahrhunderts." NZFM 127 (1966): 175-178.
Discusses Reger's relationship to other composers (particularly Brahms, R. Strauss, and Schönberg) and the musical features of Reger's style: chromatic harmonies, rhythmic idiosyncrasies, and the extreme range of dynamics found in many of the composer's works.

B64 Braungart, Richard. "Max Reger." Monographien Moderner Musiker, Band II: 20 Biographien zeitgenössischer Tonsetzer mit Portraits. Leipzig: C.F. Kahnt, 1907: 197-214.
Contains biographical overview and brief section on each genre of composition.

B65 -----. "Max Reger: Sätze aus einem Essay." Musikalische Rundschau 1 (1905): 71-73.

B66 -----. "Regeriana." M 3 (1903/04): 173-176.
A very favorable essay on the creative output of Reger that is written from a philosophical/cultural standpoint. "In Reger I see now a frankly typical example of the positive creative techniques of the musical instinct, certainly seldom existing in such intensity....Reger's music knows no sentimentality; it is of the freshest wholesomeness."

B67 Brennecke, Ernest. "The Two Reger-Legends." Musical Quarterly (1922): 384-396.
Brennecke presents an even appraisal of Reger's career and argues for a middle ground between the two Reger "legends" (i.e., unrecognized genius and pedantic failure): "Both of the legends are merely legends: both are false; for this man was neither God nor Insect, as he is alternately painted, but a fascinating personality possessing both godlike and spiderish attributes: a com-

bination of amazing strength and equally amazing weakness, of charm and repulsiveness, for which a nervous age like the present should really make some show of interest, and perhaps also of gratitude." [p. 396]

B68 Brent-Smith, Alexander. "Max Reger." The Musical Times 66:988 (1925): 497-499.

B69 Brodde, Otto. "Max Reger und der evangelische Kirchenchor." Der Kirchenchor 33:2 (1973): 23-27.

B70 -----. "Max Reger: Zur 50. Wiederkehr seines Todestages." Der Kirchenchor 26 (1966): 18-23.

B71 Bücken, Ernst. "Vom Sinn der Regerschen Kunst." AMZ 55:23 (1928).

B72 Burnett, J. "Max Reger: A Centenary Appraisal." Your Musical Cue 1:2 (1973): 11-15.

B73 Burwick, Hildegard. "Max Regers Sendung." AMZ 65 (1938): 295ff.

B74 Busch, Fritz. "Begegnung mit Dirigenten." MU 12 (1958): 718-721.
Details Reger's work as the conductor of the Meiningen Hofkapelle Orchestra and as guest conductor of other ensembles. Also includes sections on Fritz Steinbach, Arthur Nikisch, and Gustav Mahler.

B75 Busch, Hermann J. "Max Reger und die Orgel seiner Zeit." MK 43 (1973): 63-73.
Busch explores the problem of performance practice in Reger's organ music by examining the actual organs Reger played on during his lifetime. Includes lists of organ stops found on the organs under discussion.

B76 Cadenbach, Rainer. "Momento und Momentum: Der Gedanke an den Tod in der Musik Max Regers." Vergänglichkeit und Denkmal: Beiträge zur Sepulkralkultur (1985): 239-246.
Discusses the concept of death in Reger's Opp. 100, 128, 4/5, 12/1, 13/13, 17/4, 12, 15, 30, 40/2, 144b, 71, 24, 125, 119, 110/3, 147/1, 108, 124, 136, 101, 132, 133, 114, and selected chorales.

B77 Cahn-Speyer, Rudolf. "Eine Erwiderung an Herrn Dr. Carl Mennicke." MW 29:12 (1908)
On Reger's article "Degeneration and Regeneration in Music."

B78 -----. "Offener Brief an Herrn Dr. Carl Mennicke." MW 29:17 (1908).

B79 Chantavoine, Jean. "Max Reger in Frankreich." AMZ 41 (1914): 29ff.

B80 Cherbuliez, A.-E. "Max Reger und die Meiningen Hofkapelle." SMZ 59 (1919): 283-284; 61 (1921): 338-339, 350, 370.

B81 -----. "Reger und die Meiningen Hofkapelle." SMZ 59 (1920): 27ff.

B82 Chop, Max. "Was wird aus Regers Erbe?" SMW 76:35/36 (1919).

B83 Cords, Gustav. "Max Reger." Deutscher Musiker-Zeitung 47:21 (1916).

B84 Crankshaw, G. "Advocacy for Reger." Music & Musicians 14 (1966): 56.

B85 Crew, Sidney. "Reger's Pianoforte Music." MO (1912): 761-763.

B86 -----. "The Tragedy of Max Reger." New Music Review and Church Music Review 30 (1931): 45-48.

B87 Czach, Rudolf. "Max Reger zum Gedächtnis." Oraganum 36: 18 (1936).

B88 Daffner, Hugo. "Unterricht bei Max Reger." M 13:8 (1926).

B89 Dahlhaus, Carl. "Warum ist Regers Musik so schwer verständlich?" NZFM 134 (1973): 134.
Dahlhaus asserts that Reger's music is difficult to understand not because its harmonic structure is complicated, but that the complex harmonies cause alterations in the other aspects of the music. "Reger is a composer ...who listeners in strong measure...reject."

B90 Dauffenbach, Wilhelm. "Marien-Sololieder." MS 63 (1933): 97-100.

B91 David, Hans. "Max Reger." Melos 6 (1927): 210-214.
A balanced appraisal of Reger's oeuvre. "Reger's music, growing out of the 19th century, points significantly away from its time. In many works Reger aims at a quite lighter style. Already the serene Quartet, Op. 54/2 (A Major) displays a noticeable looseness of voice treatment."

B92 Demuth, Norman. "Max Reger: A Plea." MO (November 1929): 148.

Demuth praises the orchestral works and pleads for wider dissemination, yet disparages the chamber and organ works.

B93 Denecke, Heinz Ludwig. "Max Regers Sonatenform in ihrer Entwicklung." Festschrift Fritz Stein zum 60. Geburtstag (1939): 26-32.
A study of the development of sonata form in Reger's music. Works examined include Opp. 28, 72, 102, & 107. Reger's use of "classical" procedures is examined in light of the influence on his music of Wagner and Bruckner.

B94 Desderi, Ettore. "La Musica per pianoforte e per organo di Max Reger." RMI 34 (1927): 399-411.

B95 -----. "L'opera sinfonica di Max Reger." RMI 31 (1927).

B96 Dessauer, Heinrich. "Alles um ein Konzert oder Max Reger als Konzertveranstalter." SMW (1923): 1141-1143.

B97 Dettelbach, Hans Herbert. "Entwicklungswege des deutschen Liedes." M 18 (1926): 733-740.

B98 Diez, Werner. "Sehnsucht nach der Vergangenheit: Bemerkungen zum deutschen Kunstlied am Ende der Romantik." NZFM 130 (1969): 239-244.
Diez views Reger as being moderately within the mainstream of the traditions of the German lied, although in a very personal sense, especially in regard to the Voklslied.

B99 Dilsner, Laurence. "Reger Can Be for Anyone." Clavier 12:4 (1973): 11-12, 20-28.
Dilsner lists a variety of Reger compositions for use by beginning piano students. On pp. 20-28 the following works are reproduced: Albumblatt, Op. 36; Miniatur-Gavotte (1898); Was die Grossmutter erzählt, Op. 17; Erster Streit, Op. 17; Das tote Vöglein, Op. 17; Weihnachtstraum, Op. 17; Praise to the Lord! the Almighty, the King of Creation, Op. 135a/15; and A Mighty Fortress, Op. 135a/5.

B100 -----. "Reger's Brief but Prolific Life." Clavier 12:4 (1973): 10.
This is a good one-page overview of Reger's life and career for junior and senior high students.

B101 Doppelbauer, Josef Friedrich. "Max Reger zum Gedenken." Sigende Kirche 20 (1972/73): 118-121.

B102 Dorfmüller, Joachim. "Heinrich Riemann--Zeitgenosse und

Vorbild Max Regers: Ein Würdigung seines Lebens und Schaffens anlässlich der 75. Wiederkuhr seines Todestages am 24. Mai 1981." MK 51 (1981): 128-132. A reappraisal of Riemann's career. Riemann's Phantasie über den Choral "Wie schön leuchtet der Morgenstern", Op. 25 served as the model for Reger's Opp. 40/1 & 2 and 52/1-3.

B103 Dorfmüller, Kurt. "Absolute Musik nach Wagner." Musik in Bayern I: Bayerische Musikgeschichte: Überblick und Einzeldarstellungen (1972): 339-347. Reger's penchant for absolute music is traced back to the influence of J.S. Bach.

B104 Dorschfeldt, Gerhard. "Die letzten Stunden mit Reger." NMZ 37 (1916): 272ff.

B105 -----. "Eine lustige Fahrt mit Max Reger nach Braunschweig." NMZ 37 (1916): 299.

B106 -----. "Reger als Lehrer." NMZ 37 (1916): 210.

B107 Draeseke, Felix. "Die Konfusion in der Musik." NMZ 28:1 (1906): 1-7.

B108 Drengemann, Heinz-Rüdiger. "'Reger neobarock.' Antwort auf die Stellungnahme von H. Lohmann." K 25 (1974): 58-61.

B109 Dreyer, Karl. "Max Reger: Ein deutscher Kämpft um sein Werk." Die Musik im Kriege (1943): 52.

B110 Dürr, Alfred. "Vor dem Tribunal der Orgelbewegung. Un das Orgelschaffen Max Regers." MK 22 (1952): 98-102.

B111 -----. "Zur geistlichen Musik Max Regers." Reliogiöse Musik in nicht-liturgischen Werken von Beethoven bis Reger. Regensburg: Gustav Bosse Verlag, 1978: 195-219. Detailed discussion including an examination of Reger's religious views, his sacred music, and a style comparison between Reger's and Heinrich Riemann's chorale fantasias on "Wie schön leucht't uns der Morgenstern."

B112 E.H. "Max Reger und die Kritiker." [N]ZFM 108 (1941): 37-38. Contains a previously unpublished letter from Reger to the pianists Pauline von Erdmannsdörfer-Fichtner in which the composer rebuts a local critic's assertion that the Op. 64 Piano Quintet is a "problematic" work. Reger goes on to state that the Op. 72 Violin Sonata contains clearly defined themes, but will probably be critcized anyway at its premiere.

B113 Ebbeke, Klaus. "Max Reger als Bearbeiter Bachscher Werke." MK 51 (1981): 121-128.
A thorough examination of Reger's arrangements of works by J.S. Bach. "Reger appears to desire to endow [Bach's works] with inner tension, strength of voice leading, and expression."

B114 Eck, Konrad. "Die Hiller-Variationen--eine Reger-Erinnerung." M 23 (1931): 271-274.
An account of the composition of Op. 100. "Brahms finished his first symphony at the age of 43. Reger died at the age of 43."

B115 Egenberger, R. "August Schmid-Lindner zu Max Reger." Mitteilungsblatt der Joseph-Haas-Gesellschaft 14 (1955): 8ff.

B116 Ehrenforth, Karl Heinrich. "Max Reger: Variationen und Fuge über ein Thema von W.A. Mozart für grosses Orchester op. 132 (1914)." Musik und Bildung 5:12 (1973): 673-676.

B117 Elsenheimer, Nicholas J. "Max Reger--An Unknown Master Musician of the Post-Wagner Period." The Catholic Choirmaster 20 (1934): 201-203.

B118 Engelfred, Abele. "Arte contemporanea: Max Reger." RMI 13 (1906): 546-551.

B119 Fiebig, Paul. "Den Romantiker neu entdecken...Gespräch mit Hans Zender über die Komponisten Reger und Pfitzner." NZFM 143:4 (1982): 17-20.

B120 Fiedler, Max. "Über Regers Orchesterwerke." SMW 74: 24/25 (1916).

B121 Fischer, Kurt von. "Bemerkungen zum ersten Satz des Klaviertrios op. 102 von Max Reger." Studi Musicali 9: 1 (1980): 151-159.

B122 Fischer, Walter. "Max Reger als Orgelkomponist." AMZ 32:30-33 (1905).

B123 Fleischer, Hugo. "Brahms-Einflüsse bei Reger." ME 8:12/13 (1919).

B124 Fortner, Wolfgang. "Zu Helmut Walchas Aufsatz 'Regers Orgelschaffen kritisch betrachtet.'" MK 22 (1952): 52-55.

B125 Franke, Friedrich. "Max Reger." NMZ 42 (1922): 247.

B126 Freihammer, F. "Offener Sprechsaal: Unter Verantwortung des Einsenders." AMZ 33 (1906): 216.
Highly critical article on Reger and his supporters. Reger's handling of dissonance is labeled a "sin against art" and the composer is called "the end of music."

B127 Frenzel, Robert. "Neue Orgelkompositionen von Max Reger." MGKK 8:1 & 4 (1903).

B128 Frey, Martin. "Die Taktart im ersten Satze von Beethovens C-moll Symphonie." M 9 (1910): 64-70.
Addresses, among other things, Reger's concern about conflicts between the phrasing and metrical impulse of the first movement of Beethoven's 5th Symphony.

B129 Friedland, Martin. "Zum Reger-Problem." AMZ 49:25/26 (1922).

B130 Friedrich, W. "Max Reger und wir: Zu seinem 25. Todestag." Musik in Jugend und Volk 4 (1941): 98.

B131 Frotscher, Gotthold. "Max Reger der Kirchenmusiker: Zu seinem 20. Todestag." MK 8:3 (1936).

B132 Gale. "The Strauss and Reger Race." Musical Courier 51 (1908): 18.

B133 G.B. "Breitkopf & Härtel. Liszt-Reger: Der heilige Franziskus von Paul auf den Wogen schreitend." Arss Organi 28 (1980): 63-64.

B134 Georgii, Walter. "Die Klaviermusik der letzten Jahrzehnte." NMZ 44 (1923): 230-232.

B135 Gehrenbeck, David. "A Liturgical Index to Max Reger's Opus 67." The American Organist 16:12 (1982): 50-51.
This is a listing of the correct placement within the liturgical calendar of the 52 chorale preludes of Op. 67. This article was written as an addendum to Michael Krentz's article "Max Reger's Opus 67" in The American Organist 16:8 (1982): 34-36.

B136 Gess, Wolfgang Friedrich. "Max Regers Werke für die Violine allein." NMZ 44:12 (1923).

B137 -----. "Max Regers Werke für Violine und Klavier." NMZ 43:5/6 (1921).

B138 Ghislanzoni, A. "La rivalorizzazione romantica della

fuga." RMI 53 (1951): 116-124.

B139 Gideon, Henry L. "The Musical Trinity of Leipsic [sic]: Nikisch, Reger, Straube." The Musician 15:2 (1910).

B140 Gilbert, V. de. "Max Reger." Revista Musical Catalana 4 (1907): 41.

B141 Grabner, Hermann. "Die Bedeutung Max Regers für die Kunst der Gegenwart." Deutsch Musikjahrbuch 4 (1926): 18-25.

B142 -----. "Das Klaviermusik Max Regers." Das Klavierspiel 3:1 (1961): 1-8.

B143 -----. "Der letzte Dirigent der Meininger Hofkapelle: Max Reger zum Gedächtnis." Der Musik-Woche 4:21 (1936): 6-8.

B144 -----. "Max Reger als Lehrer." Das Klavierspiel 2:5 (1960): 3-7.

B145 -----. "Max Regers Werk in der Gegenwart." [N]ZFM 114 (1953): 135-139.
Grabner says that at first glance Reger does not appear to be as modern a composer as Mahler, Strauss, or Pfitzner, but this is belied by an examination of Reger's harmonic idiom. Confusion about Reger's place in music history results from the composer's restriction on musical expression and the emphasis placed upon baroque contrapuntal forms. A number of compositions (Op. 128, the Romantic Prelude, the Symphonic Prologue, Op. 116, and Op. 60 among others) are discussed.

B146 -----. "Reger in Meiningen." NMZ 37 (1916): 295ff.

B147 -----. "Regers 'Sinfonietta.'" [N]ZFM 94 (1927): 9: 481-488, 10: 553-557, 11:620-623.
On Op. 90.

B148 Grace, H.. "The Late Max Reger as Organ Composer." MT (June 1916): 282-284.

B149 Gräner, Georg. "Max Reger." ME 5 (1914): 108.

B150 Grassmann, H.H. "Max Reger und das Lied." SMW 96 (1938): 409.

B151 -----. "Vor 25 Jahren starb Max Reger." Die Tonkunst 14 (1941): 131-132.

B152 Gress, Richard. "Zu Max Regers Gedächtnis." NMZ 47 (1966): 316-318.

B153 Guber, Ria. "Die Max-Reger Stadt Weiden." Sauerländischer Gebirgsbote 4 (1966): 80-81.

B154 Günther, Ernst. "Max Reger als Liederkomponist." NZFM 69 (1902): 326-328.

B155 Günther, Siegfried. "Max Reger und die Schaffenden der Gegenwart." AMZ 55:45 (1928).

B156 H. "Max Reger--ein Expressionist." NMZ 41 (1920): 248ff.

B157 Haas, Joseph. "Ansprache aus Anlass des 40. Todestages von Max Reger." Mitteilungsblatt der Joseph-Haas-Gesellschaft 20 (1957): 10ff.

B158 -----. "Elsa Reger: Vortrag beim Bayerischen Volksbildungsverband." Reden und Aufsätze. Mainz: Schott: 132-133.
Reminiscences of Reger's widow and her book, Mein Leben mit und für Max Reger.

B159 -----. "Etwas über Max Reger und die Instrumentalform." NMZ 37 (1916): 278-280.

B160 -----. "Max Reger" Veröffentlichungen des Max-Reger-Instituts Vol. I. (1949): 5-13.
Brief dedication to the memory of Reger on the composer's 75th birthday.

B161 -----. "Max Reger als Lehrer." Reden und Aufsätze. Mainz: Schott: 78-85.
Reprint of article in Richard Würz, Regers Personlichkeit (Munich: Halbreiter).

B162 -----. "Max Regers Werk heute." Reden und Aufsätze. Mainz: Schott: 110.
A very brief discussion of the position and influence of Reger's music in the present day. A contrast is made with the critical reception accorded to Richard Strauss' works.

B163 -----. "Meinen Lehrmeistern zum Gedenken." [N]ZFM 115 (1954): 129-132.
Contains Haas' memories of Reger as a teacher in Munich as well as letters to Haas from both Reger and Richard Strauss.

B164 -----. "Der Meister Max Reger: Vortrag in Weiden 1948." Reden und Aufsätze. Mainz: Schott: 99.
A brief address on Reger's place in music history. "The Reger problem is like the starry skies."

B165 -----. "Worte des Gedenkens an Max Reger." Mitteilungsblatt der Joseph-Haas-Gesellschaft 23 (1957): 1-6.

B166 -----. "Worte des Gedenkens an Max Reger: Ansprache bei der Enthüllung des Max-Reger-Denkmals in Weiden am 12. Okt. 1957." Reden und Aufsätze. Mainz: Schott: 100-105.
A paean to Reger. "Reger was a torchbearer for culture, a bringer of light to culture." [p. 100]

B167 -----. "Zum 20. Todestag Max Regers, Gedächtnisrede 1936." Reden und Aufsätze. Mainz: Schott: 90-97.
A reflection on Reger's career on the event of the 20th anniversary of the composer's death.

B168 -----. "Zum 40. Todestag von Max Reger: Vortrag München 1956." Reden und Aufsätze. Mainz: Schott: 97-98.
Reprint of Musik im Unterricht article of Volume 48 (1957).

B169 Haberl, Ferdinand. "Max Reger--1873-1916." MS 93 (1973): 314-318.

B170 Hahn, Christof Emanuel. "Max Reger--Geistliche Vokalwerke." Singende Kirche 20 (1973): 122-125.

B171 Hahn, Gustav A. "'...aufpassen wie die Haaftelmacher.' Erinnerungen eines Musikes der Meininger Hofkapelle an den Dirigenten Max Reger." MG 18 (1968): 763-765.

B172 Hahn-Oederan, Erich. "Max Reger." ME (1911): 961-966.

B173 Halperson, Maurice. "Max Reger." Canadian Journal of Music 3 (1916): 214ff.

B174 Harburger, Walter. "Max Reger als Expressionist." Dur und Moll 1:4 (1923).

B175 -----. "Max Reger und die moderne Orgel." Organon 5 (1928): 41-44.

B176 Haselböck, Hans. "Max Reger als Orgelkomponist--noch oder wieder modern?" Osterreichische Musikzeitschrift 28 (1973): 132-140.
Haselböck concludes his article by saying that the question of whether or not Reger was a "modern" composer is largely irrelevant to a full understanding and appreciation of the composer's works.

B177 Hasse, Karl. "Achtes deutches Regerfest in Baden-Baden." [N]ZFM 99 (1932): 955-957.

Outline of the events at the 8th Reger Festival in Baden-Baden. Many works were performed including the Piano Concerto (Rudolf Serkin as soloist), Op. 90, and the Romantic Suite.

B178 -----. "Die evangelische Kirchenmusik und Max Reger." AMZ 48 (1921): 316-319.

B179 -----. "Max Reger und der deutsche Geist." Jahrbuch der deutschen Musik (1944): 112-122.

B180 -----. "Max Reger und die deutsche Orgelkunst." Freiburger Tagung für deutsche Orgelkunst, vom 27. bis 30. Juli 1925. Augsburg: Bärenreiter, 1926: 122-129. A discussion of Reger's organ music and its relationship to German organ music of the past.

B181 -----. "Max Reger und unsere Zeit." [N]ZFM 100 (1933): 205-207.
Hasse argues that Reger is an essentially German composer because, among other reasons, the control of formal means was an essential element of his music, regardless of function or genre. The use of baroque compositional features is merely a concomitant feature of romanticism (as witness a similar reverance for the past in the music of Brahms, one of Reger's chief influences).

B182 -----. "Max Reger, Festrade, gehalten beim Reger-Fest in Freiburg/Br." [N]ZFM 103 (1936): 819-824.
Dedicatory address on the 20th anniversary of Reger's death.

B183 -----. "Monumentalität, Lyrik und Kleinkunst in Max Reger's Werk." AMZ 70:6 (1943).

B184 -----. "'Neapolitanischer Sextakkord' oder 'Akkord der phrygischen Sekunde'?" Die Musikforschung 10 (1957): 295-296.
A discussion of the neapolitan 6th chord within the harmonic system established by Reger in Beiträge zur Modulationslehr. This article is a reply to Hermann Stephani's article "Stadien harmonischer Sinnerfüllung" in Die Musikforschung 9:4 (1956): 432-441.

B185 -----. "Die neuere deutsche Orgelbewegung: Eine Zusammenfassung." [N]ZFM 98:10 (1931): 857-863

B186 -----. "Regers Orchesterbehandlung vor op. 100." NMZ 44: 12 (1923).

B187 -----. "Von einen Regerianer." SMW 68 (1910): 1149-1151.

B188 Hatzfeld, Johannes. "Von katholischen Kirchenmusik: Auch eine Zeitfrage." M 8 (1908): 212-224.
In this article on the state of Catholic liturgical music at the beginning of the 20th century, Hatzfeld quotes a review by Karl Straube of Reger's Op. 61 (pp. 223-224): "Before the Caecilians of the Roman Catholic Church Max Reger makes a deep bow with his Op. 61."

B189 Haupt, Hartmut. "Max Regers symphonisches Orgelschaffen--Introduktion, Passacaglia und Fuge op. 127." MK 47 (1977): 225-232.
Excellent analysis of Op. 127 complete with a chronology of its composition. A comparative analysis of Op. 127 is made with Opp. 73 and 96.

B190 -----. "Symphonische Phantasie und Fuge op. 57--ein Markstein in Max Regers Orgelschaffen." MK 49 (1979): 120-126.
Excellent analysis of Op. 57 which takes into account the work's inspiration (the 3rd Canto of Dante's Inferno), chronology, formal structure, and influence on the composer's later works. Haupt sees the work's dualities (minor-major, subjective-objective, active-passive) as exemplifying new mature formal principles that will be further developed in the rest of Reger's organ compositions.

B191 Hecker, Joachim von. "Wie spielte Reger?" Musica Schallplatte (1959): 52-54.

B192 Hehemann, Max. "Max Reger." M 4(1904/05): 410-424.
Reger is viewed by Hehemann as continuing the evolution of classical forms that has taken place in the 19th century. Additionally, Reger is viewed as the antipode of Richard Strauss in the composition of orchestral music. Works discussed in detail are Opp. 72, 74, & 90.

B193 -----. "Max Reger als Liederkomponist." NZFM 72:44 (1905): 871-872.

B194 -----. "Max Regers Sinfonietta." Musikalische Rundschau 1 (1905): 38-40.
On Op. 90.

B195 -----. "Das Reger-Problem: Gedanken zu Guido Bagiers Reger-Buch." M 16 (1924): 233-240.
Hehemann discusses many of the problems associated with Reger's music (performance practice, formal design, harmonic and contrapuntal complexities). In his review of Bagier's biography of Reger, Hehemann points out that

Bagier's book is the first by a single author and also the first by someone who was not intimate with the composer.

B196 -----. "Regers Klaviermusik." NMZ 37 (1916): 298.

B197 -----. "Variationen um das Thema Reger." AMZ 48 (1921): 315-316.

B198 -----. "Von Max Reger dem Menschen und Künstler: Kleine Anmerkungen zu einem grossen Thema." NMZ 37 (1916): 293ff.

B199 Heldt, Gerhard. "Musik der Reger-Schüler." Bericht über den internationalen Musikwissenschaftlichen Kongress Berlin 1974. Kassel: Bärenreiter, 1980: 414-416.
A brief discussion of Reger's influence and relationship among his students, especially Joseph Haas, Hermann Unger, Karl Hasse, Hermann Grabner, Fritz Lubrich, Franz von Hoesslin, Botho Sigwart, Wilhelm Bettich, Else Wormser, Margarete von Mikusch, Karl Gemünd, Käthe Bach, Erich Anders, Othmar Schoeck, Jaromir Weinberger, Karl Hoyer, Hermann Keller, and Kurt von Wolfurt. Heldt remarks that for all of his modern tendencies, Reger was still composing within the context of 19th century music, and that Reger's later lied style shows the influence of the works of his students.

B200 Herold, Curt. "Der Einfluss Hugo Riemann's auf Max Reger." AMZ 39 (1912): 1371-1372.
A very short srticle on the influence of Riemann's theoretical teachings on Reger's music. "The characteristics of Regerian music point directly to an origin in Riemann."

B201 Herrenschwand, F. "The Organ of Max Reger." The American Organist 44 (1961): 13ff.

B202 Hermann, J. "Max Reger." Neue Christotherpe 39 (1918): 179-212.

B203 Herzfeld, Friedrich. "Max Reger. Zu seinem 20. Todestag am 11. Mai 1936." AMZ 63 (1936): 317-319.

B204 H.H. [Hermann Heyer]. "Ein neues Präludium von Max Reger. Zur Notenbeilage." AMZ 60:6 (1943).

B205 H.L. "Herzog Georg II. von Sachsen-Meiningen." NMZ 35:20 (1914).

B206 Hoffmann, Herbert Manfred. "Towards an Interpretation of

Reger's Organ Music." Diapason 63:9 (1972): 8.
This is a translation by Raymond Mabry of Hoffmann's article which first appeared in MK 37:4 (1967): 162-163. The article deals mainly with the debate concerning proper dynamics in Reger's organ music in light of the baroqueish tendencies of the organ reform movement of the late 19th/early 20th centuries.

B207 -----. "Zur Interpretation Regerscher Orgelmusik." MK 37 (1967): 162-163.
Hoffmann argues that in order to interpret Reger's organ music correctly, one must keep in mind the organs of the 19th century for which Reger was composing (which are much different from the type of organ in favor at the present time).

B208 Högner, Friedrich. "Bekenntnis zu Max Reger." K 17 (1966): 108-112.

B209 -----. "Bekenntnis zu Max Reger." MS 86 (1966): 342-347.

B210 -----. "Das Gesetz der Orgel. Max Reger und der moderne Orgel." MK 23 (1953): 94-100.

B211 -----. "Karl Straube und die missbrauchte Musikphilologie." MK 44 (1974): 280-285.
Högner disputes some of the findings of Wolfgang Stockmeier in his article "Karl Straube als Reger-interpret" (Max Reger, 1873-1916, ein Symposion). Contains interesting insights into Straube's alterations of Reger's tempo markings and performance suggestions.

B212 -----. "Max Reger und die deutsche Orgelbewegung." Ars Organi 16 (1968): 1153-1158.

B213 -----. "Max Reger und Karl Straube." Musik und Gottesdienst 27 (1973): 139-144.

B214 -----. "Zur Darstellung der Orgelwerke Max Regers." MK 41 (1971): 302-307.
A discussion of the various styles of performance of Reger's organ music, including those of the composer, of Karl Straube, and of contemporary performers. The author examines earlier styles of organplaying and also discusses the extant recorded performances of Reger at the organ.

B215 Holbrooke, Josef. "Max Reger." The Strad (1926): 167ff.

B216 Hollander, Hans. "Max Reger." The Music Review 3 (1942): 280-284.

B217 Holle, Hugo. "Max Reger: Der 100. Psalm." NMZ 43:17

(1922).
On Op. 106.

B218 -----. "Max Regers Chorwerke." [N]ZFM 100 (1933): 215-218.
A good basic overview of Reger's choral works that seeks to redress the paucity of critical and scholarly attention given them: "Reger's choral creations, in relationship to his instrumental works, have received only a small amount of attention."

B219 -----. "Max Regers Einzeichnungen in den Symphonien von Johannes Brahms." Almanach der Deutsche Musikbücherei auf das Jahr 1924/25. Regensburg: Bosse, 1924: 145-158.

B220 -----. "Max Regers 'Gesang der Verklärten.'" NMZ 44:15 (1923).

B221 Horwitz, Karl. "Neue Musik für Soloinstrumente." Melos 5 (1926): 123-134.
Discusses many of Reger's compositions for string instruments. Musical examples are given from Opp. 42 and 131.

B222 Huber, Max. "Reger und die Musik zum Gottesdienst. I. Die Konfessionen." K 21 (1970): 126-128.

B223 -----. "Warum schreib Max Reger evangelische Kirchenmusik?" Musik und Gottesdienst 22 (1968): 82-85.

B224 Huesgen, Rudolf. "Die Lebenskrise Max Regers." [N]ZFM 99 (1932): 219.

B225 Hull, A. Eaglefield. "Contemporary Organ Music: Max Reger." The Organ (1926): 91-93.

B226 Huschke, Konrad. "Max Klinger und die Musik. Teil 4: Klinger und Reger." [N[ZFM 105 (1938): 861-865.
Article deals with the influence of Max Klinger on Reger after the latter had become the music director of the University of Leipzig in 1907.

B227 -----. "Das Regerarchiv in Weimar." [N]ZFM 99 (1932): 229ff.
Discusses the holdings of the Weimar Reger Archives.

B228 -----. "Regers Nationalbewussten." AMZ 60:48 (1933).

B229 Jaeger, A.J. "Max Reger." MT 46 (1905): 326-327.

B230 Jäger, Ernst. "Ein Beitrag zum Problem 'Reger und die

Orgel.'" Musik und Gottesdienst 20:5 (1966).

B231 Jemnitz, Alexander. "Max Reger, der einsame Kollektivist." M 23 (1931): 422-430.

B232 Jensch, G. "Die Musikstadt Breslau und Max Reger." AMZ 48 (1921): 320-323.

B233 Jinkertz, Willi. "Mit Reger an Zwei Flügeln." Düsseldorf: Verlag die Faehre, 1951.
A brief account of Reger's abilities as a piano performer.

B234 Joachim, Heinz. "Reger und die deutsche Tradition." Melos 12:12 (1933).

B235 Johns, Donald. "A Survey of Contemporary Organ Music: Germany and Austria." Church Music 2 (1967): 25-28.

B236 Johnson, T.A. "The Music of Max Reger." The Music Teacher and Piano Student 31 (1952): 139.

B237 J.S.S. "Max Reger: 1873-1916." MMR 46 (1916): 546-547.
Generally praiseworthy review of Reger's career, with the standard criticism of the composer's tendency towards elaboration and devotion to J.S. Bach.

B238 Junker-Fredrikshamm. "Max Reger in seinen Briefen." SMW 80 (1922): 1067-1068.

B239 K. "Rückblick auf Reger: Zu einigen 'Da Camera'--Produktionen." Der Musikhandel 24:8 (1973): 359-360.

B240 Kalb, Friedrich. "Max Reger--Kirchenmusiker über den Konfessionen." Gottesdienst und Kirchenmusik 3 (1966): 79-86.

B241 Kaufmann, Ferdinand. "Max Regers Tantum Ergo-Kompositionen für A Cappella-Chor." MS 88 (1968): 75-78.

B242 Kaufmann, Harald. "Aushölung der Tonalität bei Reger." NZFM 128 (1967): 28-33.
A re-examination of Reger's music in view of the functional harmony theories of Riemann and Schenker.

B243 Kaufmann, H.W. "Joseph Rheinberger und Max Reger." Jahrbuch des historischen Vereins für das Fürstentum Liechtenstein 40 (1942): 251-256.

B244 Kaupert, Werner. "Reger im Meininger Schloss." MU 8 (1954): 61.

Short account of an evening of Reger's music presented at the Meiningen Palace under the auspices of the Max-Reger-Archiv. Works performed included Op. 103a and the Allegro for 2 Violins Alone, Op. post.

B245 Keller, Hermann. "Die deutsche Orgelmusik nach Reger." Freiburger Tagung für die deutsche Orgelkunst, vom 27. bis 30. Juli 1926. Augsburg: Bärenreiter, 1926: 130-8. Discusses the legacy of Reger's organ music and the prospects for developments in German organ composition.

B246 -----. "Max Regers Orgelwerke." NMZ 37 (1913): 283-287.

B247 -----. "Regers B-A-C-H-Fantasie in ihrem harmonischen Ausdruck." NMZ 44:12 (1923).
On Op. 46.

B248 Kirchberg, Klaus. "Auf dem Wege zur Neuen Musik: vor 50 Jahren starb Max Reger." Der Musikhandel 17:3 (1966): 100.

B249 Klotz, Hans. "Max Reger--Complete Works: Volume 15: Organ Works." Diapason 63:9 (1972): 8.
Translated by Raymond Mabry. This is a brief discussion of Reger's selections concerning organ types, coupling, dynamics, and tempi.

B250 -----. "The Organ Works of Max Reger: An Interpretation." The Organ Yearbook 5 (1974): 66-69.

B251 Klotz, Hans & H.M. Hoffmann. "Zur Interpretation Regerscher Orgelmusik." K 17 (1966): 8-10.

B252 Kolodin, Irving. "The Real Max Reger." Stereo Review 32:4 (1974): 104-105.
Kolodin posits the theory that Reger was possessed of three compositional personalities: song writer, contrapuntalist, and tone poet. The article includes a review of Reger recordings on the Vox and Musical Heritage Society labels.

B253 Kralik, Heinrich von. "Max Reger." ME 7:11/12 (1918).

B254 Kraus, Eberhard. "Choralvariationen für Orgel." MS 101 (1981): 163-173.

B255 Krause, Emil. "Max Reger." Die Sängerhalle 40 (1900): 30ff.

B256 -----. "Max Reger: Eine Studie." NZFM 67:14 (1900).

B257 Kravitt, Edward F. "The Orchestral Lied: An Inquiry into

its Style and Unexpected Flowering around 1900." The Music Review 37 (1976): 209-226.
Kravitt describes Reger's interest in the orchestral lied as a bridge between the composer's early chamber music and later orchestral works.

B258 Kreckel, Philip G. "Reger as I Knew Him: Personal Characteristics of the 'Bach' of the Twentieth Century." The American Organist 20 (1937): 232-234.
Kreckel, a student of Reger's at Munich, relates stories about Reger and also gives a few insights into his pedagogical methods.

B259 -----. "Reger's Organ Works: A Gold Mine of Sterling Organ Pieces for the Modern Organist." The American Organist 20 (1937): 87-88, 122-123.
A good overview of Reger's organ music with a works list arranged by the level of difficulty.

B260 Krellmann, Hanspeter. "'Ein deutscher Meister': Zum 100. Geburtstag des Komponisten Max Reger." Der Musikhandel 24:4 (1973): 153-154.

B261 Krentz, Michael E. "Max Reger's Opus 67." The American Organist 16:8 (1982): 34-36.
This is a very detailed and useful analysis of Reger's Op. 67 collection of chorale preludes. A listing of chorale preludes according to type (cantus firmus chorales, chorale canons, etc.) is also given.

B262 Krienitz, Willy. "Max Regers letztes Werk." AMZ 60:2 (1933).
About Op. 147.

B263 -----. "Max Regers letztes Werk und die Geschichte seiner Vollendung durch Florizel von Reuter." Die Musik-Woche 9 (1941): 169.

B264 Kügele, Felix Hugo. "Epilog zun Gedächtnis Max Regers." NMZ 37 (1916): 291.

B265 Kühn, Hellmut. "Im Schatten des Neuen: Hinweise auf Kammermusikwerke von Max Reger." MU 34 (1980): 463-465.
An overview of Reger's chamber music compositions. The author notes that Reger's friends and students rejected the music of Schönberg evenb though Schönberg and his followers admired Reger's works. Reger's music, therefore, tended to be outside the mainstream of the development of new music.

B266 -----. "Sang und Gegensang: Zu Regers Klarinetten-quintett opus 146." NZFM 134:3 (1973): 141-143.

Reger's Op. 146 is described as a composition with a dualistic nature, containing expressionistic and rigorously craftsmanlike elements.

B267 Kühn, Oswald. "Regers Rücktritt als Dirigent der Meininger." NMZ 35:16 (1914).

B268 Kundi, Paul. "Vergessene und verbannte Orgelkunst." Singende Kirche 16 (1969): 115-118.

B269 Kwast, James. "Abschied von Max Reger." AMZ 43:20 (1916).
Obituary.

B270 -----. "Max Regers als Kammermusik- und Klavier-Komponist." AMZ 37 (1910): 441-443.
A very laudatory accounting of Reger's chamber and piano works. "...Reger is 'The' composer of chamber music of our time."

B271 Langevin, Paul-Gilbert. "Le Centenaire de Max Reger." Le Guide Musical 60 (1973): 18-19.

B272 Laux, Karl. "Max Reger. Erinnerungen--Bekenntnis--Aufgaben." MG 23 (1973): 129-135.

B273 Law, Frederic S. "Max Reger." The Musician 10 (1905): 45.
Law attempts an evaluation of Reger's output to Op. 86 and very presciently adumbrates the arguments (both pro and con) that will surround the debate after Reger's death concerning the composer's place in music history. Law discerns an impressionistic facet in Reger's compositional style, particularly in his lieder.

B274 Lechthaler, Josef. "Max Reger zum Gedenken." Musica Divina 24 (1936): 101-104.

B275 Leib, Walter. "Max Reger: Zu seinem 20. Todestag." Süddeutsche Sänger-Zeitung 30 (1936): 140ff.

B276 Leichtentritt, Hugo. "Max Reger als Kammermusik-komponist." NZFM 72 (1905): 871.

B277 Lemacher, Heinrich. "Max Jobst. Ein Musiker der Bayerischen Ostmark." [N]ZFM 107 (1940): 69-74.
A brief biographical account of Max Jobst (along with a discussion of his music), a Reger disciple about whom little has been written.

B278 Liebscher, Arthur. "Die Variationform als Ausdrucksmittel

bei Max Reger." M 8 (1908/09): 323-340.
Examines Reger's use of the variations form, especially in the Bach, Beethoven, and Hiller Variations. (Musical examples included.) Liebscher remarks that the use of variations was held in common by the three great "B's" of music history and the author compares and contrasts Reger's use of the form with those employed by Bach, Beethoven, and Brahms.

B279 Lindner, Adalbert. "Die drei Wesenelemente der Musik Max Regers." M 23 (1931): 147-154.

B280 -----. "Max Regers erstes Klavierquintett in c-moll." NMZ 43:17 (1922).

B281 -----. "Max Regers erstes Streichquartett in d-moll." NMZ 44:12 (1923).

B282 -----. "Max Reger und sein Lehrer Adalbert Lindner." NMZ 37 (1916): 276-278.
An overview of Reger's life and career along with a discussion of Reger's course of study with Lindner and, to a lesser extent, with Hugo Riemann. Includes photos of Lindner's house in Weiden, a Lindner portrait, and the Protestant church in Weiden for which Reger was organist from 1886-1889.

B283 Lissa, Zofia. "Max Regers Metamorphosen der 'Berceuse' op. 83 von Frèdèric Chopin." Fontes Artis Musicae (1966): 79-84.

B284 Litterschied, Richard. "Meister der Jahrhundertwende: Strauss--Pfitzner--Reger--Puccini." Meister der Musik und ihre Werke. Berlin: Bong, 1939: 247-271.
A good article comparing and contrasting these four composers. Contains one musical example from the Telemann Variations (6th Episode).

B285 Lohmann, Heinz. "Bemerkungen zur Interpretation der Orgelwerke von Max Reger." MK 43 (1973): 222-233.
Detailed examination of the dynamics and changes of registration required in Reger's organ music. Reger's dynamics, which are usually considered to be excessive, are shown to follow Romantic tendencies.

B286 -----. "'Reger neobarock.' Eine Stellungnahme." K 24 (1973): 172-176.

B287 -----. "Überlegungen zur Interpretation der Orgelwerke von Max Reger." MS 93 (1973): 93-97.

B288 Lohmer, Theodor. "Elsa Reger." [N]ZFM 112 (1951): 302.

Obituary for Elsa Reger, the composer's widow.

B289 Lowe, George. "The Piano Works of Reger." MO (1915): 909.

B290 -----. "The Songs of Max Reger." MO (1910): 88ff.

B291 Lüpke, G. von. "Hausmusik von Max Reger." NMZ 27 (1906): 345-347.
A discussion of the piano works, Opp. 82 and 89.

B292 McCredie, Andrew. "Modern Chamber Music from Strauss to Stockhausen." The Canon 16:5/6 (1962/63): 3-12.

B293 Maass, Albert. "Die musikalische Stellung Max Regers." NMZ 46 (1924): 46.

B294 Mahnke, Allan. "Max Reger's Introduction, Variations and Fugue in F-Sharp Minor, Op. 73." The American Organist 17:4 (1983): 46-48.
Op. 73 is discussed in great detail concerning performance practice and formal structure.

B295 Marsop, Paul. "Max Reger." Musikalische Runbdschau 1:2 (1914).

B296 -----. "Max Reger. Ein Vorversuch." AMZ 39 (1912): 3-6.
Marsop's essay concerns Reger and his place in music history. In comparing Reger to Richard Strauss, Marsop says that while Strauss' art points to the future, Reger's begins in the 21st century and goes to the 18th century and proceeds further back.

B297 -----. "Vom Geistreichen in der Musik: Zwanglose Briefe eines älteren Aesthetikers." M 1 (1902): 943-957.
In this examination of wit in music, Marsop states that Reger's approach to musical wit has something in common with that of Hugo Wolf's. [p. 952]

B298 Matthews, J. "The Organ Works of Max Reger." MO (1909): 545ff.

B299 Mehl, Johannes G. "Nachwort des Schriftleiters." Gottesdienst und Kirchenmusik 3 (1966): 87.

B300 Mendelssohn-Bartholdy, Edith. "Max Reger." NMZ 37 (1916): 271.

B301 Mennicke, Carl. "Max Reger als Retter in der Not!" NZFM 75 (1908): 1-3.

B302 -----. "Offener Brief an Herrn Rudolf Cahn-Speyer." MW 39:12 (1908).

B303 Mephistopheles [pseudonym]. "Die 144. Kakophonikerversammlung in Bierheim: Ein Reformkasperspiel in drei Erhebungen." M 8 (1909): 225-241.
A farcical dramatic roman à clef on the musical tendencies of the early 20th century. Characters include "His Majesty Richard II, chosen ruler of cacophony" (an obvious reference to Richard Strauss); the "diplomatic Max, crown prince and automobile owner" (Max Reger, the chromatic harmonist); and the "contrapuntal Max, a lifeless spirit" (a Döppelgänger of the diplomatic Max and a reference to the contrapuntal aspect of Reger's compositional style.

B304 Mersmann, Hans. "Max Reger und unsere Zeit." Veröffentlichungen des Max-Reger-Instituts Vol. I Bonn: Dümmlers Verlag, 1949: 14-23.
Brief discussion of Reger's place in music history.

B305 -----. "Regers Harmonik." AMZ 48 (1921): 325ff.

B306 Messner, Josef. "Max Reger." ME 9:19 (1918): 646-651; 9:20 (1918): 685-691; 9:22 (1918).

B307 Metzger, Hans Arnold. "Max Regers geistliche Chorwerke und sein Orgelschaffen." MK 36 (1966): 213-224.
An excellent overview of Reger's church music. Contains musical examples from Opp. 135b, 65, and 52/2. Also contains a discussion of problems of rhythm and registration for performer's of Reger's organ music.

B308 Meyerstein, E.H.W. "Reger." The Music Review 6 (1945): 171.

B309 Michaeli, Otto. "Nachruf an Max Reger." NMZ 37 (1916): 272.

B310 -----. "Wer ist der Text dichter von Regers 'Schelm'? Eine Umfrage." NMZ 42:20 (1921).

B311 Michel, Paul. "Max Reger als Förderer der Schul- und Laienmusikerziehung." Musik in der Schule 24:10 (1973): 393-397.
Michel examines Reger's contributions to the improvement of music teacher training and the music the composer wrote specifically for children.

B312 -----. "Max Regers Lehrerpersönlichkeit." Musik in der Schule 17:6 (1966): 244, 253-260.

B313 -----. "Max Regers musikpädagogische Auffassungen." Beiträge zur Musikwissenschaft 8 (1966): 259-288.

B314 Mies, Paul. "Zu Stil und Auffassung bei Richard Strauss und Max Reger." Colloquium Leos Janacek et Musica Europaea (1970): 303-306.

B315 Millo, S.K. "Londoniana." MW 39 (1908): 198. Contains Op. 17,523.

B316 Mitchell, Donald. "Contemporary Chronicle: The Case of Max Reger: I." MO 76 (1953): 539-541.

B317 -----. "Max Reger." Mandrake [Oxford University] 2 (1946): 25-33.
A lament on Reger's music not being performed as much as it once was. "His [Reger's] music is the satisfying expression of a complete musical personality and as such is confident and self-assured. Yet in his later works there is a sense of inner-weariness, and this weariness is visible even in the fugue of the Mozart Variations with its final fortissimo." [p. 33]

B318 -----. "Max Reger (1873-1916): An Introductory Portrait." The Music Review 12 (1951): 279-288.
Mitchell attempts to assess Reger's place in music history from the perspectives of the composer's contemporaries and present-day critics.

B319 Mitscherlich-Claus, Luise & Harald Kümmerling. "Schubert, Brahms und Reger: Eine Sinndeutung von Regers Silhouetten." [N]ZFM 114 (1953): 148-151.
Compares Reger's Op. 53 to selected piano compositions of Schubert, Brahms, Schumann, and Chopin. The authors point out Reger's efforts at paraphrasing the works of earlier composers.

Mitteilungen der Max-Reger-Gesellschaft (1921-1941)

Volume 1 (1921):

B320 Reger, Elsa. "Wie ich Max Reger kennenlernte." p. 3

B321 Hasse, Karl. "Modulation oder Tonalitätserweiterung." pp. 3-7.
Discusses the modulatory procedures of Reger which the author says follow an inner logic of expression and clarity.

B322 Haas, Joseph. "Eine unbekannte Choralkantate Regers." p. 8.

B323 Busch, Fritz. "Zum Vortrag der Mozart-Variationen von Max Regers." pp. 8-10.
A brief discussion of Op. 132 with comments on each

variation.
B324 Lindner, Adalbert. "Reger-Literatur." pp. 10-11.
Outdated, not useful for current research.
B325 Busch, Fritz & Edith Mendelssohn-Bartholdy. "Von der Arbeit der Max-Reger-Gesellschaft. Geschäftsbericht für das Jahr 1920." pp. 11-13.
A precise report for the Reger Society of the years 1919 and 1920.
B326 Thiele, Adalbert. "Rechnungsbericht für das Jahr 1919 und 1920." p. 13.
Financial report of the Reger Society for 1919 and 1920.
B327 Stein, Fritz. "Helft dem Max Reger-Archiv!" p. 14.
A short account of the activities of the Reger Archives in Jena (research, collections, sponsoring of concerts, Reger monuments).
B328 Nagel, Willibald. "Die Reger-Interpreten." p. 15.
A list of people performing Reger's works.

Volume 2 (1921):
B329 Michaeli, Otto. "An Max Reger." p. 2.
B330 Hasse, Karl. "Warum wollte und konnte Max Reger den letzten Schritt zu Richard Strauss nicht tun." pp. 3-5.
A discussion of Reger's use of the idea of program music and its relationship to that of Richard Strauss'.
B331 Grabner, Hermann. "Aus meinem Meiningen Tagebuch." pp. 6-9.
Grabner's Meiningen diary from the Fall of 1912 to the summer of 1913. Contains many personal observations of Reger.
B332 Lindner, Adalbert. "Max Regers Verhältnis zum evangelischen Choral und katholischen Kirchenmusik." pp. 9-12.
A fairly detailed examination of Reger's church works for both Protestant and Catholic liturgies.
B333 Nagel, Willibald & Adolf Spemann. "Besprechungen." pp. 12-14.
Reviews of four-hand arrangements of Opp. 133 and 146 and several books on Reger.
B334 Busch, Fritz & Adolf Spemann. "Von der Arbeit der Max-Reger-Gesellschaft." p. 14.
B335 Nagel, Willibald. "An alle Regerfreunde." p. 14.
B336 Stein, Fritz. "Helft dem Max-Reger-Archiv!" p. 15.
B337 Nagel, Willibald. "Reger-Interpreten." p. 16.
List of performers specializing in the works of Reger.

Volume 3 (1923):
B338 Nagel, Willibald. "Zu Regers 50. Geburtstag." p. 1
B339 Busch, Fritz. "Max Reger als Dirigent." p. 2.
Busch is generally approving of Reger as a conductor, especially of the Meiningen years.
B340 Hasse, Karl. "Regers 'Gesang der Verklärten.'" pp. 3-4.
"Reger, the great idealist, brings to the period of the

'Gesang der Verklärten' and the 'Sinfonietta' a colossal strength to abandon all routine, and 'only make music.'"

B341 Schulz-Dornburg, Rudolf. "Uber Regers Sinfonietta Opus 90." pp. 4-7.
A detailed discussion of Op. 90, especially in regards to instrumentation and expressive concerns.

B342 Moeschinger, Albert. "Max Reger redivivus: Eine Aufdeckung." pp. 7-8.
Concerns Helmut Gropp's Horn Sonata, Op. 5 which was plagiarized from Reger.

B343 Sbach, Georg. "Max Reger in Kolberger Dom." pp. 8-9.
Concerns Reger's performances at the organ in the Holberg Cathedral during the summers of 1905 and 1907.

B344 Stark, Ernst. "Regers Hausorgel." pp. 9-10.
Very brief discussion of Reger's practice organ--"half organ, half harmonium."

B345 Nagel, Willibald. "Das Reger-Fest in Breslau." pp. 10-11.
Opp. 108, 77, 118, 107, 121, 146, 128, & 106 performed.

B346 -----. "Sonstige Regerkonzerte seit 1. Dez. 1921: Versuch u. Anfang einer Statistik." pp. 11-12.
Lists performances of Reger compositions from December 1921 to October 1922.

B347 -----. "Geplante Veranstaltungen für 1923 anlässlich des 50. Geburtstages von Max Reger (19 März 1923)." pp. 12-13.
Lists Reger festivals (11) in 1923.

B348 -----. "Vom Max Reger Archiv." p. 13.

B349 -----. "Besprechungen." pp. 14-15.
Reviews of Eugen Segnitz's Max Reger and Max Reger-Brevier, edited by Adolf Spemann.

B350 Nagel, Willibald & Viktor Junk. "Max Reger-Brevier: Im Auftag der Max Reger-Gesellschaft hrsg. v. Adolf Spemann, Stuttgart 1923." p. 15.

B351 Nagel, Willibald. "Reger-Interpreten." pp. 15-16.

B352 Spemann, Adolf & Fritz Busch. "Von der Arbeit der Max Reger-Gesellschaft.

Volume 4 (1924):

B353 Straube, Karl. "Max Reger." pp. 1-2.

B354 Gatscher, Emanuel. "Einige Bemerkungen zum Studium Regerscher Orgelwerke." pp. 2-8.
A very general introduction to the performance of Reger's organ music.

B355 Holle, Hugo. "Reger als Liederkomponist." pp. 8-12.
Good, general discussion of Reger's song output. The author stresses that Reger's songs must be thought of in the general sense of "compositions" instead of "lieder."

B356 Unger, Hermann. "Regers Hausmusik." pp. 12-14.
A discussion of Reger's music that was meant for amateurs, e.g., Opp. 82, 103, 89, 77, etc.

B357 Hernried, Robert. "Erinnerungen an Max Reger." pp. 14-18.

Reminiscences of Reger in Weiden, Traunstein, & Hamburg.
B358 Rabich, Ernst. "Erinnerungen an Reger." pp. 18-21.
B359 Swoboda, Heinrich. "Zu Regers Variationsstil"; "Analyse der Bach-Variationen Opus 81." pp. 21-24.
Swoboda sees Reger's variation style as deriving from his predilection for the chorale fantasy and chorale variations procedures.
B360 Holle, Hugo. "Erläuterungen zur Lustspiel-Ouvertüre op. 120, zum Violinkonzert op. 101 und zur Romantischen Suite op. 125." pp. 24-30.
A discussion of thematic development in the three works.
B361 Richard, August. "Vom Max Reger-Archiv." pp. 30-32.
B362 Junk, Viktor. "Das zweite Reger-Fest in Wien." pp. 32-33.
Opp. 108, 123, 128, 132, 119, 162 [sic, 126], 27, 46, 59, 65, 74, & 77a were performed.
B363 Holle, Hugo. "Reger-Konzerte." pp. 34-38.
B364 Keller, Hermann. "Neue Literatur über Reger, Guido Bagier, Max Reger, Stuttgart, 1923." pp. 38-39.
B365 Holle, Hugo. "Hermann Unger, Max Reger, Bielefeld 1924." p. 39.
B366 Unger, Hermann. "Hermann Keller, Reger und die Orgel." pp. 39-40.
B367 Holle, Hugo. "Reger-Interpreten." pp. 40-42.

Volume 5 (1926):
B368 Stein, Fritz. "Zur Entstehungsgeschichte des 100. Psalms: Persönliche Erinnerungen von Fritz Stein." pp. 1-8.
Traces the development of the idea of Reger's 100th Psalm from 1905 to its completion.
B369 Reger, Max. "Max Reger über die Aufführung des 100. Psalms: Aus einem Brief an K. Straube." p. 8.
Taken from Max Regerbrevier, edited by Adolf Spemann.
B370 Pisk, Paul A. "Regers Modulationslehre und die neue Harmonik." pp. 8-9.
In discussing Reger's Beiträge zur Modulationslehr, Pisk says that two especially important points in the composer's manner of modulation are brevity and clarity.
B371 Gatscher, Emanuel. "Über Aufgaben und Ziele der Reger-Biographie." pp. 9-12.
Gatscher's article, concentrating on the collection of source materials, etc., is somewhat dated for current research. Some of his remarks on biographical methodology are still valid.
B372 Hess, Ludwig. "Vom Liederkomponisten Reger." pp. 12-13.
Brief examination of Reger's songs and a few of the singers who performed them.
B373 Reger, Max. "Max Reger über seine Liedertexte: Berichtet von Hermann Unger." p. 13.
From Max Regerbrevier, edited by Adolf Spemann.
B374 Hehemann, Max. "Zum Regerfest in Essen." pp. 13-15.
B375 Reger, Max. "Max Reger über sich und eigene Werke." pp. 16-17.

From Max Regerbrevier, edited by Adolf Spemann.
B376 Blessinger, Karl. "Emanuel Gatscher: Die Fugentechnik Max Regers." pp. 17-18.
Book review.
B377 Holle, Hugo. "Reger-Konzerte." pp. 18-22.
List of performances of Reger's works in 1924 and 1925 with addenda from the years 1919-1923.
B378 -----. "Reger-Interpreten." pp. 22-24.

Volume 6 (1927):
B379 Harburger. "Reger und das irrationale Weltbild." pp. 1-5.
A defense of Reger's modulation theories in light of the "atonality" of modern music.
B380 Blessinger, Karl. "Zur Metrik Max Regers." pp. 5-9.
A discussion of the overall metrical design in such works as Opp. 81, 99, 36, 76, 100, 115, 20, 46, 89, 118, and 45.
B381 Holle, Hugo. "Sinfonietta op. 90." pp. 9-12.
Explanation of formal and thematic development in Op. 90.
B382 -----. "Der 100. Psalm op. 106." pp. 13-17.
Explanation of formal and thematic development in Op. 106.
B383 Martin, Friedrich. "Vom Reger-Archiv in Weimar." pp. 17-18.
B384 Holle, Hugo. "Reger-Konzerte." pp. 18-20.
List of performances of Reger's works in 1926 and 1927 with addenda from 1920, 1923, and 1925.
B385 -----. "Reger-Interpreten." pp. 20-22.

Volume 7 (1928):
B386 Friedland, Martin. "Der Mensch Reger: Ein psychologischer Versuch." pp. 1-5.
Among other things, Friedland examines Reger's intellectual and analytical abilities stemming from the composer's youthful mathematical abilities.
B387 Pisk, Paul. A. "Max Regers Klavierstil." pp. 5-8.
Pisk argues that Reger's piano works embody a new piano style that must be mastered.
B388 Holle, Hugo. "Reger-Konzerte." pp. 10-11.
List of performances of Reger's works in 1927 and 1928 with addenda from the years 1922-1926.
B389 -----. "Reger-Interpreten." pp. 12-14.

Volume 8 (1932):
B390 Hase, Hellmuth von. "An unsere Mitgleider." p. 1.
B391 Poppen, Hermann Meinhard. "Reger als Erscheinung zwischen den Zeiten." pp. 2-11.
Poppen views Reger as existing between two style periods and embodying dual style characteristics in his music, much as Robert Schumann embodied aspects of both

"Eusebius" and "Florestan."

B392 Hasse, Karl. "Max Regers Orgelmusik und die neuere Orgelbewegung." pp. 11-15.
A discussion of Reger's organ music in view of the modern tendency towards baroque performance practice, dynamics, and registration.

B393 Rehberg, W. "Reger als Klavierkomponist." pp. 15-17.
Rehberg views Reger as belonging with Schumann and Brahms as "a master of the largest formats [genres] for the piano."

<u>Volume 9 (1933)</u>

B394 Eucken, Rudolf. "Persönliche Erinnerungen an Max Reger." pp. 1-5.

B395 Dittmar, K. "Das Max Reger-Archiv in Weimar." pp. 6-11.

B396 Hasse, Karl. "Zur Frage der Umurbeitung und Ergänzung Regerscher Werke." pp. 11-18.
Concerns unedited and variant versions of Reger's works.

B397 -----. "Hans von Dettelbachs <u>Breviarium Musicae</u>." pp. 21-25.
Book review.

<u>Volume 10 (1933)</u>:

B398 Hoffmann, Hans. "Zu Max Regers Sonate op. 72 für Violine und Klavier in C-dur." pp. 1-7.
Discusses thematic and formal development in Op. 72. Hoffmann says that traces of Opp. 74, 73, and 81 may be heard in the sonata.

B399 Schmidt, Karl. "Max Reger als Organisator." pp. 8-11.
Details Reger's organizing abilities as a youthful performer and as a conductor.

B400 Hasse, Karl. "Wie Regers 60. Geburtstag begangen wurde: Eine Übersicht." pp. 11-13.

B401 -----. "Ergänzte und umgearbeitete Werke Max Regers." pp. 14-16.
A continuation of B396.

B402 Dittmar, K. & Karl Hasse. "Mitteilungen und Bemerkungen." pp. 16-20.

<u>Volume 11 (1933)</u>:

B403 Lindner, Adalbert. "Max Regers Klavierspiel." pp. 1-6.
Reger's teacher explains the manner in which Reger was taught piano and examines the literature that Reger played as a youth and young adult.

B404 Huesgen, Rudolf. "Die Zusammenhänge der Künstlerischen Jugendentwicklung Max Regers." pp. 6-12.
An examination of Reger's development as an artist in light of the influence of Riemann's teaching and the body of music that formed the repertoire of Reger's youth.

B405 Dittmar, K. "Max Reger und die Meininger Hofkapelle."

pp. 12-16.
Dittmar discusses Reger's years as conductor of the Meiningen Hofkapelle Orchestra. Of interest are the very large number of concerts Reger performed with the orchestra and with other ensembles. [120 planned performances in the Winter of 1912 alone.]

Volume 12 (1934):

B406 Schmid-Lindner, August. "Mit Max Reger im Gefolge J.S. Bachs." pp. 2-4.
Reminiscences of Reger as editor of J.S. Bach's keyboard works.

B407 Hösl, Joseph. "Mein Verhältnis zu Max Reger." pp. 4-13.

B408 Gemünd, Willy. "Aus Max Regers Wiesbadener Zeit." pp. 13-15.

Volume 13 (1936):

B409 Stein-Czerny, Margarete. "Reger fantasiert auf der Orgel." p. 1.

B410 Nedden, Otto zur. "Max Reger als Liederkomponist." pp. 2-4.
Overview of Reger's song output. The author deems particularly praiseworthy "Schlichte Weisen" which he views as a point of calmness between the stormy works of "the upward mobility of his [Reger's] genius" and the composer's fourth style period.

B411 Wagner, Hermann. "Ein Besuch bei Adalbert Lindner." pp. 4-7.
An examination of Lindner's influence on Reger.

B412 Hasse, Karl. "Mitteilungen und Bemerkungen." pp. 8-10.

Volume 14 (1937):

B413 Nedden, Otto zur. "Max Reger als Liederkomponist." pp. 1-3.
A continuation of B410.

B414 Bücken, Ernst. "Zum Wort-Ton-Problem im Liede Regers." pp. 3-4.
Discusses the many problems posed by the relationship between the words and the music in Reger's songs, which were exacerbated by the breakdown in the declamatory style of text setting in vogue around the turn of the century.

B415 Arend, Max. "Max Reger in Wiesbaden 1892/93." pp. 4-8.

B416 Hasse, Karl. "Max Reger und die 'Neue Klassik.'" pp. 8-12.
Discusses Reger's music in view of the 'neo-classic' movement of the 1920'2 and 1930's as exemplified by the works of Stravinsky from this period.

B417 Dittmar, K. "Max Reger in der Plastik." pp. 12-15.
Discusses sculptures of Reger. Contains photographs of a Reger bust and the Reger monument in Meiningen.

<u>Volume 15 (1939)</u>:

B418 Schreyer, Hans. "Die mütterlichen Ahnen des Meisters." pp. 1-3.
Gives an account of Reger's maternal ancestors.

B419 Maur, Sophie. "Persönliche Erinnerungen an Max Reger." pp. 3-9.
Reminiscences of Reger at several festivals in 1910, and an account of a composition with the composer.

B420 Stoverock, Dietrich. "Das Werk Max Regers in der Schule." pp. 9-11.
A discussion of the use of Reger's compositions in music courses.

B421 Hasse, Karl. "Neue Bücher über Max Reger." pp. 11-15.
Reviews of Reger books by Lindner, Stein, and Brand.

<u>Volume 16 (1940)</u>:

B422 Hasse, Karl. "Zum Eintritt ins 25. Jahr der Max-Reger-Gesellschaft." pp. 1-2.

B423 Dittmar, K. "Altes und Neues aus dem Reger-Archiv." pp. 3-5.

B424 Maur, Sophie. "Persönliche Erinnerungen an Max Reger." pp. 6-10.
Reminiscences of Reger during the Summer of 1909 in Ostsee at Kolberg, specifically about op. 114.

B425 Nedden, Otto zur. "Gedanken zu Paul Hindemiths Lehre vom Tonsatz." pp. 11-13.
A view of Hindemith's <u>Lehre vom Tonsatz</u> taken from the perspective of Reger's <u>Beiträge zur Modulationslehre</u>, especially with regard to "musical logic."

B426 Unger, Hermann. "Reger-Episoden." p. 14.

B427 Hasse, Karl. "Regers Harmoniesystem." pp. 14-17.
A discussion of Reger's system of harmonic relationships and chordal movements.

B428 -----. "Max Regers nachgelassener Requiem-Satz." pp. 17-20.
An analysis and explanation of Reger's Requiem, Op. post.

B429 Reichelt, Johannes. "Im Reger-Archiv." pp. 21-25.

<u>Volume 17 (1941)</u>:

B430 Maur, Sophie. "Persönliche Erinnerungen an Max Reger." pp. 1-7.
Reminiscences of Reger when Maur was a private student of the composer in Leipzig.

B431 Keller, Hermann. "Erinnerungen an Max Reger." pp. 7-10.

B432 Grabner, Hermann. "Aus Regers Kompositionsunterricht." pp. 10-13.
A discussion of Reger's harmonic pedagogical methods with examples of exercises.

B433 Hasse, Karl. "Gegenstimme." pp. 13-20.
A re-examination of Reger's music at the occasion of the 25th anniversary of the composer's death. "Even though

Reger at this time has been dead for 25 years, his music is still a part of the living present."

Mitteilungen des Max-Reger-Instituts (1954-1974)

Volume 1 (1954):

B434 Mersmann. "Zum Geleit." p. 1.

B435 Hasse, Karl. "Max Reger: Vortrag, gehalten zu seinem 80. Geburtstag in Kassel." pp. 3-8.

B436 Engländer, Richard. "Max Reger und Karl Straube." pp. 8-14.
Contains good insights into the relationship between Reger and his friend Karl Straube. One interesting point that is brought out is that Straube did not consider the influence of Bach upon Reger to be as spontaneous or as narrowly defined as generally thought.

B437 Otto, Eberhard. "Max Reger--Vermächtnis und Verpflichtung: Rede im Rahmen einer Gedenkfeier der städtischen Musikschule Weiden anlässlich des 80. Geburtstages am 19 März 1953." pp. 14-19.
Commemorative speech.

B438 Fellerer, Karl Gustav. "Joseph Haas. Zum 75 Geburtstag des Meisters am 19 März 1954." pp. 20-21.
Commemorative essay on Haas, one of Reger's students.

Volume 2 (1954):

B439 Schreiber, Ottmar. "Fritz Steins Thematischer Reger-Katalog. Zum 75. Geburtstage seines Verfassers." pp. 2-7.
Contains some corrections to the Stein catalog.

B440 Blessinger, Karl. "Max Reger und die Orgel." pp. 7-11.
"A true successor to Reger in organ music has not been found." [p. 11]

B441 Walter, Rudolf. "Die Formtypen von Max Regers Choralvorspielen." pp. 12-16.
Walter delineates and elaborates upon five types of chorale preludes composed by Reger.

B442 Schreiber, Ottmar. "Schallplatten mit Werken von Max Reger." pp. 18-20.

Volume 3 (1955):

B443 Hasse, Karl. "Max Regers unvollendetes 'Vater unser' für zwölfstimmigen Chor a cappella und seine Ergänzung." pp. 2-9.
Very fine article tracing the origin and development of Reger's unfinished "Vater unser" from 1909.

B444 Hallwachs, Karl. "Meine Erinnerungen an Max Reger." pp. 10-18.

B445 Wirth, Helmut. "Notizen zu Regers Klavierwerk." pp. 19-23.
"Framed on Beethoven and the romantics in lessons with Adalbert Lindner, Reger remained--not only in his

keyboard music--indebted to these masters throughout his life." [p. 19]

B446 Schreiber, Ottmar. "Verzeichnis der in Musikalienhandel erhältichen Werke Regers." pp. 25-28.

B447 -----. "Schallplatten mit Werken Regers." p. 28.

Volume 4 (1956):

B448 Hasse, Karl. "Zum 40. Todestag Max Regers." pp. 2-5.

B449 Mendelssohn-Bartholdy, Edith. "Erinnerungen an Max Reger." pp. 6-9.

B450 Schleder. "Max Reger und Coburg." pp. 9-19.
Discusses Reger's relationship with the artistic life of Coburg while he was director of the Meiningen Orchestra.

B451 Holtschneider, Carl. "Rückblick auf das Erste Deutsche Regerfest (Dortmund)." pp. 19-23.

Volume 5 (1957):

B452 Leupold, Ulrich S. "Max Regers Responsorien." pp. 2-7.
An examination of Reger's responsories for Lutheran services dated Leipzig, September 1914. Included is the music for one of the responsories with an English setting of the text. The autograph of this work is found in the Krauth Memorial Library in Philadelphia, PA.

B453 Schreiber, Ottmar. "Unbekannte geistliche Reger-Chöre." pp. 8-26.
Excellently detailed article on unknown Reger responsories. Included are many musical examples with English texts.

B454 Stein, Fritz. "Regers Geburtsort?" pp. 26-30.

B455 Hasse, Karl. "Offener Brief an Hermann Stephani." pp. 31-34.

B456 Marx, Joseph. "Zu Max Regers 40. Todestag: Ein Klavierabend Hans Webers in Wiener Brahmssaal." p. 34.

B457 Hasse, Karl. "Eine verspätete 'Gegenstimme.'" pp. 35-36.

B458 Stögbauer, Isidor. "Musiktage der Reger-Stadt Weiden." pp. 36-37.

B459 Schreiber, Ottmar. "Regers Klavierspiel auf Schallplatten." pp. 37-38.

Volume 6 (1957):

B460 Schreiber, Ottmar. "Zum Werdegang von Regers Mozart-Variationen." pp. 2-17.
Traces the development of Op. 132 from 1914 and elaborates on the changes of instrumentation, tonality, and variation order that accompanied the composition of this work.

B461 Strecker, Willy. "Max Reger in London." pp. 17-21.
An account of Reger's 1909 concert tour of London.

B462 Hasse, Karl. "Zu einem neuen Reger-Buch." pp. 21-26.
A review of Eberhard Otto's Max Reger, Sinnbild einer Epoche.

B463 Bunk, Gerard. "Begegnung mit Max Reger." pp. 26-30.
B464 Otto, Eberhard. "Hans Koessler--Praeceptor Hungariae." pp. 30-34.
B465 Trenktrog, Karl Hasse, & Hermann Stephani. "Stimmen und Berichte: 'Neapolitanischer ' oder 'Phrygischer' Akkord?" pp. 34-37.
B466 Schreiber, Ottmar. "Um Regers Orgelschaffen: Besprechung einer Rostocker Orgelvesper Wolfgang Aulers durch die Norddeutsche Zeitung, Rostock, vom 25. 10. 1956." pp. 37-38.
B467 K.O. "Eine Lanze für Max Reger." p. 38.
B468 Högel, Max. "Das Hohelied der Ottobeurer Orgel-Trias." pp. 38-39.
B469 Ramge, Heinz. "Zwei Orchesterwerke Max Regers auf Langspielplatten." pp. 39-40.

Volume 7 (1958):
B470 Haas, Joseph. "An Karl Hasse." p. 2.
B471 Stein, Fritz. "Karl Hasses Dienst an Max Reger." pp. 3-5.
B472 Nedden, Otto zur. "Karl Hasse: Zum 75. Geburtstag am 20 März 1958." pp. 5-8.
B473 Laux, Karl. "Für Karl Hasse: Ein Geburtstagsblatt aus der Heimat." pp. 8-9.
B474 Hasse, Karl. "Max Reger und die grossen deutschen Meister." pp. 9-12.
A discussion of Reger's music within the context of the traditions established by the great German composers of the classic and romantic eras.
B475 Klotz, Hans. "Gedanken zur Orgelmusik Max Regers." pp. 12-14.
A discussion of Reger's organmusic and problems of dynamics and interpretation for modern performers.
B476 Sievers, Gerd. "Zur Harmonik Regers." pp. 15-20.
An examination of harmonic practices in Opp. 132, 46, 51/6, 82/II/4, 13/9, 82/I/5-7, and 82/II/10.
B477 Wolfrum, Karl. "Ein Tag mit Reger." pp. 21-28.
B478 Schreiber, Ottmar. "Max Regers erste Lieder." pp. 28-29.
B479 Lentz, Ellen. "Einige Erinnerungen an Reger," pp. 29-30.
B480 Wehmeyer, Grete. "Viola d'amour: Lieder Max Regers auf einer Langspielplatte der DGG." pp. 30-31.
B481 Schreiber, Ottmar. "Verzeichnis der Werke von Karl Hasse." pp. 31-34.

Volume 8 (1958):
B482 Schröder, Cornelia. "Regers Kammermusik und ihre Bedeutung für unsere Zeit." pp. 2-5.
The author views Reger's chamber music accomplishments to be of the utmost importance and to be less problematical than the composer's other compositions.
B483 Sievers, Gerd. "Zur Harmonik Regers." pp. 5-12.
Examines harmonic practices in Opp. 51/4, 14b, 48/6,

49/1, 52/1, 55/9 & 10, 57, and 62/5.
B484 Unger, Hermann. "Echte und Unechte Reger-Anekdoten." pp. 12-16.
B485 Schreiber, Ottmar. "Der Reger-Maler Franz Nölken." pp. 16-23.
Article on the life and career of the painter of one of the best known portraits of Reger.
B486 Erler-Schnaudt, Anna. "Erinnerungen an Reger." pp. 23-24.
B487 Conta, Cläre von. "Erinnerungen an Reger." pp. 24-26.
B488 Lumnitzer-Kühns, Magda. "Aus meinen Erinnerungen." pp. 26-27.
B489 Baresel, Alfred. "Max Regers 'Berchtesgadener Psalm.'" pp. 27-30.
On. Op. 106.
B490 Fast, A. "Aus dem Schatten ins hellst Licht: Regers sämtliche Orgelwerke erklangen in Halle." pp. 30-32.
B491 R.P. "Ein Grazer Klavierabend Hans Webers." pp. 32-33.
B492 Ramge, Heinz. "Neue Reger-Schallplatten." pp. 33-35.

Volume 9 (1959):
B493 Mersmann, Hans. "An Joseph Haas." p. 2.
B494 Stein, Joseph. "An Joseph Haas." p. 3.
B495 Laux, Karl. "Joseph Haas, Schüler, Freund und Sachwalter Max Regers." pp. 3-7.
B496 Otto, Eberhard. "Hermann Unger zun Gedenken." pp. 7-8.
B497 Baresel, Alfred. "Max Reger als Lehrmeister am Leipziger Konservatorium (1907-1916)." pp. 8-11.
Discusses Reger's pedagogical procedures. In analysis classes Reger utilized his own works and those of Brahms, Mahler, and Strauss.
B498 Taube, Charlotte. "Quasi improvisato." pp. 11-14.
Reminiscences in the form of a parody.
B499 Schreyer, Hans. "Wo ist Max Reger geboren?" pp. 14-17.
B500 Schreiber, Ottmar. "Zur Datierung der ersten Reger-Lieder." pp. 17-18.
B501 Fischer-Schlotthauer, Fritz. "Erinnerungen an Jugendtage Max Regers." pp. 18-19.
B502 Drescher, K. "Ein Posener Konzert Max Regers." pp. 20-21.
B503 Ramge, Heinz. "Eine neue Langspielplatte mit. op. 125 und op. 132." pp. 25-27.

Volume 10 (1959):
B504 Mersmann, Hans, Friedrich Blume, Carl Wendling & others. "An Fritz Stein." pp. 2-6.
B505 Moser, Hans Joachim. "Der Regerfreund Fritz Stein als Förderer der Musiker." pp. 6-8.
B506 Söhngen, Oskar. "Max Reger und die Kirchenmusik." pp. 8-13.
Makes several interesting points, the most notable of which is that by remaining true to the concept of "absolute" music, Reger performed an invaluable service in the cause of liturgical music.

B507 Grabner, Hermann. "Regers Opus 108." pp. 13-17.
Discusses the origin and evolution of the Symphonic Prologue to a Tragedy.

B508 Hasse, Karl. "Max Regers Schriften." pp. 17-26.
Discusses and examines Reger's prose writings (essays, articles, reviews, and letters).

B509 Schreiber, Ottmar. "Ein unveröffentlicher Bläserserenadensatz Max Regers." pp. 26-33.
Examines an uncompleted movement for 2 flutes, 2 oboes, 2 clarinets, 2 bassoons, and 4 horns.

B510 Ohlhoff, Gerhard. "Ottomar Güntzel und das Max Reger-Archiv in Meiningen." pp. 34-35.

B511 Würz, Richard. "Die Frühzeit Max Regers im Spiegel Münchener Erinnerungen." pp. 35-39.

B512 Otto, Eberhard. "Zur Neueinrichtung des 100. Psalms." pp. 39-43.

B513 -----. "Eine Lanze für Regers op. 140!" pp. 43-44.

B514 Schreiber, Ottmar. "Regers opus 73 auf einer amerikanischen Schallplatte." pp. 44-45.

Volume 11 (1960):

B515 Fellerer, Karl Gustav. "Joseph Haas." pp. 2-3.

B516 Otto, Eberhard. "Karl Hasse." pp. 3-7.

B517 Mies, Paul. "Brahms-Bearbeitungen bei Max Reger." pp. 7-17.
Examines Reger's arrangements of compositions by Brahms and discusses the history of arranging and transcribing. Considered are: (1) orchestral arrangements of lieder; (2) solo piano arrangements of lieder; and (3) piano arrangements of symphony movements.

B518 Stein, Fritz. "Max Regers Balletsatz 'Pantalon.'" pp. 17-18.

B519 Sievers, Gerd. "Regers zweihändige Klavierkompositionen: Form- und stilkritische Unterschung." pp. 18-27.
A thorough examination of Reger's corpus of solo piano works. Compositions are grouped by affective types (humorous, improvisatory, etc.).

B520 Fleischer, Hans. "Johanna Senfter." pp. 28-29.

B521 Bronnenmeyer, W. "Wiedener Musiktage 1960." pp. 29-30.

B522 Oehlmann, Werner & Walter Kaempfer. "Ein Rückblick auf die Reger-Konzerte der Berliner Bach-Reger-Woche im Juni dieses Jahres." pp. 30-32.

B523 Handke, Erna. "Vom Reger-Spiel auf unseren Orgeln." pp. 32-35.

B524 Rohnstock, Sofie. "Erinnerungen an Max Reger." pp. 35-38.

B525 Raphael, Günter. "Friedrich Högners Reger-Spiel auf einer Schallplatte." pp. 38-39.

Volume 12 (1961):

B526 Schafgans, Theo & Else Bunk. "Die letzten Poträtfotos von

Max Reger." pp. 2-5.

B527 Moser, Hans Joachim. "Hermann Grabner fünfundsiebzigjährig zum 12. Mai 1961." pp. 5-9.

B528 Raphael, Günter. "Reger und seine Stellung in der evangelischen Kirchenmusik." pp. 9-14.
A consideration of Reger's role in the renaissance of Protestant church music.

B529 Sievers, Gerd. "Regers zweihändige Klavierkompositionen: Form- und stilkritische Untersuchung." pp. 14-23.
A continuation of B519.

B530 Westphal, Helmut. "Die Regersche Kammermusik im Rahmen der Hausmusik von Liebhabern." pp. 23-26.
Considers Reger's chamber music and its value for performance by amateurs.

B531 Högner, Friedrich. "Günter Raphael." pp. 27-30.

B532 Kiesler, Irene. "Meine Erinnerungen an der Regerhaus." pp. 30-33.

B533 Reger, Max. "Aus Max Regers Tischrede beim Festbankett des Dortmunder Regerfestes 1910." pp. 33-34.

B534 Schroeder, Rudolf. "Max-Reger-Fest Dortmund 1960." pp. 34-36.

B535 Poppe, Paul. "Wiedener Musiktage 1961." pp. 36-37.

B536 Otto, Eberhard. "Das Max-Reger-Museum in Weiden." pp. 38-41.

B537 Ramge, Heinz. "Reger-Werke auf CANTATE-Schallplatten." pp. 41-44.

B538 Wehmeyer, Grete. "Unvergänglich--unvergessen." pp. 44-46.
On Reger's songs.

Volume 13 (1962):

B539 Söhngen, Oskar. "Fritz Stein zum Gedächtnis: Trauerrede." pp. 3-6.

B540 Hedemann, Justus Wilhelm. "In memoriam: Aus jungen Jahren." p. 6.

B541 Grabner, Hermann. "Meine Erinnerungen an Fritz Stein." pp. 6-9.

B542 Stein, Fritz. "Die Briefe der Eltern Max Regers an Heinrich Geist." pp. 9-19.

B543 Becker, Alfred. "Max Regers Verhältnis zu seinen nächsten Verwandten und zu Weiden." pp. 19-29.

B544 Schreiber, Ottmar. "'Freier Jenaischer Stil'--Regers Violinsonate op. 139.
Extensive tracing of Op. 139 from its inception in the early part of 1915. Contains color facsiimiles of the original drafts and sketches.

B545 Otto, Eberhard. "Max Reger--unerreichbar für die Jugend?" pp. 56-60.
Concedes the inaccessibility of much of Reger's music for young players; however, suggested works by Reger for intermediately skilled performers are named.

B546 Pisk, Paul. A. "Reger-Aufführung in USA." p. 60.

B547 Lauer, Erich. "Palma von Paszthory." pp. 60-61.

B548 Groell, H. "Johanna Senftner." pp. 61-62.
B549 Schreiber, Ottmar. "Reger-Werke in Neudrucken." pp. 62-64.
B550 Ramge, Heinz. "Reger-Werke auf CANTATE-Schallplatten." pp. 64-67.

Volume 14 (1963):
B551 Keller, Hermann. "Max Reger--Werk und Persönlichkeit." pp. 2-4.
B552 Schreiber, Ottmar. "Max Reger in unserer Zeit." pp. 5-12. An examination of Reger's place in music history and his importance for modern musicians.
B553 Hasse, Karl. "Meine Begegnung mit Max Reger." pp. 12-15.
B554 Bosch, Werner. "Wie Regers Orgelspiel für die Nachwelt festgehalten wurde." pp. 16-19. Details how Reger's organ playing was preserved on a type of "player-organ."
B555 Schaarwächter, Gerda. "Die Orgelfuge bei Max Reger: Fragen der Struktur und Interpretation." pp. 19-26. An examination of fugal techniques in Reger's organ works Opp. 129/9, 29, 65, 27, 57, 7, 16, 46, 60, 59, 80, 85, and 30.
B556 Hoffmann, Herbert Manfred. "Gedanken zur heutigen Interpretation Regerschen Orgelmusik." pp. 26-28.
B557 Walther, H. "Max Reger in Griessen." pp. 28.
B558 Marckwaldt, Ernst. "Weidener Musiktage 1962 und 1963." pp. 29-30.
B559 Otto, Eberhard. "Charlotte Brock-Reger." pp. 31-32.
B560 Braungart-Lautenbach, G. "Richard Braungart." p. 31.
B561 Ramge, Heinz. "Neue Reger-Schallplatten." pp. 32-37.

Volume 15 (1966):
B562 Reger, Max. "Hugo Wolfs Künstlerischer Nachlass." pp. 2-44. Reprint of Reger's essay. Facsimile with transcriptions.
B563 Wolfrum, Philipp. "Am Sarge Max Regers. Gedächtnisrede." pp. 44-47.
B564 Hanschke, Paul. "Max Reger: Versuch einer ersten Hinführung." pp. 47-55.
B565 Bagier, Guido. "Zwei Ausserungen zum Thema 'Max Reger und die Gegenwart.'" pp. 55-58. Responses of Karl Böhm and Elly Ney.
B566 Steinmetz, Wilhelm. "Dem Andenken an Frieda Kwast-Hodapp. Auszüge aus Briefen der grossen Pianist an ihre Freudin Frau Eva Rieppel." pp. 59-66.
B567 Otto, Eberhard. "Hermann Grabner, der jugendliche Achtziger." pp. 66-69.
B568 Steinmetz, Wilhelm. "Regers Krankheit: Zu einem Kapitel aus dem Buch von Dieter Kerner Krankheiten grosser Musiker." pp. 69-73.

B569 Schreiber, Ottmar. "Übersicht über die seit 1945 in den Musikalienhandel gekommenen Originalkompositionen Max Regers." pp. 74-79.

Volume 16 (1966):
B570 Fellerer, Karl Gustav, Hawart von Franquè, Hellmuth von Hase, and others. "An Hans Mersmann." p. 1.
B571 Mersmann, Hans. "Max Reger in Tradition und Moderne." pp. 2-7.
B572 Valentin, Erich. "Regers Kunst wird lange bleiben." pp. 7-10.
B573 Schreiber, Ottmar. "Max Regers Künstlerische Welt." pp. 10-17.
Discusses the artistic milieu in which Reger worked. Schreiber quotes Albert Schweitzer's description: "A modern artist in an unmodern man."
B574 Grabner, Hermann. "Regers 'Modulationslehre.'" pp. 18-19.
B575 Walter, Rudolf. "Regers evangelisches Kirchenmusikschaffen und seine Ursachen." pp. 19-34.
Examines the origins of the great quantity of Protestant church music by Reger (who was Catholic).
B576 Otto, Eberhard. "Richard Strauss und Max Reger--Antipoden oder Gesinnungs verwandte?" pp. 35-38.
Examines the relationship between these two composers who are often presented as representing two style tendencies in late romantic music, but were, in reality, admirers of each other's works.
B577 Niemann, Helmut. "Max Regers Konzerterfolge in Russland." pp. 59-65.
B578 Rösner, Helmut. "Eine neue Reger-Bibliographie." pp. 65-67.
B579 Liebe, Annelise. "Max Regers geistliche Werke in der Musikkritik 1966." pp. 67-70.
B580 Rösner, Helmut. "Süddeutsche Max-Reger-Tage 1966--Ein Fazit." pp. 70-77.
B581 Otto, Eberhard. "Ein erheiterndes Reger-Verdikt." pp. 77-81.
B582 Wirth, Helmut. "Schallplatten zum Reger-Jahr 1966." pp. 81-87.

Volume 17 (1968):
B583 Geffert, Hans. "Zur Dynamik der Regerschen Orgelwerke." pp. 1-6.
B584 Haupt, Hartmut. "Max Regers letztes Orgelwerk, op. 135b." pp. 6-12.
B585 Kraus, Eberhard. "Max Regers Briefe an Joseph Renner." pp. 12-25.
Contains Rager's letters to the organist and composer Joseph Renner.
B586 Bagier, Guido. "Erinnerung an eine Reger-Uraufführung." p. 26.
Reminiscences of the premiere of Op. 102.

B587 Backers, Cor. "Erfolgreiche Reger-Konzerte in Holland." pp. 28-29.
B588 Wirth, Helmut. "Neue Schallplatten mit Orgelmusik von Max Reger." pp. 29-31.
B589 -----. "Eine Schallplatte mit drei Sonaten für Violine Solo aus op. 91 von Max Reger." pp. 32-33.

Volume 18 (1971):
B590 Schreiber, Ottmar. "Hans Mersmann zun Gedächtnis." pp. 1-6.
B591 Grabner, Hermann. "Erinnerungen an Max Reger." pp. 6-15.
B592 Wuensch, Gerhard. "Spielformen in Regers Klaviermusik." pp. 16-29.
Divides Reger's keyboard music into two groups: (1) the idiomatic group; and (2) the purely autonomous musical group.
B593 Mirbach, Erich. "Hans von Ohlendorff." p. 28.
B594 Irmen, Hans-Josef. "Max Regers Beziehungen zur Bachsen Kontrapunktschule in München." pp. 29-37.
Contains many of Reger's letters.
B595 Wirth, Helmut. "Max Reger und Edvard Grieg." pp. 38-47.
Discusses the influence of Grieg on Reger's music, particularly in Opp. 13, 17, 18, 36, 53, and 64.
B596 Haas, Rosalinde. "Das Problem einer werkgetreuen Interpretation der Orgelkompositionen von Max Reger." pp. 48-50.
B597 Baumann, Max, Helmut Wirth, & Heinz Ramge. "Neue Schallplatten." pp. 50-66.

Volume 19 (1973):
B598 Söhngen, Oskar. "Max Reger heute." pp. 1-11.
An assessment of Reger's position in music history and posthumous reputation.
B599 Högner, Friedrich. "Max Reger, der heimliche Sieger." pp. 11-15.
An assessment of Reger's posthumous reputation in which the author claims that the composer has finally triumphed over his critics.
B600 Wunderlich, Heinz. "Zur Interpretation von Regers Symphonischer Phantasie und Fuge op. 57." pp. 15-25.
B601 Haupt, Helmut. "Max Regers Orgelvariationen op. 73." pp. 26-33.
B602 Schreiber, Ottmar. "Zur Frage der gültigen Fassung von Regers Orgel-Opus 135b." pp. 34-38.
An attempt to reconstruct the authentic form of Op. 135b.
B603 Würtz, Roland. "Max Reger in Mannheimer Briefsammlungen." pp. 38-50.
B604 Fritz, Nicolas. "Max Reger in französischen Urteil." pp. 51-57.
French reaction to Reger's compositions.

B605 Tautenhahn, Willy. "Regers Musik in Schweizerkritiken bis 1916." pp. 57-76.
A very thorough assessment of Swiss critical reaction to Reger's works.

Volume 20 (1974):

B606 Popp, Susanne. "Reger-Rezeption 1973." pp. 1-24.
A very thorough examination of critical and historical reaction, and scholarly and performing activities, of Reger's works in the year of the centennial of the composer's birth.

B607 Schürmann, Hans G. "Max Reger und die Schallplatte 1973." pp. 24-30.

B608 Walter, Rudolf. "Entstehung, Uraufführung und Aufnahme von Max Regers op. 127." pp. 30-53.
A very complete article on the origin, premiere performance, and critical reception of Op. 127. Contains organ registrations and specifications for the organ of the Jahrhunderthalle in Breslau and reprints of reviews of the premiere.

B609 Schreiber, Ottmar. "Die Skizzen zu Regers Mozart-Variationen." pp. 54-73.
Contains sketches of Op. 132 and philological background.

B610 Schaltuper, Julia. "Notizen zu Max Reger." pp. 73-77.

B611 Langevin, Paul-Gilbert. "Max Reger: Plädoyer zum hundertsten Geburtstag." pp. 77-81.

B612 Samama, Leo. "Max Reger in den Niederlanden." pp. 81-99.
Examines critical reception of Reger's works in Holland from 1905-1916.

B613 Guggenheim, Paul. "Max Reger: Würdigung eines amerikanischen Verehres." pp. 99-101.

B614 Schreiber, Ottmar. "Das Max-Reger-Institut." pp. 101-104.

B615 Dürr, Alfred. "Buchbesprechung: Günther Stange, Die geistesgeschichtlichen und religiösen Grundlagen im kirchenmusikalischen Schaffen Max Regers, Diss. Leipzig 1966." pp. 104-105.

B616 Sievers, Gerd. "Buchbesprechung." pp. 106-108.
Review of August Schmid-Lindner's Ausgewählte Schriften.

B617 Wehmeyer, Grete. "Buchbesprechung." pp. 108-109.
Review of Helmut Wirth's Max Reger in Selbstzeugnissen und Bilddokumenten.

Volume [Sonderheft] (1973):

B618 Ramge, Heinz. "Max Regers Orchesterwerke." pp. 1-6.

B619 Weinitschke, Ludwig Ernst. "Max Regers Chorwerke." pp. 7-15.

B620 Wirth, Helmut. "Die Kammermusik von Max Reger." pp. 16-22.

B621 Wehmeyer, Grete. "Der Liederkomponist Reger." pp. 23-27.

B622 Geffert, Hans. "Die Orgelwerke von Max Reger." pp. 28-33.

B623 Sievers, Gerd. "Die Klavierkmpositionen Max Regers." pp.

34-43.

B624 Schreiber, Ottmar. "Veröffentlichungen des Max-Reger-Instituts/Elsa-Reger-Stiftung/Bonn." p. 44.

B625 -----. "Werkliste." pp. 45-66.
Also contains a discography.

B626 -----. "Notenverzeichnis." pp. 67-89.

B627 -----. "Schallplattenverzeichnis." pp. 90-100.

B628 Mittmann, Paul. "Gustav Robert-Tornow: Max Reger und Karl Straube." M 7 (1906/07): 46-49.
Essay-review of Tornow's book dealing woith the relationship between Reger and the Thomaskantor Karl Straube. Mittmann has some reservations about the narrow range of Tornow's study and the conclusions reached by the author.

B629 Mojsisovics, Roderich von. "Max Regers Orgelwerke." MW 37:37-40 (1906).

B630 Müller, Friedrich August. "Max-Reger-Gedenken: Archiv und Museum in Meiningen." Musikblätter 13 (1948): 21-22.

B631 Müller, Fritz. "Aus Max Regers Briefen. Zur 20. Wiederkehr von Regers Todestag, dem 11. Mai 1916." [N]ZFM 103 (1936): 549-551.
Amusing anecdotes about Reger as gleaned from his letters. Some of Reger's wit and self-deprecation comes to the fore: "My name is Reger, not Professor."

B632 -----. "Max Reger und Karl Straube. Zur 70. Wiederkehr der Geburtstag bieder Meister." [N]ZFM 110 (1943): 108-110.
Concerns Reger's relationship with the great organist and Thomaskantor Karl Straube. Straube was one of Reger's foremost advocates and interpretors and premiered many of the composer's organ works. The article mentions specific performances and also includes quotations from the correspondence between the two men.

B633 Müller-Hartmann, Robert. "Reminiscences of Reger and Strauss." Music and Letters 29 (1948): 153-157.

B634 Müller-Reuter, Theodor. "Max Reger als Orchester-komponist." NZFM 72 (1905): 863-865.
On Op. 90.

B635 Nachbar, Franz. "Worte der Erinnerung: Gesprochen an Regers Bahre." NMZ 37 (1916): 270.

B636 Nagel, Willibald. "Musik-Kultur. Ketzerische Sommer-Gedanken." NMZ 34:1 (1912).

B637 Nagel, Willibald. "Rede auf Max Reger: Geh. in der offtl. Trauerfeier im K. Konservat. zu Stuttgart am 30. Mai 1966." NMZ 37 (1916): 273-276.

B638 Nedden, Otto zur. "Karl Hasse. Zu seinem 60. Geburtstag am 20. März 1943." [N]ZFM 110 (1943): 110-113. Biographical article on Hasse, a Reger associate. Mention is made of Hasse's latest work, the Symphonic Suite for Orchestra in F Major, Op. 65, the first movement of which features the B-A-C-H motive, used often by Reger.

B639 Nef, Karl. "Max Reger." SMZ 41:28 (1901).

B640 Neubeck, Ludwig. "Persönliche Erinnerungen an Reger." AMZ 43:27 (1916).

B641 Neuhaus, Max-Chr. "Max Reger." Le Courrier Musical [Paris] 14:17/18 (1911): 560-562; 14:19 (1911): 599-601.

B642 Newman, Ernest. "The Songs of Max Reger." The Musician 10 (1905): 454-455.
A generally unfavorable review of Reger's lieder output. While Newman occasionally praises certain Reger songs, he says of them in general that "gradually we come to the conclusion that after all Max Reger is not a born song-writer, and that, if the truth were told, he is doing the form rather more harm than good by the way he handles it."

B643 Niemann, Walter. "Max Reger." NMZ 37 (1916): 296ff.

B644 -----. "Max Reger." NZFM 83:20 (1916).

B645 -----. "Max Reger als Klavierkomponist." NZFM 72:44 (1905).

B646 -----. "Max Reger in seinen neuen Orgelwerken." SMW 62:27/28 (1904).

B647 Northcott, B. "Case of Neglect." Music & Musicians 19 (1971): 26-28.

B648 Oesterheld, Herta. "Bericht: Max-Reger-Kolloquium in Meiningen." Beiträge zur Musikwissenschaft 16:2 (1974): 154-156.

B649 -----. "Um ein wahres Regerbild." MG 16 (1966): 334-337.

B650 Ohlekopf, R. "Zum 25. Todestag Max Regers." SMW 99 (1941): 174.

B651 Otto, Eberhard. "Adalbert Lindner: Der Lehrer und

Sachwalter Regers." Musikblätter 10 (1956) 173-177.
Memorial article on Reger's teacher Lindner on the 10th anniversary of his death.

B652 -----. "Dichter in Bayern und ihre Komponisten." Musik in Bayern 18/19 (1979): 95-109.
Reger's settings of Rückert's poems are examined.

B653 -----. "Männer um Max Reger. 1. Hans Kössler." Musikblätter 11 (1957): 167-169.

B654 -----. "Männer um Max Reger. 2. Fritz Stein." Musikblätter 11 (1957): 241-245.

B655 -----. "Männer um Max Reger. 3. Karl Hasse." Musikblätter 12 (1958): 33-35.

B656 -----. "Max Reger: Brücke zwischen drei Jahrhunderten." [N]ZFM 114 (1953): 133-134.
"Reger's greatness, just as that of Brahms, [was] not only in the imitation of old masters, but in discerning newer ranges of emotional expression...."

B657 -----. "Max Reger und die letzten Dinge." MU 20 (1966): 130-131.
Discusses Reger's Opp. 144-147.

B658 -----. "Neue Kontroverse um Reger." Musikblätter 6 (1952): 109ff.

B659 -----. "Regers geistiges Fundament." Musikblätter 7 (1953).

B660 -----. "Der Tod eines grossen Meisters: Zum 40. Todestag Max Regers." Musikblätter 10 (1956/57): 25ff.

B661 -----. "Wer war hier leicht fertig?" Musikblätter 11 (1957): 269-272.

B662 P. "Die Meininger Hofkapelle unter Reger." NMZ 33:7 (1912).

B663 Paetow, Walter. "Max Reger." AMZ 37 (1910): 439-441.
A brief examination of Reger's historical position as of 1910, and a discussion of assumptions about Reger held by his detractors and supporters. As reported by Paetow, Reger is said to have remarked, "I find only a small following, but what does that mean to me? I find myself in the best company." Includes a photograph of a bust of Reger by Theodor von Gosen.

B664 Palmer, Christopher. "Reger's Orchestral Music." MT 114 (1973): 243-244.

B665 Pankalla, Gerhard. "Max Reger." Cäcilia 43:[pp.]17-21.

B666 Pasche, Hans. "Max Reger." SMW (1923): 701-704.

B667 Paszthory, Palma Erdmann von. "Erinnerung an Max Reger." [N]ZFM 112 (1951): 596-597.
Contains some personal observations of Reger from the years 1907-1916, especially concerning Opp. 42 and 139.

B668 Petschnig, Emil. "Max Regers musikalischer Humor." AMZ 66 (1939): 101-103.

B669 Petzet, Walter. "Max Reger als Orgel- und Klavier-komponist." SMW 74:24/25 (1916).

B670 Phillips, Gordon. "The Technique of Trio-Playing Based on Reger's Compositions in Trio-Form." Organ and Choral Aspects and Prospects. New York: Hinrichsen, 1958: 81-83.
Gives a list of suggestions for the performance of Reger's organ music, especially for less advanced performers.

B671 Piccolo. "An Organist's Notebook." MT (1937): 731-733.
The author attacks the complexity and density of Reger's organ music: "Reger might fairly be called the Apostle of the Redundant: too many notes, too many dynamic indications, too many difficulties, too heavy a hand--in short, too much of everything except simplicity and beauty."

B672 Piersig, Johannes. "Der Streit um Reger." MK 24 (1954): 49-59.

B673 Pillney, Karl Hermann. "Neu instrumentierung von Regers 'Gesang der Verklärten.'" AMZ 60:26 (1933).
On Op. 71.

B674 Pinkney, Edward Maynard. "Reger--Expressionist, Karg-Elert--Impressionist?" MO 96 (1973): 255-259.
In this essay Pinkney argues that Reger should be judged within the historical context of his lifetime and that Reger's music is somewhat akin to the violently abstract paintings of the Blaue Reiter school.

B675 Pisk, Paul A. "Die Klavierwerke Max Regers." SMZ 68:25 (1928).

B676 -----. "Max Reger: An Appreciation." Diapason 64:6

(1973): 14.
Pisk presents a tribute to Reger and a discussion of his musical forms and procedures.

B677 Poppen, Hermann. "Linien zur Gegenwart." M 23 (1931): 263-265.
Discusses Reger's works and notices a line of development that leads up to the music of the present day.

B678 -----. "Max Reger als Erscheinung des Ubergangs: Zum 80. Geburtstag." Die Musikleben 6 (1953).

B679 -----. "Max Reger in unserer evangelischen Kirchenmusik." Evangelische Kirchenmusik 30 (1953).

B680 -----. "Max Reger und Philipp Wolfrum." NMZ 44:12 (1923).

B681 Prince, Philip. "Reger and the Organ." Diapason 64:4 (1973): 1ff.
In addition to an historical survey of Reger's organ music, Prince discusses the organs on which Reger performed and lists their specifications, thereby providing invaluable insights into the proper registration of the composer's music.

B682 Pringsheim, Heinz. "Plagiatschnüffler." AMZ 50:15 (1922).

B683 Quoika, Rudolf. "Max Regers Orgelschaffen--Heute? Eine Stellungnahme für Max Reger." MK 22 (1952): 57-61.
Examines the historical importance of Reger's organ music and his influence as father of the modern organ movement.

B684 -----. "Zur Asthetik der Orgelwerke Max Regers." Ars Organi 14 (1966): 937-948.

B685 Rahner, Hugo Ernst. "Das Religiöse in Werk und Stil Max Regers. Zum 100. Geburtstag des Komponisten am 19. März 1973." MS 93 (1973): 84-93.

B686 Rebling, Oskar. "Regers Orgelwerk für eine Gesamtaufnahme gegliedert." K 10 (1959): 148-150, 193-195.

B687 Redlich, Hans F. "Max Reger." Monatsschrift für katholische Kirchenmusik 13 (1932): 118-122.

B688 Reger, Elsa. "Max Regers Tod." Das Orchester 7 (1930): 273ff.

B689 -----. "Schaffensintentionen Max Regers." M 23 (1931):

280.

B690 Reibnitz-Maltzan, Luise von. "Max Reger als Mensch." M 23 (1931): 28.

B691 Reiche, W. "Max Regers Hausmusik und leichte Chormusik." Musik in Leben (1925): 133.

B692 Rettich, Wilhelm. "Max Reger als Lehrer: Erinnerungen zum 50. Todestag." Musik im Unterricht 57 (1966): 335-337.

B693 Reuter, Florizel von. "Mein Bekenntnis zu Regers Violinkonzert." M 23 (1931): 265-266.
Discusses the aesthetic and personal impact of Op. 101.

B694 -----. "Nochmals: Fall Reger-Reuter." AMZ 60:11 (1933).

B695 -----. "Nochmals: Regers letztes Werk: Eine Erwiderung." AMZ 60:5 (1933).

B696 Rexroth, Dieter. "Max Reger: Zwischen Fortschritt und Reaktion: Zum 100. Geburtstag." HiFi Stereophonie 12:3 (1973): 261-266.

B697 Richard, August. "Max Reger." Die Tonkunst (1936): 210.

B698 -----. "Zu Max Regers Gedächtnis." Das Orchester 3:10 (1926): 109-110.

B699 -----. "Zu Max Regers 10 Todestag--Reger-Feier in Weimar." Zeitschrift für evangelische Kirchenmusik 4:5 (1926).

B700 Riemann, Hugo. "Degeneration und Regeneration in der Musik." Max Hesses Deutscher Musiker-Kalendar für das Jahr 1908 23. Jg. Leipzig: 1908: 136-138.

B701 -----. "Kunst und Künstler." NMZ 29:4 (1907): 87.

B702 Riemann, Ludwig. "Reger und die Tonalität." NMZ 37 (1916): 287.

B703 Riemer, Otto. "Vom alten Brahms zum jungen Reger." AMZ 65 (1938): 293-295.

B704 Robert-Tornow, Gustav. "Zur Beurteilung der Kunst Max Regers." M 7 (1907): 3-9.

B705 Rosenfeld, Paul. "An Erudite Composer." The New Republic 9:106 (1916): 47-48.
Rosenfeld delivers a scathing attack on the music of the recently deceased Reger. According to Rosenfeld, "It

was in the dust of the library that Reger existed." No intelligent musical analysis is attempted in this bitterly-worded ad hominen attack.

B706 Rowley, Alec. "The Organ Music of Reger." MO (1930): 816.

B707 Sack, Irene. "Max Regers zweite Seele." M 23 (1931): 279ff.

B708 Schaub, Hanns F. "Gustav Cords--70 Jahre alt." [N]ZFM 107 (1940): 710.
Brief mention of the 70th birthday of Cords, who was a student of Reger's. Also includes a short biography.

B709 Schenker, Heinrich. "Ein Gegenspiel: Max Reger, op. 81, Variationen und Fuge über ein Thema von Joh. Seb. Bach für Klavier." Das Meisterwerk in der Musik: Ein Jahrbuch 2 (1926): 171-192.

B710 Scherber, Ferdinand. "Degeneration und Regeneration." NMZ 29 (1908): 233-236.

B711 -----. "Künstler und Publikum--Fall Reger." SMW (1916): 453ff.

B712 Schibli, Sigfried. "Reger-Interpretation auf der Werkorgel." MG 27 (1973): 152-153.

B713 Schmid-Lindner, August. "Max Reger als Sachwalter seines Werkes." M 23 (1931): 261-263.

B714 Schmidt, Karl. "Reger-Orchester." Zeitschrift für Kirchenmusiker 12 (1930): 29.

B715 -----. "Regers erste Konzertfahrten." M 23 (1931): 277.

B716 Schmidt, Peter. "Noch ein Wort zum Reger-Problem." Das Musikleben 5:10 (1952): 305.

B717 Schmitz, Arnold. "Max Reger zur 75. Wiederkehr seines Geburtstags." Das Musikleben 1 (1948): 45-49.

B718 Schober, J. "Max Regers Choralfantasien." MGKK 4:11 (1899).

B719 Schreiber, Ottmar. "Elsa Reger zum Gedächtnis." Mitteilungsblatt der Joseph-Haas-Gesellschaft 7 (1952): 12ff.

B720 -----. "Max Reger and Contemporary German Musical Life." Canon 16:5/6 (1963).

B721 -----. "Max Reger, einer der unseren: Zur hundertsten Wiederkehr seines Geburtstages." MU 27 (1973): 130-132. Lavish tribute to Reger as man and composer. Schreiber is especially appreciative of Reger's chamber music.

B722 -----. "Max Regers musikalischer Nachlass." Berichte über den Internationalen Musikwissenschaftlichen Kongress Wien 1956 Graz: Verlag Hermann Böhlaus, 1958. A consideration of the legacy of Reger's compositions, particularly those of his last years. Contains musical examples.

B723 -----. "Der Reger-Maler Franz Nölken." Die Gesellschaft 6 (1959): 1-4.
Very brief article on the painter of Reger's best-known portrait.

B724 -----. "Reger und die Musik zum Gottesdienst. II. Regers Responsorien." K 21 (1970): 128-129.

B725 Schü, K. "Max Reger schreibt über sein Violinkonzert." M 23 (1931): 278.

B726 Schumacher, Gerhard. "Wer ist Max Reger?" MK 51 (1981): 113-120.
In attempting to come to terms with the many facets of Reger's personality and compositional style, Schumacher says that the composer remained an individualist and, in many respects, an enigma.

B727 -----. "Zur Geschichtlichkeit evangelischen Kirchenmusik im 20. Jahrhundert (Schluss): Zu einigen Neuenausgaben der letzten Jahre." MK 40 (1970): 277-284.
Discusses some of Reger's sacred compositions, in particular the Vater unser for 12-voice a cappella choir and the Requiemsatz, Op. 145a. [p. 281.]

B728 Schuhmann, Bruno. "Max Reger in Memoriam." Pacific Coast Musician 5 (1916): 36.

B729 Schultze, A. "Betrachtungen über die Abstammung Max Regers." M 31 (1939): 607-609.

B730 Schulz-Dornburg, Rudolf. "Über Regersche Orchestermusik." Deutsches Musikjahrbuch (1925): 135-141.

B731 Schunemann, Robert. "Max Reger, 1873-1916." Diapason 64:4 (1973): 2.
A short tribute and retrospective review of the composer's life and career.

B732 Schütz, Franz. "Die Orgelwerke Max Regers." Musica

Divina 9 (1923): 95-99.

B733 Schweizer, Gottfried. "Die Diskussion um Max Reger." [N]ZFM 113 (1952): 347-348.
Contains the results of a discussion between Schweizer and Helmut Walcha concerning Reger's organ works and their interpretation, especially via Karl Straube.

B734 Schwers, Paul. "Max Reger." AMZ 43:20 (1916).

B735 -----. "Unsere Strauss-Rundfrage." AMZ 39 (1912): 1058-1076.
Responding to questions about Richard Strauss, Reger remarked, "Richard Strauss is for me the shining realization of the art prepared by Franz Liszt."

B736 Segnitz, Eugen. "Über Max Regers Lebenswerk." [N]ZFM 90:6 (1923): 124-126.

B737 Senfter, Johanna. "Erinnerungen an Reger." NMZ 37 (1916): 294ff.

B738 Seydewitz, Margarete von. "Reger im eigenen Heim." NMZ 37 (1916): 310ff.

B739 Seywald, G. "Max Reger." Die Scholle 12:11 (1936): 1-10.

B740 Siber, J. "Reger und die Violine." AMZ 68 (1941): 201.

B741 Siedentopf, Henning. "Das Motiv B-A-C-H und die Neue Musik: Dargestellt an Werken Regers, Schönbergs und Weberns." MU 28 (1974): 420-422.
Discusses Op. 46. Siedentopf says that the B-A-C-H motive is not just an outer motive in Op. 46, but is intrinsic to the construction of the work.

B742 -----. "Der Nachlass des Musikgelehrten Josef Sittard." Die Musikforschung 26 (1973): 350-352.
A short discussion of the career of the music scholar Josef Sittard whose son Alfred was a very important organist and enthusiastic supporter of Reger's works.

B743 Siegele, Ulrich. "Zehn Thesen zur musikalischen Physiognomie Max Regers." NZFM 134 (1973): 430.
Siegele posits 10 ideas in an aphoristic fashion that he feels will aid in explaining Reger's compositional and formal idiosyncrasies (e.g., "Tradition as approached by Reger, is an immanent tradition of music....").

B744 Sievers, Gerd. "Max Regers Kompositionen in ihrem Verhältnis zu der Theorie Hugo Riemanns." Die Musikforschung 3 (1950): 212-223.

Sievers discounts the influence of Riemann's teachings on Reger: "All in all, one cannot see in the composer Max Reger, [in] his greatness and individuality... aspects of the theories of his former teacher Hugo Riemann."

B745 Simon, Eric. "The Clarinet Works of Max Reger." The Clarinet 20 (1955): 12-14.
Simon presents a very basic overview of Opp. 49/1 & 2, 107, and 146, and Albumleaf & Tarantella.

B746 Simon, James. "B-A-C-H." M 9 (1909): 226-232.
Discusses the B-A-C-H motive since the death of J.S. Bach and its use by Reger in Op. 46.

B747 Slonimsky, Nicolas. "Musical Oddities." The Etude 64 (1951): 5.
Anecdote about Reger's marriage.

B748 Söhngen, Oskar. "Fritz Stein zum 75. Geburtstag." K 5 (1954): 173-176.

B749 -----. "Max Reger gestern--heute--morgen. Vortrag auf den Max-Reger-Tagen 1973 in Frankfurt am Main, 9. September 1973." K 24 (1973): 168-172.

B750 -----. "Max Reger und Hermann Grabner: Ihre Bedeutung für die evangelsiche Kirchenmusiker." K 7 (1956).

B751 _____. "Max Regers Stellung in der kirchenmusikalischen Entwicklung." MK 13 (1941).

B752 Sorabji, K.S. "The Organ Works of Reger." Around Music (1936).

B753 Spannunth, August. "Reger und sein Werk." SMW 74:24/25 (1916).

B754 Sparks, Dan. "Max Reger, A Brief Look at his Life and Clarinet Works." The Clarinet 10:2 (1983): 32-33.
Brief overview of Reger's music for clarinet, along with some biographical material.

B755 Spitta, Friedrich. "Max Reger und die Monatsschrift für Gottesdienst und kirchliche Kunst." MGKK (1916): 286.

B756 -----. "Max Regers Verhältnis zum evangelischen Choral und zur katholischen Kirchenmusik." MGKK (1922): 121.

B757 Springer, Max. "Altes und Neues über Max Reger." Musica Divina 11 (1923): 31-35.

B758 -----. "Max Reger." Musica Divina 4 (1916): 139.

B759 Stahl, Heinrich. "Max Reger, der Weltkrieg und die Engländer." [N]ZFM 107 (1940): 670, 672.
Discusses the patriotic works of Reger composed during World War I. Highly tendentious.

B760 Stein, Erwin. "Mahler, Reger, Strauss und Schönberg: Kompositions-technische Betrachtungen." Jahrbuch 1926 der Universal Edition (1926): 63-78.

B761 Stein, Fritz. "Erinnerungen an Max Reger." [N]ZFM 100 (1933): 1-8.
Contains Stein's memories of Reger as a friend and as a hard-working composer.

B762 -----. "Der Freund und Vorkämpfer Max Regers: Erinnerungen an Karl Straube." [N]ZFM 114 (1953): 139-148.
Describes the close personal friendship and professional relationship between Reger and Straube.

B763 -----. "Eine Max-Reger-Erinnerung." Gestalt und Glaube--Festschrift für Oskar Söhngen zum 60. Geburtstag am 5. Dez. 1960 Berlin: Verlag Merseburger, 1960.
Stein's memories of Reger's composing such works as Opp. 131a & b in the year 1914.

B764 -----. "Max Regers letzte Werke." NMZ 37 (1916).
A brief article on Reger's works of the years 1914-1916 (from approximately Op. 131 onwards).

B765 -----. "Max Reger und Max Seiffert." MU 12 (1958): 259-261.
A brief article on the relationship between Reger and Seiffert containing a previously umpublished letter from 1894 from Reger to Seiffert concerning questions of musical form.

B766 -----. "Eine unbekanntes Sinfonie-Fragment Max Regers." M 23 (1931): 254-256.

B767 -----. "Regers letztes Werk." AMZ 60:4 (1933).

B768 Stein, F.A. "Zwei Ostermotetten von Reger und Goller." MS 93 (1973): 106-111.

B769 Steinmetz, Wilhelm. "Sinnbild einer Epoch: Zum 100. Geburtstag von Max Reger am 19. März 1973." Kurz und Gut 7:10 (1973): 30-37.

B770 Stephan, Rudolf. "Max Reger und die Anfänge der Neuen

Musik." [N]ZFM 134 (1973): 339-346.
Address given in Weiden at the 100th anniversary celebration of Reger's birth. Examines Reger's influence on Arnold Schönberg and Josef Matthias Hauer, and [his] relationship to such composers as Richard Strauss and Gustav Mahler.

B771 -----. "Max Reger und die Anfänge der Neuen Musik. Vom musikalischen Denken: Gesammelte Vorträge Mainz: Schott, 1985.
Reprint of B770.

B772 Stephani, Hermann. "Stadien harmonischer Sinnerfüllung." Die Musikforschung 9:4 (1956): 432-441.

B773 Sternberg, L. von. "Mit Max Reger in Wiesbaden." SMW (1932): 173.

B774 Stier, Alfred. "Reger und die klassische Orgel." Zeitschrift für Kirchemusiker 22 (1940): 7.

B775 Stockmann, Bernhard. "Die Kirchenmusik Max Regers und ihr theologischer Hintergrund." NZFM 125 (1964): 553-559.
An excellent and very complete discussion of Reger's church music (both Protestant and Catholic) and its position in 20th century liturgical practices. "Through his organ music and sacred choral music, he [Reger] prepared the way for the liturgical renewal of our time."

B776 -----. "Max Reger--Ausklang der romantischen Tradition." NZFM 127 (1966): 170-175.
Reger's works are described as the furthest extension of musical forms initiated in the 18th century. "...Reger's works lead away from the assumptions of functional harmony instruction."

B777 Stockmeier, Wolfgang. "Umschau: Prussisch-Bayerisches" MK 45 (1975): 129.
Contains a response to Friedrich Högner's article, "Karl Straube und die missbrauchte Musikphilologie," MK 44 (1974): 280-285. Högner's article was a response to Stockmeier's article, "Karl Straube als Reger-Interpret" that appeared in Max Reger 1873-1916. Ein Symposion.

B778 Stoecklin, Paul de. "Musiciens contemporains: Max Reger." Courrier Musical 9 (1906): 229-231.

B779 Storer, H.J. "Organ Compositions of Max Reger." Choir and Choral Magazine 6 (1906): 3ff.

B780 Strakele, H. "Anekdoten um Max Reger." MU 8:6 (1955):

14ff.

B781 Straube, Karl. "Max Reger." NMZ 21 (1900): 267.

B782 -----. "Max Regers Orgelkompositionen und Bearbeitungen." MGKK (1901): 210-212.

B783 Stuckenschmidt, Hans Heinz. "Zwischen Tradition und Erneurung: Notizen über Max Reger." Hausmitteilungen des Musikverlages Bote & Bock 25 (1966): 2-6.

B784 Sumner, W.L. "Some Organ Centenaries 1973." MO 96 (1973): 473-475.
Anecdotal account of Reger's life with a brief discussion of some of his organ works.

B785 Supper, Walter. "Max Reger und der Jugendstil...." Ars Organi 21 (1973): 1858-1864.

B786 Suter, Ernst. "Max Reger als Chorkomponist." Der Chor 6 (1954): 168ff.

B787 Szmolyan, Walter. "Bemerkungen zum Schönberg-Verein." Osterreichische Musikzeitschrift 36 (1981): 154-157.
Short article about the concerts of Schönberg's Society for the Private Performance of Music which often featured Reger's music. Reger's Romantic Suite, Op. 125 was arranged for chamber orchestra for use by the Society.

B788 -----. "Die Konzerte des Wiener Schönberg-Vereins." Osterreichische Musikzeitschrift 36 (1981): 82-104.
A complete listing of all of the programs of Schönberg's Society for the Private Performance of Music, including those featuring Reger's compositions.

B789 Teibler, Hermann. "Max Reger." MW 35 (1904): 3ff, 47ff, 67ff.

B790 Therstappen, Hans Joachim. "Das Barock Regers." Deutsche Musikkultur 6 (1942): 143-148.

B791 -----. "Das Regerbild der Gegenwart. Zum 25. Todestag." AMZ 68 (1941): 145.

B792 -----. "Über die Grundlagen der Form bei Max Reger." Festschrift Fritz Stein zum 60. Geburtstag Braunschweig: Litolff, 1939: 71-82.
A general discussion of form in Reger's music. Reger's straightforward approach to form is contrasted with the "pseudo-monumentality" of Mahler.

B793 Thienhaus, Erich. "Zum Problem Reger und die Orgel." MK 22 (1952): 104-106.

B794 Thiessen, Heinz. "Aus dem Berliner Musikleben: Betrachtungen I. Max Reger." ME 8:2 (1917).

B795 Thiessen, Karl. "Max Reger und seine Kammermusikwerke." NMZ (1905).

B796 Tiedemann, Hans-Joachim. "Scherz und Spott in der absoluten Musik. Versuch eriner Auseinandersetzung mit musikalischer Satire und Parodie." Musik im Unterricht 58 (1967): 322-329.

B797 Torbė, Jakob. "Der Liedstil Max Regers: Ein Gedenkblatt zum 60. Geburtstag (19. März)." M 25:6 (1933).
This article provides a balanced assessment of Reger's lieder output and attempts to place the composer's contribution to the genre within the development of the lied in general during the 19th century. Many contemporary opininions of Reger, both pro and con, are presented. Torbė considers Reger's songs to be examples of the full evolution of the lied. In his opinion, Reger's songs follow a line of development first enunciated by Hugo Wolf. This fully eveolved type of lied is called the "symphonic lied" by Torbė.

B798 Trevor, C.H. "The Organ Music of Max Reger and Its Performance." Organ and Choral Aspects and Prospects New York: Hinrichsen, 1958: 78-81.
Deals with the problems of tempi and dynamics in Reger's organ music.

B799 -----. "Reger's Organ Compositions: The Complete List." Organ and Choral Aspects and Prospects New York: Hinrichsen, 1958: 83-85.
Lists organ works chronologically with title, opus number, and English and American publishers.

B800 Truscott, Harold. "Max Reger." The Music Review 17 (1956): 134-152.

B801 -----. "Reger's 'Symphonischer Prolog.'" MMR 89 (1959): 214-221.
Truscott describes Reger's symphonic style as "musical prose" and discusses the modulatory nature of the Symphonic Prologue to a Tragedy.

B802 Unger, Hermann. "Max Reger als Kammer- und Orchesterkomponist." SMW (1920): 669-710.

B803 -----. "Max Reger als Lehrer." Musik im Unterricht 45

(1954): 78-79.
A brief discussion of Reger as a teacher. Reger's kindness to his students is emphasized.

B804 -----. "Max Reger in unserer Zeit." AMZ 60 11 (1933).

B805 -----. "Reger-Episoden." AMZ 48 (1921): 323-325.

B806 -----. "Unbekannte Reger-Bildnisse." [N]ZFM 99 (1932): 227-229.
A description of 3 recently discovered Reger portraits: (1) an oil painting by Asta von Pirch, a cousin of Reger's wife; (2) a portrait by Hans Blitz from the Summer of 1903; and (3) a portrait by Franz Nölken from the Summer of 1913.

B807 -----. "Zum 50. Geburtstag Max Regers am 19. März." NMZ 44:12 (1923): 177-178.

B808 Unger, Max. "Zur neueren Reger-Literatur." [N]ZFM 90:6 (1923): 131-132.
Unger discusses biographies and monographs about Reger by Adalbert Lindner, Hermann Poppen, Hermann Unger, Eugen Segnitz, Hermann Grabner, Richard Würz, and Josef Haas.

B809 Valentin, Erich. "'Wir brauchen nötigst viel, viel Mozart!' Introitus zum Reger-Jahr 1973.' Acta Mozartiana 20:1 (1973): 1-2.

B810 Varges, Kurt. "Max Reger und der Geist seiner Orgelmusik." K (1926): 1128-1130.

B811 Vogel, Johann Peter. "Reger und Pfitzner: Improvisation zum Werke zweier gegensätzlicher Zeitgenossen." Mitteilungen der Hans-Pfitzner Gesellschaft 31 (1973): 2-4.

B812 Vollenwyder, Erich. "Max Regers Orgelschaffen." MG 27 (1973): 26-29.

B813 Wagner, Herbert. "Der Bonner Organist Willy Poschadel." Bonner Geschichtsblätter 19 (1965): 163-195.
Extensive article on one of Reger's champions. Contains organ specifications and registrations.

B814 Walcha, Helmut. "Max Regers Orgelschaffen kritisch betrachtet." MK 22 (1952): 2-14.

B815 -----. "Noch ein Wort zur Aussprache." MK 22 (1952): 106-110.

B816 Waldstein, Wilhelm. "Max Reger." Osterreichische Musikzeitschrift 18 (1963): 115-119.
Waldstein attempts to define Reger's place in music history. "Max Reger has a firm place in music history, but his work today is hardly more [than] alive."

B817 Walker, Ernest. "An Introduction to Reger for Pianists." The Music Student 6 (1914): 8.

B818 Walker, Frank. "The History of Wolf's Italian Serenade." The Music Review 8 (1947): 161-174.
Deals with Reger's editing and arranging of this work.

B819 Walter, Rudolf. "Gedanken zur Interpretation der Oregl-werke Max Regers." Kirchenmusikalische Mitteilungen 12 (1973): 3-20.

B820 -----. "Gerechtigkeit für Regers Orgelschaffen." Das Musikleben 5 (1952): 136-140.

B821 -----. "Die Gesangbuchquellen der Choral bearbeitungen Max Regers." Kirchenmusikalisches Jahrbuch 36 (1952): 64-76.

B822 -----. "Max Reger und die Orgel um 1900." MK 43 (1973): 282-289.
Detailed account of Reger's organ music with particular attention paid to the organs that Reger was familiar with and how these instruments influenced his compositional style.

B823 -----. "Max Regers Choral vorspiele in ihrer Auseinander-setzung mit geschichtlichen Vorbildern." Kirchenmusikalisches Jahrbuch 38 (1954): 94-107.

B824 -----. "Max Regers Choralvorspiele op. 67 und 79b in ihrem Verhältnis zu J.S. Bach und vorbachischen Meistern." Kirchenmusikalisches Jahrbuch 37 (1953): 103-114.

B825 -----. "Max Regers Verhältnis zu den Kirchenmusikern seiner Zeit." Die katholische Kirchenmusik 4 (1966): 185-197.

B826 -----. "Die Melodiequellen von Regers Choralbearbeit-ungen." K 11 (1960): 185-193.

B827 Waltershausen, Hermann W. von. "Regers Instrumentations-kunst." M 23 (1931): 257-260.
Discusses Reger's manner of orchestration. Examines the use of the chamber style of many of Reger's orchestral works.

B828 Waters, Charles F. "The Present Neglect of Max Reger." The Organ (1926): 221-224.

B829 Weigl, Bruno. "Max Reger als Orgelkomponist." Die Orgel 9:7/8 (1909).

B830 -----. "Max Reger-Richard Strauss." MW 41 (1910): 239ff.

B831 Weiher, Anton. "Regers Klaviermusik. Neue Musikzeitschrift 2 (1948): 81-86.

B832 Weinitschke, Ludwig Ernst. "Max Regers Chorwerke." NZFM 134:3 (1973): 136-140.
Weinitschke examines "O Haupt voll Blut und Wunden," Vater unser, 100th Psalm, Die Nonnen, Latin Requiem (1914), and 8 Sacred Songs (1914). The influence of J.S. Bach and Caecilianism on Reger's choral music is discussed.

B833 -----. "Max Regers geistliche Chorwerke." MK 44 (1974): 10-16.
Examines Reger's works for both the Lutheran and Catholic liturgies. Concerning his own religious beliefs Reger remarked: "I am Catholic to my finger-tips." [p. 11]

B834 Weiss-Aigner, Günter. "Max Reger und die Tradition: Zum Violinkonzert a-Dur opus 101." NZFM 135 (1974): 614-620.
An examination into Reger;s Op. 101 and its relationship to the tradition of violin music of the 18th and 19th centuries (especially that of Mozart, Beethoven, and Brahms). A very intensive analysis of Op. 101 is undertaken. Thematic material listed on p. 616.

B835 Well, Philippus. "Das Reger-Archiv in Meiningen." MG 11 (1961): 733ff.

B836 Wellesz, Egon. "Analytische Studie über Max Regers 'Romantische Suite.'" Zeitschrift für Musikwissenschaft 4:2 (1921).

B837 -----. "Reger." The Music Review 17 (1956): 272.
[Letter to the editor]
Wellesz responds to an article on Reger by Harold Truscott [B800], particularly Truscott's assertion that "the loudest criticisms of Reger come from those who are ardent atonalists."

B838 Weyer, Martin. "Aktuelle Probleme des Regerspiels, dargestellt an der Choralfantasie op. 30." Ars Organi 23 (1975): 2209-2215.

A discussion of performance problems in Op. 30. Suggested registrations are given.

B839 -----. "Condensation of Martin Weyer: Die deutsche Orgelsonate von Mendelssohn bis Reger. Ph.D. Diss. Köln 1969." Die Musikforschung 23 (1970): 467.
Brief outline of Weyer's dissertation. The first section of the work deals with an historical examination of the romantic organ sonata, while the second section contains an important discussion of sonata movements and cycles.

B840 -----. "Joseph Rheinberger als Orgelkomponist." MK 36 (1966): 11-16.
Includes brief remarks about Rheinberger's influence on Reger for whom the latter dedicated one of the numbers of his Op. 67 to the older composer.

B841 Widmann, Joachim. "Max Reger." MK 36 (1966): 203-213.
Good overview of Reger's life and works. Mentions the yearly payment to Reger of 10,000 marks from Edition Peters.

B842 Wilson, Mortimer. "Max Reger." Musical Courier 59 (1916): 10.

B843 -----. "Max Reger: By His Pupil." The Music Student (1917): 153-156.

B844 Windische, Fritz Fridolin. "Regers Verhältnis zur Tonalität." Melos 1:4 (1920).

B845 Wiora, Walter. "Schule des Triospiels." Die Ausbreitung des Historismus über die Musik Regensburg: Gustav Bosse Verlag, 1969: 107-109.
A brief section on this controversial work, in which Reger and Karl Straube added a third voice to Bach's 2-Part Inventions.

B846 Wirth, Helmut. "Johannes Brahms und Max Reger." Brahms-Studien 1 (1974): 91-112.
Traces Brahms' influence on Reger by use of comparative analysis of the music of both composers.

B847 -----. "Max Reger et son oeuvre." Mélanges d'histoire et d'esthétique musicale 2 (1955): 213-220.

B848 -----. "Max Reger in his Works." MMR (1948): 143-149.
Wirth lists Reger, Busoni, and Schönberg as the three driving forces behind the new music of the early 20th century. Reger's creative life is divided into three periods: (1) to 1900; (2) 1900-1908; and (3) 1908-1916.

B849 -----. "Max Reger und die Hausmusik." Der Musiker 9 (1956): 73ff.

B850 Witt, Bertha. "Max Reger: Zum 20. Todestag am 11. Mai." SMW 94 (1936): 293ff.

B851 Wolf, Gary. "The Piano Works of Max Reger." The Music Director (1966): 11.

B852 Wormser, Else. "Max Reger in Meiningen." NMZ 33 (1912): 16.

B853 Wright, Craig. "Rare Manuscripts at Harvard." Current Musicology 10 (1970): 25-33.
Wright presents a listing of the important music manuscripts found at the Harvard University Library, among which the autograph manuscript of Reger's song Dein Auge, Op. 35/1 is included.

B854 Wuensch, Gerhard. "Max Reger's Choral Cantatas." Music (AGO) 6:2 (1972): 32-33, 56.
Reger's involvement in the renewal of Lutheran church music, inspired by Friedrich Spitta, is discussed, in particular the four cantatas composed from 1903-1905.

B855 Wunderlich, Heinz. "Gedanken eines Reger-Interpreten 1966." K 17 (1966): 64-69.

B856 -----. "Zur Bedeutung und Interpretation von Regers Orgelwerken: Ein Beitrag zum Regerjahr 1973." MK 43 (1973): 7-16.
Discusses various interpretations of Reger's organ music, particularly those of Karl Straube. Includes musical examples indicating Straube's phrasing and registration of several of Reger's works.

B857 Würz, Richard J. "Modulation und Harmonik bei Max Reger." MW (1907): 859ff.

B858 Wyly, James. "Further Thoughts Towards an Interpretation of Reger's Organ Music." Diapason 63:10 (1972): 2.
Wyly argues that the dynamic markings in Reger's organ music can be effectively realized on all organs, even mechanical Werkprinzip organs.

Bibliographies

B859 Gray, Michael H. & Gerald D, Gibson. Bibliography of Discographies Volume I: Classical Music, 1925-1975. New York: R.R. Bowker Co., 1977, pp. 108-109.

Lists 11 Reger discographies.

B860 Kraus, Egon. "Bibliographie: Max Reger." _Musik und Bildung_ 5:12 (1973): 677-681.

B861 Rösner, Helmut. _Max-Reger-Bibliographie: Das internationale Schrifttum über Max Reger 1893 bis 1966_. Bonn: Dümmlers Verlag, 1968. Volume 5 of Veröffentlichungen des Max-Reger-Institutes Elsa-Reger-Stiftung Bonn.
Rösner has done an admirable job of tracing down the vast majority of writings by and about Reger for the period of 1893 to 1966. Especially noteworthy are the many reviews of performances of Reger's music that have been tracked down by the indefatigable Rösner. Many articles and books have been overlooked. No annotations. Indices provided. Some of Rösner's citations are incomplete or inaccurate. This work is particularly valuable for its citations of articles and reviews in very obscure or defunct publications which are virtually inaccessible outside of Europe. These publications include: _Aarhus Stiftstidende_, _Der Alb-Bote_, _Abendzeitung_, _Altkatholisches Volksblatt_, _Austria Musik-Kurier_, _Allgemeine Thüringische Landeszeitung_, _Der Aufschwung_, _Der Aufstieg_, _Der Auftakt_, _Augsburger Abendzeitung_, _Allgemeine Zeitung_ (Munich), _Berliner Aftenavis_, _Bavaria_, _Bayerland_, _Blätter des Bayreuther Bundes_, _Bielefelder Blätter für Theater und Kunst_, _Berliner Börsenzeitung_, _Benediktinische Monatsschrift_, _Blätter für Haus- und Kirchenmusik_, _Badische Neueste Nachrichten_ (Karlsruhe), _Bollettino bibliografico musicale_, _Breslauer Zeitung_, _Die Bergstadt_, _Bayerische Staatszeitung_ (Munich), _Berliner Tageblatt_, _Badische Volkszeitung_ (Karlsruhe), _Bühne und Welt_ (Berlin), _Berliner Zeitung am Morgen_, _Christlisches Kunstblatt für Kirche, Schule und Haus_, _Der Chorleiter_, _Neue Christotherpe_, _Die Christengemeinschaft_, _Chemnitzer Tageblatt_, _Comoedia_, _Coburger Tageblatt_, _Daheim_, _Dansk Musiktidsskrift_, _Danziger Neueste Nachrichten_, _Deutsch-akademische Rundschau_, _Deutsche Allgemeine Zeitung_, _Der deutsche Erzieher_, _Duisburger Forschungen_, _Der deutsche Gedanke_, _Donau-Kurier_ (Ingolstadt), _Duitse Kroniek_, _Dansk Kirchenmusiker-Tidende_, _Deutsche Kultur-Wacht_, _Deutscher Merkur_, _Dresdener Anzeiger_, _Dresdener Neueste Nachrichten_, _Deutsche Rundschau_, _Deutsche Sängerbundes-Zeitung_, _Deutsche Stimmen_ (Pressburg), _Deutsche Akademiker-Zeitung_, _Deutsche Tonkünstlerzeitung_, _Deutsches Tageszeitung_, _Deutsche Volksbildung_, _Deutsche Verlagsanstalt_, _Deutscher Wille_, _Deutscher Welt_, _Deutsche Zeitung_, _L'Echo de Paris_, _Der Engländer_, _Erlanger Tagblatt_, _Esslinger Zeitung_, _Der Friedenssaal_, _Freie deutsche Bühne_, _Der Fichtelgebirgsbote_, _Fränkische

Landeszeitung, Fränkische Presse, Die Freistatt, Fränkische Heimat, Fränkische Kurier, Fränkische Tagespost, Frankenwald, Fränkischer Tag, Frankfurter Zeitung, Die Gesellschaft, Gema-Nachrichten, Germania, Das Goetheanum, Göttinger Tageblatt, Geigerspiel-Rundschau, Glaube und Heimat, Hellweg, Hamburger Fremdenblatt, Hamburgischer Correspondent, Die Hilfe, Hamburger Konzert- und Theaterzeitung, Hamburger Nachrichten, Hochland, Heimatbuch Oberpfalz, Heidelberger Tageblatt, Hör zu!, Instrumentenbau-Zeitschrift, Das innere Reich, L'Intransigeant, Internationale Reformzeitschrift für Gesang, Klavier und Geige, Illustreret Tidende, Illustrierte Zeitung, Jenaische Zeitung, Kunstblatt der Jugend, Klüter Blätter, Konservative Monatsschrift, Die Kulturwarte, Kölnische Volkszeitung, Der Kunstwart, Die Libelle, Leipziger Musik- und Theaterzeitung, Leipziger Neueste Nachrichten, Leipziger Volkszeitung, München-Augsburger Abendzeitung, Der März, Magdeburger Zeitung, Le Matin, Musikblätter des Anbruch, Mittelbayerische Zeitung, Medlemsblad for Dansk Organist- og Kantorforening, Mitteilungen des Landesverbands bayerischer Tonkünstler, Münchner Merkur, Musik-Mappe, Münchner Mosaik, Münchner Neueste Nachrichten, Main-Post (Würzburg), Der Musiksalon, Monatsschrift für Schulegesang, Monatsschrift des Schweizerischen Studentenvereins, Münchner Telegramm-Zeitung, Die Musikantengilde, Münchner Zeitung, National-Zeitung, Neue Bahnen, Neue Leipziger Tageszeitung, Nuova Musica, Neue musikalische Presse, Nürnberger Nachrichten, Nordisk Musikkultur, Neue Presse (Coburg), Die neue Rundschau, NS-Kurier, Neues Sächsisches Kirchenblatt, Nationalsozialistliche Monatshefte, Der Neue Tag, Neues Tagblatt, Nürnberger Zeitung, Nimm und Lies, Nord und Süd (Berlin), Neues Wiener Journal, Neues Wiener Tagblatt, Neue Zeit, Die neue Zeit, Neue Zürcher Zeitung, Osterreichische Rundschau, Oberhessischer Anzeiger, Die Oberpfalz, Ostwacht, Pädagogische Blätter, Propyläen, Paris-Soir, Prager Tageblatt, Das Reich, Rheinische Blätter, Die Redenden Künste, Der Rundfunk, Rheinische Musik- und Theaterzeitung (Cologne), Rheinisch-Westfälische Zeitung (Essen), Rheinischer Merkur, Rhein-Neckar-Zeitung, Die Rheinpfalz, Ruch Muzyczny (Krakow), Der Roland von Berlin, Reclams Universum, Regensburger Woche, Der Siebenstern, Saarbrücker Zeitung, Sächsiste Zeitung, Der Sammler, Der Schlüssel, Sclesisches Blatt für evangelische Kirchenmusik, Schönere Zukunft, Schwabenspiegel, Schwäbische Donau-Zeitung, Schwäbische Landeszeitung, Schwäbische Post, Skizzen, Stuttgarter Nachrichten, Sonntagsblatt (Augsburg), Stadtanzeiger Köln, Die Stimme Frankens, St. Petersburger Zeitung, Strassburger Post, Stuttgarter Zeitung, Stimmen der

Zeit, Süddeutsche Monatshefte, Süddeutsche Zeitung, Sängerzeitung Thüringen, Der Türmer, Tages-Anzeiger, Tübinger Chronik, Das Thüringer Fähnlein, Thüringer Lehrerzeitung, Thüringische Monatsblätter, Terzo Programmo, Tägliche Rundschau (Berlin), Die Umschau, Unser Bayern, Ur nutidens musikliv (Stockholm), Urania, Die Volksbühne, Volksbühnenblätter, Velhagen & Klasings Monatshefte, Vossiche Zeitung, Die Woche, Die Weltbühne, Weimarer Blätter, Das Werk, Westfälisches Magazin, Westfälische Zeitung, Wachtfeuer, Westermanns illustrierte deutsche Monatshefte für das gesamte geistige Leben der Gegenwart, Westfälische Neueste Nachrichten, Die Wochenpost, Die Wochenschau, Württemburgisches Schulwochenblatt, Weekblad voor Muziek (Amsterdam), Weltwach der Deutschen, Weser-Zeitung, Der Zwiebelturm, Zeitschrift für kirchenmusikalische Beamte, Die Zeit (Berlin), and Die Zeitwende (Munich).

B862 Schreyer, Hans. Ahnenliste Max Reger. Kallmünz: M. Lassleben, 1959.
Lists Reger's ancestors alphabetically.

B863 Shigihara, Susanne. Max Reger Bibliographie: Das internationale Schriftum über Max Reger von 1967 bis 1981. Bonn: Dümmlers Verlag, 1983. Volume 9 of Veröffentlichungen des Max-Reger-Gesellschaft Elsa-Reger-Stiftung Bonn.
This excellent volume is a continuation of B861. Shigihara has included a listing of Reger literature from 1967-1981, a list of pre-1966 material overlooked by Rösner in B861 (along with corrections), and a list of special materials held by the Max-Reger-Institut in Bonn. The bibliography is listed alphabetically by author (instead of being grouped under genre as is the case with B861) and does not include annotations. Indices provided. Listings of difficult to obtain journals outside of Europe include: Börsenblatt für den deutschen Buchhandel, Blätter für Haus- und Kirchenmusik, Daheim, Deutsche Kultur-Wacht, Deutsche Tonkünstler-Zeitung, Deutsche Volksbildung, Die Freistatt, Die Gesellschaft, Die Meinat, Illustriertes Salonblatt, Magyar Zene (Budapest), Musik in Württemberg, Neue Musikalische Presse, Die Oberpfalz, Siona, Sovetskaya Muzyka (Moskow), Urania, and Der Zwiebelturm.

B864 Strassl, Alois. "Max Regers Werk und Persönlichkeit im Spiegel der Literatur." Osterreichische Musikzeitschrift 18 (1963): 137.
Very brief annotated bibliography on Reger.

Biographies

B865 Amory, A.H. Max Reger: Korte Levensschets. Amsterdam: Alsbach, 1916.

B866 Böttcher, Georg. Max Reger. Braunschweig: Bartels, 1919.

B867 Brand, Erna. Max Reger in Elternhaus. Munich: Langen-Müller, 1938.
An account of Reger's childhood and his relationship with his parents.

B868 Brand-Seltei, Erna. Max Reger: Jahre der Kindheit. Wilhelmshaven: Heinrichshofen, 1968.
Deals with Reger's life, schooling, and career to 1890. Also contains several Reger letters.

B869 Braungart, Richard. Freund Reger. Regensburg: Gustav Bosse Verlag, 1949.
Braungart's memories of Reger. Also contains an examination of many of Reger's compositions.

B870 Brock, Charlotte [Lotti Reger]. Max Reger als Vater: Erinnerungen von Charlotte Brock. Marburg: Braun, 1936.
A brief account of the Reger household.

B871 Hasse, Karl. Max Reger. Leipzig: Siegel, 1921.

B872 -----. Max Reger. 2 Volumes. Dortmund: Verlag W. Crüwell, 1951.
Contains excerpts from Reger's writings and reminiscences of Reger by many people associated with the composer. Also, an overview of the composer's life and works. Contains many musical examples.

B873 -----. Max Reger: Entwicklungsgang eines deutschen Meisters. Leipzig: Friedrich Brandstetter, 1946.
Hasse concentrates on the formative musical experiences of Reger's youth (hearing performances of Die Meistersinger and Parsifal at the age of 15, etc.), and the composer's experiences in Weiden, Munich, Leipzig, and Meiningen.

B874 Isler, Ernst. Max Reger. Zurich: Art Institut Orell Füssli, 1917.
Isler concentrates on Reger's critical reception in Switzerland and presents several chapters on the overall development of his music, the organ works, piano works, other instrumental works, songs and choral music, chamber music, and the orchestral music.

B875 Kallenberg, Siegfried. Max Reger. Leipzig: Verlag Philipp Reclam, 1929.
Very short biography. Contains some good remarks on Reger as a performer.

B876 Lindner, Adalbert. Max Reger: Ein Bild seines Jugendlebens und künstlerischen Werdens. Stuttgart: Engelhorn, 1922.

B877 Müller von Asow, Erich H. Max Reger und seine Welt. Berlin: Alfred Metzner, 1944.
A short monograph on Reger's life and career which gives the basic details. Includes many illustrations including the paintings by Arnold Böcklin which inspired Reger's Böcklin Suite, Op. 128, one of the composer's few attempts at program music.

B878 Otto, Eberhard. Max Reger als Mensch. Weiden: Verlag Knauf, 1966.
Gives details of Reger's family tree as well as delving into the work and personal habits of the composer.

B879 -----. Max Reger--Sinnbild einer Epoche. Wiesbaden: Breitkopf & Härtel, 1957.

B880 Poppen, Hermann. Max Reger: Leben und Werk. 2nd edition. Wiesbaden: Breitkopf & Härtel, 1947. [1st ed. 1918]
A sympathetic portrait of Reger and his music. Contains work lists (in opus numer order and by genre) and a brief bibliography.

B881 Reger, Elsa. Mein Leben mit und für Max Reger. Leipzig: Koehler & Amelang Verlag, 1930.
Contains Frau Reger's reminiscences of the composer along with discussions of moot of his works. Also contains photos of the Reger family and circle of acquaintances not found elsewhere.

B882 Segnitz, Eugen. Max Reger: Abriss seines Lebens uns Analyse seiner Werke. Leipzig: Historia-Verlag, 1922.
By one of Reger's close associates. Contains chapters on each major field of Reger's work.

B883 Stein, Fritz. Max Reger. Potsdam: Athenaion, 1939.

B884 -----. Max Reger 1873-1916: Sein Leben in Bildern. Leipzig: Bibliographisches Institut, 1946.

B885 Stein, Max Martin. Der Heitere Reger: Heiteres von und um Max Reger. Wiesbaden: Breitkopf & Härtel, 1969.
Contains numerous anecdotes and caricatures of Reger.

B886 Taube, Lotte. Max Regers Meisterjahre (1909-1916). Berlin: Bote & Bock, 1941.
Contains a chapter on each year from 1909-1916. Quotations from Reger's letters and writings are interspersed throughout the text.

B887 Unger, Hermann. Max Reger. Leipzig: Velhagem & Klasing, 1924.
Standard biography of Reger. Contains copious musical examples and photographs. No bibliography or footnotes.

B888 -----. Max Reger: Darstellung seines Lebens, Wesens und Schaffens. Munich: Drei Masken, 1921.
Examines Reger's life and works. Contains chapters on each of the major categories of compositions in which Reger composed. Also contains useful chapters on Reger's critical reception and his relationship to his time and to the future.

B889 Wirth, Helmut. Max Reger in Selbstzeugnissen und Bilddokumenten. Hamburg: Rowohlt, 1973.
Excellent short biography of Reger featuring excerpts from the composer's letters and writings. Also features a very large selection of photographs. Includes timetable of Reger's life, a selection of writings about Reger by important composers and performers, worklist, bibliography, and discography.

Books-General

B890 Abendroth, Walter. Vier Meister der Musik: Bruckner, Mahler, Reger, Pfitzner. Munich: Prestel, 1952.
Abendroth concentrates on the forms and compositional techniques employed by Reger in his music. Reger is referred to as a "Janus-faced" composer, alternately looking to the past and the future in his compositions. The chapter on Reger also contains a useful comparison and contrast between Reger and Bruckner.

B891 Albrecht, Christoph. Interpretationsfragen: Probleme der kirchenmusikalischen Aufführungspraxis von Walter bis Reger (1524-1916). Göttingen: Vandenhoeck & Ruprecht, 1982.
Contains an examination of performance problems (dynamics, tempi, organ registrations, form, etc.) in Reger's sacred music.

B892 Altmann, Wilhelm. Kleiner Führer durch die Streichquartette für Haus und Schule. Berlin: Deutscher Musikliteratur-Verlag, 1950.
Opp. 109 and 121 are briefly examined. [pp. 137-139]

B893 Arens, Hans, ed. Der grosse Europäer Stefan Zweig. Frankfurt: Fischer, 1981.
Contains a letter from Reger to Zweig dated March 29, 1907. [p. 80]

B894 Aulich, Bruno & Ernst Heimeran. Das stillvergnügte Streichquartette. Munich: Heimeran, 1936.
Contains brief descriptions of Opp. 54, 74, 109, and 121. [pp. 129-131]

B895 Austin, William. Music in the 20th Century. New York: W.W. Norton & Co., 1966.
Austin gives a very accurate and factual summary of Reger's life and compositional methods. Reger's position in music history is posited with that of Fauré. Mention is also made of students and composers influenced by Reger.

B896 Barlow, Harold & Sam Morgenstern. A Dictionary of Musical Themes. Revised edition. New York: Crown Publishers, Inc., 1975.
This work provides movement and thematic incipits for Reger's Opp. 130, 82/5, 123, 146, 87/2, 77a, and 103a. [pp. 379-380]

B897 Bauer, Rudolf. Das Konzert: Lebendige Orchestermusik bis zur Gegenwart. Berlin: Safari-Verlag, 1955.
Contains section on Reger. [pp. 501-513]

B898 Beaufils, Marcel. Le Lied romantique allemand. 4th edition. Paris: Gallimand, 1956.
Pages 294-299 deal briefly with Reger's lieder. The author remarks on Reger's overwhelming concern with the musical rather than the textual aspects of his songs and their harmonic complexity. "His [Reger's] chorales may be placed at the opposite end of the world of chorales, and his 'popular' songs at the opposite end of the universe of folklore."

B899 Beaumont, Antony. Busoni the Composer. Bloomington: Indiana University Press, 1985.
Quotes from Reger's highly favorable review of Busoni's Konzertstück in the AMZ (July 1894): 401.

B900 Bekker, Paul. Neue Musik. Berlin: Reiss, 1919.
A considerable portion of Bekker's exposition is given over to a discussion of Reger's compositional practices.

B901 Berrsche, Alexander. Trösterin Musika. Munich: Callwey, 1942.
Contains critical discussion and commentary on a large number of Reger's works, including Opp. 124, 86, 2, 71,

127, 146, 114, 64, 123, 106, 144, 95, 90, 74, 109, 118, 125, 108, 128, 141b, 81, 100, 132, 140, 101, 41, & 137.

B902 Bloch, Ernst. Geist der Utopie. Frankfurt: Suhrkamp. 1973.
Brief remarks on Reger's use of older musical forms, and on Opp. 106 and 128. [p. 89]

B903 Blom, Eric. A General Index to Modern Musical Literature in the English Language. New York: Da Capo, 1970 [1927].
Blom lists several articles and sections from books in English concerning Reger and his music. [p. 119]

B904 Brandl, Willy. Scherzo: Heiteres aus der Welt der Musik. Esslingen: Bechte Verlag, 1951.
This collection of amusing stories and aphorisms about famous composers and musicians contains a number of selections concerning Reger.

B905 Brod, Max. Max Brod Streitbares Leben: Autobiographie 1884-1968. Frankfurt: Insel Verlag, 1979.
Brod, best known as the translator of Janacek's libretti, was a Reger enthusiast. Contains a short chapter about Brod hosting Reger in Prague when the composer came to the city for a performance of his works.

B906 Bücken, Ernst. Führer und Probleme der neuen Musik. Cologne: Tonger, 1924.
Contains a section entitled "Die Grundlagen der Kunst Max Regers."

B907 Busch, Grete. Fritz Busch: Dirigent. Frankfurt: S. Fischer, 1970.
Discusses the life and work of Fritz Busch who often conducted Reger's works.

B908 Carner, Mosco. Alban Berg: The Man and the Work. 2nd revised edition. New York: Holmes & Meier, 1983.
Briefly discusses the overwhelming presence of Reger's compositions in theprograms of the Society for the Private Performance of Music.

B909 Dahlhaus, Carl. Die Musik des 19. Jahrhunderts. Wiesbaden: Akademische Verlagsgesellschaft Athenaion, 1980.
Dahlhaus makes comparisons of Reger's music to that of Wolf and Szymanowski, particularly in regards to the use of variations and rhythmic structure. Reger's Symphonic Prologue to a Tragedy and Strauss' 'Elektra' are regarded as high water marks in the artistic development

of both composers after which, in Dahlhaus' opinion, both composers turned away from modern techniques.

B910 Danuser, Hermann. Musikalische Prosa. Regensburg: Gustav Bosse, 1975. Volume 46 of Studien zur Musikgeschichte des 19. Jahrhunderts.
In the chapter "Der Ausdruck musikalische Prosa im Reger-Kreis" (pp. 119-124), the various ways in which the term "musical prose" has been applied to Reger's music by his biographers and analysts are examined. Includes a brief discussion of Opp. 43, 66, 64, 82,, 74, and 73. "Max Reger is the first composer in music history in whose works...the term 'musical prose' was explicitly referred to in the positive sense."

B911 Dettelbach, Hans von. Breviarium Musicae: Probleme, Werke, Gestalten. Darmstadt: Wissenschaftlichen Buchgesellschaft, 1958.
Pages 262-272 on Reger.

B912 -----. Breviarium Musicae: Werke, Probleme, Gestalten. Graz: Stiasny Verlag, 1967.
Contains a chapter on Reger (pp. 208-224) which deals extensively with the formal aspects of the composer's music, especially his use of variations techniques.

B913 Dopheide, Bernhard. Fritz Busch: Sein Leben und Wirken in Deutschland mit einem Ausblick auf die Zeit seiner Emigration. Tutzing: Hans Schneider, 1970.
Contains much information about Busch's conducting of Reger compositions. Includes lists of Reger's works conducted by Busch.

B914 Dümling, Albrecht. Lasst euch nicht verführen: Brecht und die Musik. Munich: Kindler Verlag, 1985.
Reger's influence on Kurt Weill is mentioned. (p. 137)

B915 Ebert-Stockinger, Klara. Helden des Willens: Lebenswerke aus neuerer Zeit. Stuttgart: Strecker & Schröder, 1928.
Pages 178-194 on Reger.

B916 Einstein, Alfred. Nationale und universale Musik. Zurich: 1958.
Pages 121-127 on Op. 108.

B917 Espina, Noni. Repertoire for the Solo Voice. Metuchen, N.J.: Scarecrow Press, 1977.
This book contains an annotated listing of 19 Reger lieder. Poets are listed as well as indications of range and degree of difficulty. [pp. I:567-569]

B918 Fellerer, Karl Gustav. Orgel und Orgelmusik: Ihre

Geschichte. Augsburg: Filser, 1929.

B919 Frotscher, Gotthold. Geschichte des Orgelspiels und der Orgelkomposition. 2 Volumes. Berlin: Hesse, 1936. Contains many good comments on Reger's organ playing and compositions for the organ.

B920 Gould, Glenn. The Glenn Gould Reader. New York: Alfred A. Knopf, 1985.
Reger is mentioned several times. "...Schoenberg in his later years developed the rather Max Reger-like trait of employing all constituent factors of a chord whenever possible." [p. 212]

B921 Gurlitt, Willibald. Hugo Riemann (1849-1919). Mainz: Akademie der Wissenschaften und der Literatur, 1951. Riemann's instruction of Reger (who is described as Riemann's favorite student) is discussed. [p. 24]

B922 Harburger, Walter. Form und Ausdrucksmittel in der Musik. Stuttgart: J. Engelhorn, 1926.
Contains an examination of Reger's use of dynamics as a means of artistic expression (pp. 119-139, "Die moderne Melodik: Die Atonalen und die Regersche Dynamik"). Harburger states: "But Reger, in my opinion, is close to being the first expressionist (while also keeping to a unity with the classical tradition via Brahms)...." [p. 134]

B923 Hase, Oskar von. Breitkopf & Härtel: Gedenkschrift und Arbeitsbericht. Volume 2. Wiesbaden: Breitkopf & Härtel, 1968.
Contains an account of Reger's dealings with the Breitkopf & Härtel publishing company concerning the publication of Opp. 19, 23, and 126, and Reger's arrangements of the works of other composers. Includes a letter from Reger (May 23, 1907) to the company. [pp. 544-546]

B924 Hase-Köhler, Else von, ed. Heldburg, Freifrau von (Ellen Franz). Gemahlin des Herzogs Georg II. von Sachsen-Meiningen: Fünfzig Jahre Glück und Leid. Ein Leben in Briefen aus den Jahren 1873-1923. 5th edition. Leipzig: Koehler & Amelang, 1926.
Contains several letters to Reger and his wife.

B925 Hasse, Karl. Ausgewählte Aufsätze. Regensburg, 1934.

B926 Hasse, Karl. Von deutschen Meistern: Zur Neugestaltung unseres Musiklebens im neuen Deutschland. Regensburg: Bosse, 1934.
Contains a short chapter on Reger (pp. 120-131) which

examines several facets of the composer's work, particularly the organ music.

B927 -----. Von deutscher Kirchenmusik. Regensburg: Bosse, 1936.
Contains the essay "Max Reger und die deutsche Orgelkunst" (pp. 110-124) in which an attempt is made to place Reger's religious music within the history of German church music in general.

B928 Held, Christoph & Ingrid. Karl Straube: Wirken und Wirkung. Berlin: Evangelische Verlagsanstalt, 1976.
Excellent biography of the Thomaskantor and Reger-enthusiast. Due to their close collaboration for many years there are numerous sections on the composer.

B929 Heldt, Gerhard. Das deutsche nachromantische Violinkonzert von Brahms bis Pfitzner. Regensburg: Gustav Bosse, 1973.
Contains a brief examination of the origin and form of Op. 101.

B930 Hilmar, Ernst, ed. Arnold Schönberg Gedenkausstellung 1974. Vienna: Universal Edition, 1974.
Contains several letters of Schönberg in which Reger is mentioned as well as two articles about the Society for the Private Performance of Music that deal with works by Reger which were performed by that organization.

B931 Horsley, Imogene. Fugue: History and Practice. New York: The Free Press, 1966.
Horsley discusses the fugal finales in Reger's Opp, 108 and 132. [pp. 368ff]

B932 Hughes, Gervase. Sidelights on a Century of Music (1825-1924). London: 1969.
Pages 188-194 on Reger.

B933 Jöde, Fritz. Die Kunst Bachs dargestellt an seinen Inventionen. Wolfenbüttel: 1926.
Includes a chapter entitled "Regers Orgelbearbeitung der Bachschen Inventionen." [pp. 199-223]

B934 Kerner, Dieter. Krankheiten Grosser Musiker. 2nd edition. Stuttgart: Friedrich-Karl Schattauer Verlag, 1967.
The chapter on Reger (pp. 141-161) contains an extensive examination of Reger's medical problems, a medical history of the composer's family, and biographical insights into the origins of Reger's later medical conditions, particularly smoking and drinking which appear to stem from the years of study with Riemann

(which the composer referred to as the "Storm and Drinking" years).

B935 Klaus, Kenneth B. The Romantic Period in Music. Boston: Allyn and Bacon, 1970.
Klaus presents a strong defense of Reger as a composer and contends that the vast majority of Reger's critics have never come into contact with anu of the composer's works. Musical examples taken from Opp. 132 and 82.

B936 Kolneder, Walter. Anton Webern: An Introduction to His Works. Translated by Humphrey Searle. Berkeley: University of California Press, 1968.
In several instances Kolneder discusses Reger's influence on Webern. Webern's Op. 23/1 is compared to Reger's Schlichte Weisen. [p. 124]

B937 Kötzsche, Richard. Geschichte der Universitäts-Sängerschaft zu St. Pauli in Leipzig 1822-1922. Leipzig: 1922.
Includes a chapter entitled "Der Paulus unter Max Regers und Friedrich Brandes' Leitung bis Ende Juli 1914." [pp. 416-467]

B938 Kraft, Zdenko von. Grosse Musiker: Berühmte Tonsetzer als Menschen. Munich: J.F. Lehmann, 1961.
The chapter on Reger (pp. 378-387) deals almost exclusively with Reger's personality and homelife. In the chapter on Hugo Wolf, the relationship between Wolf and Reger is briefly discussed.

B939 Kretzschmar, Hermann. Kirchliche Werke. 5th edition. Leipzig: Breitkopf & Härtel, 1921. Volume II of Führer durch den Konzertsaal.
A brief discussion on Op. 106 and the chorale cantatas. [pp. 443-445, 608-609]

B940 Krug, Walter. Die neue Musik. Zurich: Eugen Rentsch, 1920.
The section on Reger (pp. 44-56) traces the development of romanticism through Reger's works.

B941 Kusche, Ludwig. Musik und Musiker in Baiern. Munich: Süddeutscher Verlag, 1963.
Briefly considers Reger and his work (especially in comparison to that of Richard Strauss) in an attempt to determine Reger's place in music history.

B942 Lang, Paul Henry. Music in Western Civilization. New York: W.W. Norton & Co., 1941.
Lang views Reger's contrapuntal writing as "pseudo-polyphony", the result of rapidly shifting harmonies.

Lang also considers Reger to be the German counterpart to Debussy inasmuch as the two composers utilized harmonies in a non-functional manner.

B943 Laux, Karl. Joseph Haas. Düsseldorf: Progress-Verlag, 1954.

B944 -----. Joseph Haas: Leben und Werk. Leipzig: 1957.

B945 -----. Joseph Haas: Porträt eines Künstlers, Bild einer Zeit. Mainz: 1931.

B946 Leichtentritt, Hugo. Music, History, and Ideas. Cambridge University Press, 1947.
Leichtentritt describes the great success of Reger's compositions during the years 1909-1914, stating: "No composer of the present time can boast of even a slight approach to Reger's triumphal presentation of his own works during those luxurious prewar years." [pp. 249-250]

B947 Lewinski, Wolf-Eberhard von. Ludwig Hoelscher. Tutzing: Hans Schneider, 1967.
Contains some insights on Hoelscher's performance of Reger's cello sonatas. [pp. 29ff]

B948 Louis, Rudolf. Die deutsche Musik der Gegenwart. Munich: Müller, 1909.
Brief discussion of Reger's music, particularly in comparison to that of Richard Strauss.

B949 Lukas, Viktor. Orgelmusikführer. Stuttgart: Reclam, 1963.
Contains a brief description of the more important organ compositions of Reger (with musical examples). [pp. 180-193]

B950 Machlis, Joseph. Introduction to Contemporary Music. New York: W.W. Norton & Co., 1961.
Machlis gives the standard account of Reger's life with the caveat that the composer's music is for native consumption only. The author does, however, mention Reger's influence on Hindemith. [pp. 105-107]

B951 Malsch, Rudolf. Geschichte der deutschen Musik: Ihre Formen, ihr Stil und ihre Stellung im deutschen Geistes- und Kulturleben. Berlin: Lichterfelde, 1928.
Brief discussion of Reger's music. Gives some musical examples. [pp. 337-340]

B952 Marteau, Blanche. Henri Marteau: Siegeszug einer Geige. Tutzing: Hans Schneider, 1971.
Contains much useful information about the collaboration

between Reger and Henri Marteau who premiered the composer's Violin Concerto, Op. 101.

B953 Mayer, Ludwig K. Die Musik des 20. Jahrhunderts: Von der Nachromantik bis in die neueste Zeit. Zurich: Leitner. Briefly discusses Reger's harmonic practices and makes a comparison to other composers. Mentions some of Reger's most important works.

B954 Mellers, Wilfrid. Romanticism and the 20th Century. London: Rockliff, 1957. Mellers views Reger's use of contrapuntal forms to control his chromaticism as being somewhat reminiscent of procedures employed earlier by Liszt. Also includes Meller's well known statement that "...Reger is most impressive when he is least in awe of Bach...." [pp. 193-196]

B955 Mersmann, Hans. Eine deutsche Musikgeschichte. Potsdam: Sans-souci-Verlag, 1934. A very brief overview of the career of Reger is given. Also contains several musical examples and caricatures of Reger. [pp. 481-484]

B956 -----. Die moderne Musik seit der Romantik. Potsdam: Athenaion, 1927.

B957 -----. Die Kammermusik. Leipzig: Breitkopf & Härtel, 1930. Volume III of Führer durch den Konzertsaal. Reger's Opp. 77, 42, 91, 117, 54, 74, 109, 121, 1, 3, 5, 28, 41, 49, 72, 78, 107, 93, and 103 are examined, some in detail. [pp. 132-150]

B958 Meyer, Wilhelm. Charakterbilder grosser Tonmeister: Persönliches und Intimes aus ihrem Leben und Schaffen. Band 4: Chopin, Brahms, Bruckner, Reger. Bielefeld: V & K, 1920.

B959 Moldenhauer, Hans & Rosaleen. Anton Webern: A Chronicle of His Life and Work. New York: Alfred A. Knopf, 1979. In his recollections of Webern, Karl Amadeus Hartmann says of his teacher: "He esteems Reger highly, and it is very enjoyable to take apart under his guidance the String Quartet in F Sharp Minor."

B960 Moser, Hans Joachim. Das deutsche Lied seit Mozart. Zurich: Atlantis Verlag, 1937. In the section on Reger's songs Moser comments on the prolific nature of Reger's song output and makes a brief comparison with the songs of Strauss, Wolf, and Pfitzner. [pp. 301-304]

B961 -----. Die evangelische Kirchenmusik in Deutschland. Berlin: Verlag Carl Merseburger, 1953.
Good overview of motets, religious songs, and organ music. Explains about Reger's indebtedness to both Bach and Brahms. Musical examples taken from Opp. 110/3, 46, and 135b. [pp. 255-264, 446-450]

B962 -----. Geschichte der deutschen Musik vom Auftreten Beethovens bis zur Gegenwart. 2nd edition. Stuttgart: Cotta, 1928.
Pages 436-449 on Reger.

B963 -----. Kleine deutsche Musikgeschichte. Stuttgart: Cotta, 1949.
Pages 302-306 on Reger.

B964 -----. Musikgeschichte in hundert Lebensbildern. Stuttgart: Reclam, 1952.
Pages 887-893 on Reger.

B965 Müller-Blatau, Joseph. Geschichte der Fuge. 3rd expanded edition. Kassel: Bärenreiter, 1963.
Discusses Reger's use of fugal techniques in Opp. 46, 54, 57, 81, 86, 96, 100, 109, 131b, 132, 135, and 141b. [pp. 120-121]

B966 Nardone, Thomas R. Organ Music in Print. Philadelphia: Musicdata, Inc., 1975.
Nardone lists in alphabetical order the organ music of Reger that is in print. Also includes publishers and addresses. [pp. 184-185]

B967 Nef, Karl. Geschichte der Sinfonie und Suite. Leipzig: Breitkopf & Härtel, 1921.

B968 Nelson, Robert U. The Technique of Variation: A Study of the Instrumental Variation from Antonio de Cabezon to Max Reger. Berkeley: University of California Press, 1962.
Examines Reger's use of the variations form in Opp. 127, 96, 100, 132, 134, and 117/4.

B969 Newman, William S. The Sonata Since Beethoven. 2nd edition. New York: W.W. Norton & Co., 1972.
This book contains an excellent overview of Reger's considerable sonata output and includes a very useful discussion of the composer's harmonic theories as well. A complete list of all of Reger's sonatas is given. Newman's documentation is outstanding and his assessment of Reger's sonatas is highly favorable (calling Reger "the most important composer of sonatas" of central Germany during the late-romantic era). [pp. 432-442]

B970 Niemann, Walter. Die Musik der Gegenwart. Berlin: Schuster & Loeffler, 1921.
Contains the chapter "Die Weiterentwicklung des Brahmsischen Klassizimus zur Moderne Max Regers" (pp. 153-171) in which the influence of Reger is traced as well as Reger's continuation of the Brahmsian tradition of classical-romanticism.

B971 -----. Die Musik seit Richard Wagner. Berlin: Schuster & Loeffler, 1913.
Contains the chapter "Der Zerfall des Brahmsischen Klassizismus in modernes Barock" (pp. 196-210) in which Reger's neo-baroque and neo-classic tendencies and their influence on later generations are discussed.

B972 Pahlen, Kurt. Sinfonie der Welt. Zurich: Schweizer, 1967.
Contains brief verbal descriptions of Opp. 90, 93, 95, 100, 101, 108, 114, 123, 125, 128, and 130. [pp. 253-56]

B973 Petersen, Barbara A. Ton und Wort: The Lieder of Richard Strauss. Ann Arbor: UMI Research Press, 1980.
Contains discussions of some of Reger's songs, particularly those in which the same texts were set by both Reger and Strauss. (See especially pp. 81-89, "The Treatment of Identical Texts by Strauss and Reger.")

B974 Piersig, Johannes. Das Fortschrittsproblem in der Musik un die Jahrhundertwende. Regensburg: Gustav Bosse Verlag, 1977. Volume 53 of Studien zur Musikgeschichte des 19. Jahrhunderts.
In section III/2 (pp. 121-145), "Die Zerfall der funktionellen Harmonik", Reger's role in the transition from "functional" tonality to atonality is assessed. Piersig comments on the harmonic basis of Reger's counterpoint which is referred to as "Scheinpolyphonie".

B975 Quoika, Rudolf. Albert Schweitzers Begegnung mit der Orgel. Berlin: Merseburger, 1954.
Contains some of Schweitzer's insights into Reger's organ music. Organ registrations are given.

B976 Raupp, Wilhelm. Max von Schillings: Der Kampf eines deutschen Künstlers. Hamburg: Hanseatische Verlag, 1935.
Although Schillings is often presented as an artistic antipode to Reger, the former's Prologue to Sophocles' "Oedipus Rex" inspired Reger's Op. 108. Reger's thoughts on Schillings are examined, particularly in pp. 93-94.

B977 Reichelt, Johannes. Erlebte Kostbarkeiten: Begegnungen mit Künstlern in Bekenntnisstunden. Leipzig: Payne, 1936.
The chapter on Reger (pp. 51-70) concentrates on the composer's relationship to the music of J.S. Bach.

B978 Reiser, Rudolf. Alte Häuser-Grosse Namen. München. Munich: Bruckmann, 1978.
On pp. 142-145 is a short article and photograph of Reger's house on Viktor-Scheffel-Strasse where the composer lived ca. 1905-1906.

B979 Reuter, Florizel von. Great People I Have Known. Waukesha, Wisconsin: The Cultural Press, 1961.
Contains Reuter's memories of Reger. [pp. 102-107]

B980 Roberts, Kenneth. A Checklist of Twentieth-Century Choral Music for Male Voices. Detroit: Information Coordinators, Inc., 1970. Volume 17 of Detroit Studies in Music Bibliography.
Roberts recommends for performance Reger's Requiem and the Chorale-Cantata for Christmas.

B981 Rosen, Charles. Arnold Schoenberg. New York: The Viking Press, 1975.
Rosen briefly discusses Reger's influence on Schönberg and the frequency of performance of Reger's compositions on the programs of the Society for the Private Performance of Music.

B982 Rufer, Josef. Composition with Twelve Notes Related Only to One Another. Translated by Humphrey Dearle. London: Barrie and Rockliff, 1954.
In this book Rufer, a student of Arnold Schönberg's, traces the development of dodecaphonic music from the late 19th-century chromatic harmonists to Schönberg and the Second Viennese School. The author demonstrates that 12-tone melodies are found in abundance in Reger's later music. (Examples listed are from Opp. 121, 122, & 141b.) Rufer quotes the German composer Winfried Zillig who makes the following statement supporting Reger's contribution to the development of the dodecaphonic idea: "...the twelve-note system seems to me personally to be an extraordinary expression of the search for the mysterious, strange and new--a search which can already be found in Mozart...,became the aim of Wagner and Reger and was finally attained by Schoenberg." [p. 200]

B983 Salazar, Adolfo. Music in Our Time: Trends in Music Since the Romantic Era. Translated by Isabel Pope. New York: W.W. Norton & Co., 1946.
Salazar denigrates Reger's compositions and finds value only in the composer's chamber works. According to

Salazar, Reger and his students pursued "fruitless careers" not in "the field of artistic intuitions but technical conventions." Schönberg, Busoni, Stravinsky, Hindemith, and Milhaud are likewise treated, all of whom Salazar considers to have composed into "blind alleys." [pp. 117-120, 280]

B984 Salevic, Marion. Die Vertonung der Psalmen Davids im 20. Jahrhundert: Studien im deutschen Sprachbereich. Regensburg: Gustav Bosse Verlag, 1976.
Brief discussion of some of Reger's psalm settings as well as those of his student Joseph Haas. [pp. 82-104]

B985 Schmid-Lindner, August. Ausgewählte Schriften. Tutzing: 1973.

B986 Schmidt, Christian Martin. Johannes Brahms und seine Zeit. Regensburg: Laaber-Verlag, 1983.
Makes some comparisons of the works of Brahms and Reger and the mutual interest of the two composers in new editions of earlier music.

B987 Schoenberg, Arnold. Style and Idea. Translated by Leo Black. New York: St. Martin's Press, 1975.
In the essay "Criteria for the Evaluation of Music" Schoenberg presents his now famous concept of the "developing variation" and discusses the contributions of Reger, Mahler, and himself to the establishment of this compositional procedure. Reger also features prominently in Schoenberg's most famous essay "Brahms the Progressive" in which Schoenberg demonstrates Brahms' influence over Reger, Strauss, and Mahler regarding irregular rhythmic and phrase structures. Reger's Op. 101 is used as an example. [p. 427]

B988 Schumann, Otto. Handbuch der Klaviermusik. 4th edition. Wilhelmshaven: Heinrichshofen, 1979.
Very good synopsis (with musical examples) of Reger's piano music. [pp. 547-574]

B989 Seidl, Arthur. Neuzeitliche Tondichter und zeitgenössische Tonkünstler. 2 Volumes. Regensburg: Gustav Bosse, 1926.
Contains a brief section on Reger (pp. 89-94), mostly an essay with no musical examples.

B990 Slonimsky, Nicolas. Lexicon of Musical Invective: Assaults on Composers Since Beethoven's Time. 2nd edition. Seattle: University of Washington Press, 1965.
Contains several very critical reviews, including Rudolf Louis' famous denunciation of the Sinfonietta, along

with Reger's equally famous reply. [pp. 139-142]

B991 -----. Music Since 1900. 3rd enlarged edition. New York: Coleman-Ross Co., Imc., 1949.
Mention is made of several premieres of Reger works and "A Statement of Aims" by Alban Berg for the Society for the Private Performance of Music lists works by Reger performed and rehearsed by that organization during its first few months of existence.

B992 Söhngen, Oskar. Die Wiedergeburt der Kirchenmusik: Wandlungen und Entscheidungen. Kassel: Bärenreiter, 1953.
Contains the essay "Max Regers Stellung in der kirchenmusikalischen Entwicklung [1941]" (pp. 122-146), an attempt to assess Reger's role in the development of church music in the 20th century, and also the essay "Thomaskantor Dr. Karl Straube zum 70. Geburtstag [1943]" (pp. 147-150), a tribute to Reger's close friend.

B993 Spengler, Oswald. The Decline of the West: Volume II Perspectives of World History. Translated by Charles Francis Atkinson. New York: Alfred A. Knopf, 1981.
Spengler sees a trend towards the "intellectual art of playing with expression" in the artistic creations of Reger, Kierkegaard, Theocritus, and Brentano. [pp. 136-137]

B994 Stargardt-Wolff, Edith. Wegbereiter grosser Musiker. Berlin: Bote & Bock, 1954.
Contains reminiscences of Reger by Hermann and Louise Wolff. [pp. 94, 182-184, and 222-223]

B995 Stein, Erwin, ed. Arnold Schoenberg Letters. Translated by Eithene Wilkins & Ernst Kaiser. New York: St. Martin's Press, 1965.
In a letter to Alexander Zemlinsky dated October 26, 1922, Schoenberg says of Reger: "...Reger must in my view be done often; 1, because he has written a lot; 2, because he is already dead and people are still not clear about him. (I consider him a genius.)"

B996 Stier, Friedrich. Ehrung deutscher Musiker durch die Universität Jena. Weimar: Böhlau, 1955.
Gives an account of Reger's honorary doctorate at Jena in 1908 for which Reger composed Op. 106. [pp. 41-45]

B997 Straube, Karl. Briefe eines Thomaskantors. Stuttgart: H.O. Hudemann, 1952.
Contains many letters to Reger.

B998 Stuckenschmidt, H.H. Die grossen Komponisten unseres

Jahrhunderts, Bd. 1 Deutschland und Mitteleuropa. Munich: Piper, 1970.
Contains a chapter on Reger (pp. 29-38) which features the standard biographical material and a brief discussion of the composer's music.

B999 -----. Twentieth-Century Composers, Vol. II Germany and Central Europe. New York: Holt, Rinegart and Winston, 1970.
Stuckenschmidt's brief overview of Reger's life and career is one of the most thorough and balanced available in English. Much attention is paid to the great influence Reger had upon a whole generation of composers (Second Viennese School, Hindemith, and Honegger). [pp. 31-40ff]

B1000 -----. Twentieth Century Music. Translated by Richard Deveson. New York: McGraw-Hill, 1969.
Stuckenschmidt views Reger's compositional style as a type of "musical prose" in which symmetrical phrase structures are avoided as well as the scale degrees of the various tonalities Reger employs. In this regard Reger is linked to Mussorgsky in the development of ultra-chromaticism.

B1001 Susskind, Charles. Janacek and Brod. New Haven: Yale University Press, 1985.
Brod's admiration for Reger is chronicled along with an accounting of a meeting between the two men in Prague. [p. 11]

B1002 Thomas, Ludwig. Ein Leben in Briefen [1875-1921]. Munich: Piper, 1963.
Very brief mention of Reger and his Christmas music. [pp. 328-330]

B1003 Tovey, Donald Francis. Essays in Musical Analysis. Volume IV. 2nd edition. New York: Oxford University Press, 1961. [1939]
Tovey analyses Op. 128, Reger's only overtly programmatic orchestral work, and points out, among other things, the impressionistic tendencies of the composition, especially its similarity to Debussy's La Mer. [pp. 166-169]

B1004 -----. Essays in Musical Analysis. Volume VI. 2nd edition. New York: Oxford University Press, 1963. [1939]
This book includes an insightful analysis of Op. 95. Tovey makes two interesting points: (1) Reger's compositional style is essentially improvisatory in nature; and (2) Reger's mastery of sonata form does not include a

mastery of the inherent dramatic nature of the form. [pp. 65-73]

B1005 Unger, Udo. Die Klavierfuge im zwanzigsten Jahrhundert. Regensburg: Gustav Bosse, 1956. Volume 11 of Kölner Beiträge zur Musikforschung.
Contains a discussion of fugal techniques in Reger's keyboard music, with particularly extensive treatment given to Op. 81.

B1006 Unverricht, Hubert. Geschichte des Streichtrios. Tutzing: Hans Schneider, 1969.
Reger's trios Opp. 77a, 77b, 141a, and 141b are examined. [pp. 279-282]

B1007 Voge, Richard. Fritz Heitmann: Das Leben eines deutschen Organisten. Berlin: Verlag Merseburger, 1963.
An account of one of Reger's students and most devoted promoters of the composer's organ music. (Heitmann also studied with Karl Straube.)

B1008 Vogel, Werner. Othmar Schoeck: Leben und Schaffen im Spiegel von Selbstzeugnissen und Zeitgenossenberichten. Zurich: Atlantis, 1976.
Contains several letters from Reger who was Schoeck's composition teacher at Leipzig.

B1009 Walker, Hugo. Hugo Wolf: A Biography. New York: Alfred A. Knopf, 1951.
Walker discusses Reger's editing of Wolf's Italian Serenade (pp. 309-310) and gives an overview as to Reger's contribution to the composition of the work.

B1010 Weissmann, Adolf. Die Musik in der Weltkrise. Stuttgart: Deutsche Verlagsanstalt, 1922.
Contains a chapter entitled "Von Brahms bis Reger" (pp. 118-128). A number of Reger's works are examined including Opp. 72, 106, 100, and 146.

B1011 Wellesz, Egon. Cobbett's Cyclopedic Survey of Chamber Music. 3 Volumes. London: Oxford University Press, 1930.
Reger's chamber music is discussed on pp. 277-338.

B1012 Weyer, Martin. Die deutsche Orgelsonate von Mendelssohn bis Reger. Regensburg: Gustav Bosse, 1969. Volume 55 of Kölner Beiträge zur Musikforschung.
Contains a good examination of Opp. 33 and 60 in the chapter "Regers Sonaten in ihrem Verhältnis zur romantischen Orgelsonate" (pp. 147-166). Includes extensive musical examples.

B1013 Wolgast, Johannes. Karl Straube: Eine Würdigung seiner Musikpersönlichkeit anlässlich seiner 25 jährigen Tätigkeit in Leipzig. Leipzig: Breitkopf & Härtel, 1928.

B1014 Wolters, Klaus & Franzpeter Goebels. Handbuch der Klavierliteratur Volume I: Klaviermusik zu zwei Händen. Zurich: Atlantis, 1967.
Annotated bibliography of 2-hand piano music. Contains a section on Reger (pp. 419-423). Reger's works appearing as part of anthologies are also listed.

B1015 Wulf, Joseph, ed. Musik im Dritten Reich: Eine Dokumentation. Gütersloh: Sigbert Mohn Verlag, 1963.
Brief mention of Reger on p. 43 in which Siegfried Kallenberg describes Reger as "expressionist and romantic in one person."

B1016 Yastrebtsev, V.V. Reminiscences of Rimsky-Korsakov. Edited and Translated by Florence Jonas. New York: Columbia University Press, 1985.
Rimsky-Korsakov's opinion of Reger is given on p. 396: "His [Reger's] fugues are better than his other things, but in our day the ability to write fugues more or less well doesn't indicate a real gift for composition but just the opposite. All in all, I cannot understand what there is to like about this composer."

B1017 Zillig, Winfried. Von Wagner bis Strauss. Munich: Nymphenburger Verlagshandlung, 1966.
A good discussion of Reger's music done mostly in chronological order. No musical examples. [pp. 131-144]

Discographies

B1018 Drengemann, Heinz-Rüdiger. "'Reger neobarock.' Kritische Bemerkungen zur gegenwärtigen Reger-Renaissance anlässlich neuer Schallplatten." K 24 (1973): 138-141.

B1019 Fuhrmann, Peter. "Schallplatten zum Reger-Jahr." Opernwelt 8 (1973): 47-48.

B1020 Heckenbach, Willibrod. "Diskographie der Orgelwerke von Max Reger." MS 93 (1973): 97-100.

B1021 Herand, Frank. "A Reger Discography." Diapason 62:7 (1971): 27.
Herand lists recordins of Reger organ compositions on the following labels: Da Camera, Christophorus, Psallite, Telefunken, MPS, Pelca, Electrola, Vogue, Quadriga, Polydor, Supraphon, Philips, Fona, Life, and

Aeolian-Skinner.

B1022 Konold, Wulf. "An der Schwelle zum 20. Jahrhundert: Analytische und diskografische Bemerkungen zu Regers Kammermusik." Fono-Forum (1974): 100-106.
An examination of recordings of Reger's chamber music. The music is considered chronologically.

B1023 -----. "Regers Kammermusik: Chronologie und Interpretation." Fono-Forum (1974): 216.
Lists recordings of Reger's chamber music (with the compositions listed in chronological order). Also includes a photograph of a Reger stamp from the DDR.

B1024 Pfluger, Rolf. "Diskographie der Werke von Max Reger." Osterreichische Musikzeitschrift 28 (1973): 153-156.
A very thorough discography of Reger's works as of 1973. Contains some minor errors in numbering.

B1025 Rockwell, John. "Max Reger: Windbag or Prophet?" High Fidelity 24:5 (1974): 53-59.
This article is an extended discographic essay on recordings of Reger compositions readily available ca. 1974.

B1026 Schermall, Herbert. Max Reger--Eine Diskographie. Berlin: Deutsche Musikphonothek, 1966.

B1027 Schürmann, Hans G. "Reger-Platten im Reger-Jahr: Versuch eines ersten kritischen Überblicks." MU 37 (1973): 300-303.
Annotated selective discography of Reger's music as of 1973.

B1028 Wienke, Gerhard. "Max Reger--von der Schallplatte vergessen?" Phono-Prisma 9 (1966): 34-37.

B1029 Wirth, Helmut. "Max Reger: Eine Diskographie zu seinem 50. Todestag." Fono-Forum 11 (1966): 228ff.

Dissertations

B1030 Coenen, Paul. Max Regers Variationsschaffen. Berlin, 1935.

B1031 Dejmek, Gaston Roman. Der Variationszyklus bei Max Reger. Bonn, 1930.

B1032 Gatscher, Emanuel. Die Fugentechnik Max Regers in ihrer Entwicklung. Bonn, 1922.

B1033 Gibson, Benn. The Organ Works of Max Reger: Problems Involved in Their Performance: One-Manual Organs, A Historical Survey; One-Manual Organs, A Handbook. II Performance (Organ). Northwestern, 1973.

B1034 Glaeser, Robert. Die Stilentwicklung bei Max Reger unter besonderer Berücksichtigung der Kammermusik. Vienna, 1938.

B1035 Holliman, Jamesetta V. A Stylistic Study of Max Reger's Solo Piano Variations and Fugues on Themes by Johann Sebastian Bach and Georg Philipp Telemann. New York University, 1975.

B1036 Hopkins, William Thomas. The Short Piano Compositions of Max Reger (1873-1916). Indiana, 1972.

B1037 Huesgen, Rudolf. Der junge Max Reger und seine Orgelwerke. Freiburg, 1935.

B1038 Jordahl, Robert. A Study of the Use of the Chorale in the Works of Mendelssohn, Brahms and Reger. University of Rochester, 1965.

B1039 Jung, Wilfried. Der Künstlerbrief als Informationsquelle --am Beispiel Max Reger. Seminar Project, Pädagogische Hochschule Nürnberg der Universität Erlangen-Nürnberg, 1970.

B1040 Kalkoff, Arthur. Das Orgelschaffen Max Regers im Lichte der deutschen Orgelerneuerungsbewegung. Jena, 1944.

B1041 Kostelecky, Emma. Die Sologeige bei Max Reger. Vienna, 1938.

B1042 Kranz, Maria Hinrichs. Max Reger: Piano Variations on Themes of Bach, Beethoven, Telemann. American Conservatory of Music, 1985.
This work contains a detailed discussion of the three variations sets for piano by Reger. The contrast between neo-romantic and neo-classic tendencies in these compositions is examined.

B1043 Krejnina, Julia. Maks Reger kak javlenie nemeckoj muzykal' noj Kul'tury. [Max Reger as a Manifestation of German Musical Culture] Moscow, 1976.

B1044 Langner, Thomas Martin. Studien zur Dynamik Max Regers. Berlin, 1952.

B1045 Maki, Paul-Martin. The Three Chorale-Fantasies, Op. 52 of Max Reger: Commentary and a Practical Edition (Parts and 2). Eastman, 1975.

B1046 Müller, Herbert. Studien zu Regers Personstil an Hand seiner Violin-Klavier Sonaten. Vienna, 1964.

B1047 Nelson, Robert Uriel. The Technical Development of the Instrumental Variation from Cabezon to Reger. Harvard, 1944.

B1048 Nolte, Hans. Die Meiningen Hof- und Landeskapelle in den Jahren 1880 bis 1945. Halle, 1974.

B1049 Pohl, Elisabeth. Die Harmonik in den Leidern Max Regers als Ausdrucksfaktor. Vienna, 1936.

B1050 Rahner, Hugo Ernst. Max Regers Choralfantasien. Eine Studie über Grundlagen und Werden des Regerschen Orgelstil. Heidelberg, 1936.

B1051 Ramge, Heinz. Max Regers Orchesterbehandlung, insbesondere seine Retuschen an Meininger Repertoirewerken. Marburg/Lahn, 1966.

B1052 Schmid, R. Die Linienstruktur in Regers "Schlichten Weisen". Vienna, 1929.

B1053 Schmidt, Hans. Untersuchungen zur choralbezogenen Orgelmusik seit Max Reger. Erlangen, 1952.

B1054 Schmitt, Hans. Studien zur Geschichte und Stilistik des Satzes für zwei Klaviere zu vier Händen. Saarbrücken, 1965.

B1055 Sievers, Gerd. Die Grundlagen Hugo Riemanns bei Max Reger. Hamburg, 1949.

B1056 Stange, Günther. Die geistesgeschichtlichen und religiösen Grundlagen im kirchenmusikalischen Schaffen Max Regers: Eine theologische Untersuchung. Leipzig, 1966.

B1057 Stockmeier, Wolfgang. Die deutsche Orgelsonate der Gegenwart. Cologne, 1958.
Deals with Reger's Opp. 33 and 60.

B1058 Teerisuo, Timo. Aarre Merikanannon Ooppera Juha. [Aare Merikanto's Opera "Juha"] Helsinki, 1970.

B1059 Trapp, Klaus. Die Fuge in der deutschen Romantik von Schubert bis Reger: Studien zu ihrer Entwicklung und Bedeutung. Frankfurt, 1958.

B1060 Trock, Josef. Die Orchesterwerke Max Regers. Vienna,

1937.

B1061 Troeblinger, Carl Friedrich. Die Suite im Schaffen Max Reger. Frankfurt, 1943.

B1062 Troskie, Albertus Jakobus Johannes. Die Koorwerke van Max Reger (1873-1916). [The Choral Works of Max Reger (1873-1916)] Wysbegeerte University (South Africa), 1975.

B1063 Wakely, Charles Sherwood. A Study of the Chorale Preludes of Max Reger with Reference to Those by J.S. Bach. Master of Sacred Music Thesis, Union Theological Seminary, New York City, 1954.

B1064 Walter, Rudolf. Max Regers Choralvorspiele für Orgel. Mainz, 1949.

B1065 Wehmeyer, Grete. Max Reger als Liederkomponist: Ein Beitrag zum Problem der Wort-Ton-Beziehung. Cologne, 1950.

B1066 Weyer, Martin. Die deutsche Orgelsonate von Mendelssohn bis Reger. Cologne, 1969.

B1067 Whitsitt, Don Everett. A Conductor's Analysis of Selected Choral Works of Max Reger. Indiana, 1976.

B1068 Wilhelmer, August. Die Choralfantasien Max Regers. Vienna, 1928.

B1069 Wolf, James Gary. The Solo Pianoforte Variations of Max Reger. University of Rochester, 1964.

B1070 Wolf, Margarete. Des Capriccio in Regers Klaviermusik. Vienna, 1928.

B1071 Wünsch, Gerhard. Die Entwicklung des Klaviersatzes bei Max Reger. Vienna, 1950.

Encyclopedia & Dictionary Entries

B1072 Altmann, Frank. Tonkünstler Lexikon. Wilhelmshaven: Hinrichshofen, 1971.
Very brief listing.

B1073 Baker's Biographical Dictionary of Musicians. 7th edition. pp. 1868-1870.

B1074 Moser, Hans Joachim. Musiklexikon. 4th edition. Hamburg: Sikorski, 1955.
Good general overview of Reger's life and work.

B1075 Popp, Susanne. "Reger, Johann Baptist Joseph Max." Das Grosse Lexikon der Musik. 1976.
Good short overview of Reger's life and work. Contains work list (by type), a brief list of Reger's prose writings, and a short bibliography.

B1076 Riemann Musik Lexikon. 1976.
Gives only a few works of Reger along with a bibliography.

B1077 Wirth, Helmut. "Reger, Johann Baptist Joseph Max." Die Musik in Geschichte und Gegenwart.
Contains very complete work list and bibliography. Wirth discusses Reger's circle of friends and admirers and also the composers influenced by his music.

B1078 -----. "Reger, (Johann Baptist Joseph) Max(imilian)." New Grove Dictionary of Music and Musicians.
Excellent work list, bibliography, and biography.

Festschriften

Beiträge zu Regerforschung. Festschrift aus Anlass des 80. Geburtstages des Meisters am 19. März 1953. Leipzig, 1953.

B1079 Haas, Joseph. "Das Künstler- und Menschentum Regers im eigenen Wort." pp. 7-12.

B1080 Hasse, Karl. "Max Regers musikalische Sendung." pp. 13-16.

B1081 Unger, Hermann. "Max Reger als Weggenosse Bachs und Beethovens." pp. 17-20.

B1082 Moser, Hans Joachim. "Max Regers Orchesterwerke." pp. 21-34.

B1083 Kalkoff, Arthur. "Die Orgelwerke Max Regers und die neue Orgelbewegung." pp. 35-52.

B1084 Wehmeyer, Grete. "Max Regers Auseinandersetzung mit dem Lied." pp. 53-58.

B1085 Poppen, Hermann Meinhard. "Über das Charakterische an Regers Tonsprache." pp. 59-64.

B1086 Grabner, Hermann. "Regers Bedeutung für das gegenwärtige Schaffen." pp. 65-71.

B1087 Stein, Fritz. "Max Reger als Freund." pp. 72-80.

B1088 Schmid-Lindner, August. "Aus meinem Erinnerungen an Max Reger." pp. 81-84.

B1089 Güntzel, Ottomar. "Das Max Reger-Archiv in Meiningen, seine Geschichte und Bedeutung." pp. 85-90.

Festschrift für Elsa Reger anlässlich ihres 80. Geburtstages am 25. Oktober 1950. Bonn: Dümmler, 1950. Volume 2 of Veröffentlichungen des Max-Reger-Institutes Elsa-Reger-Stiftung Bonn.

B1090 Haas, Joseph. "Zum 25. Oktober 1950." p. 5.

B1091 Wendling, Carl. "Persönliche Erinnerungen an Max Reger." pp. 5-8.

B1092 Wolffhügel, Fritz. "Persönliche Erinnerungen an Max Reger." pp. 8-10.

B1093 Würz, Richard. "Erinnerungen an Max Reger." pp. 10-13.

B1094 Lubrich, Fritz. "Erinnerungen an Max Reger.' pp. 13-19.

B1095 Zschinsky-Troxler, Elsa von. "Persönliche Erinnerungen an Max Reger." pp. 19-21.

B1096 Treichler, Hans. "Erinnerungen an Max Reger." pp. 21-24.

B1097 Muth, Fritz. "Erinnerungen an Max Reger." pp. 24-26.

B1098 Hedemann, Wilhelm. "Erinnerungen an Max Reger." pp.27-8.

B1099 Erler-Schnaudt, Anna. "Erinnerungen an Max Reger." pp. 28-30.

B1100 Schmid-Lindner, August. "Elsa Reger." p. 30.

B1101 Grabner, Hermann. "Reger und die Meininger Hofkapelle." pp. 32-37.

B1102 Unger, Hermann. "Max Reger als Naturfreund." pp. 38-41.

B1103 Stein, Fritz. "In memorium Henriette Schelle. Aus Regers Briefen an Henriette Schelle und Willi Obermeyer." pp. 42-77.

Hasse, Karl, ed. Max Reger: Mensch und Werk. Berlin: Bote & Bock, 1938. Essays from the 1938 German Reger Festival.

B1104 Hasse, Karl. "Max Reger, Mensch und Werk." pp. 5-16.

B1105 -----. "Orchesterwerke." pp. 17-32.

B1106 -----. "Vokalwerke mit Orchester." pp. 33-42.

B1107 Unger, Hermann. "Kammermusikwerke." pp. 43-50

B1108 Nedden,Otto zur. "Max Reger als Liederkomponist." pp. 51-55.

B1109 Hasse, Karl. "Werke für zwei Klavier." pp. 56-59.

B1110 Maur, Sophie. "Die Sonatinen für Klavier zu zwei Händen." pp. 60-61.

B1111 Hasse, Karl. "Orgelwerke." pp. 62-69.

B1112 "Deutsch Reger-Fest." pp. 70-71.

Karl Straube zu seinem 70. Geburtstag. Gaben der Freund. Leipzig: Koehler & Amelang, [1943]. Festschrift for Straube, the Thomaskantor and promoter of Reger's music.

B1113 Hausegger, Siegmund von. "Geleitwort zum 6. Januar 1943." pp. 7-11.

B1114 David, Johann Nepomuk. "Der Thomaskantor." pp. 12-17.

B1115 Ramin, Günther. "Karl Straube, der Pädagoge." pp. 18-25.

B1116 Schwarz, Bernhard. "Straube und die Thomasschule." pp. 26-41.
B1117 Stein, Fritz. "Max Reger und Karl Straube." pp. 42-79. Outlines the Reger-Straube relationship and discusses Straube's interpretations of Reger's organ music. Contains excerpts from a number of Reger's letters to Straube.
B1118 Thomas, Kurt. "Karl Straube als Freund der jungen Komponisten." pp. 80-89. Straube's promotion of a large number of young composers (including Reger) is discussed.
B1119 Matthaei, Karl. "Dank an Karl Straube." pp. 90-95.
B1120 Litt, Theodor. "Musik und Menschbildung." pp. 96-112.
B1121 Furtwängler, Wilhelm. "Dem Freunde." p. 113.
B1122 Kippenberg, Anton. "Gruss und Angebinde." pp. 114-130.
B1123 Beyerlein, Franz Adam. "Kleine Rückschau." pp. 131-147.
B1124 Münch, Fritz. "Karl Straube und die Bach-Pflege im Elsass." pp. 148-152.
B1125 Hasse, Karl. "Karl Straube als Orgelkünstler." pp. 153-194. Touches upon Straube's collaboration with Reger on the editing of the "Schule des Triospiels" and their mutual activities.
B1126 Gurlitt, Willibald. "Karl Straube als Vorkämpfer der neueren Orgelbewegung." pp. 195-225.
B1127 Schneider, Max. "Karl Straube als Erwecker der alten Musik." pp. 226-232.
B1128 Schnoor, Hans. "Stufen des 19. Jahrhunderts." pp. 223-260.
B1129 Mitteis, Heinrich. "Karl Straube und die Geschichte." pp. 261-277.
B1130 Haller, Johannes. "Vom Nationalen Staat: Nachlänge eines politischen Gesprächs mit Karl Straube." pp. 278-309.
B1131 Weber, Wilhelm. "Die Weltstunde: Eine weltgeschichliche Betrachtung." pp. 310-351.
B1132 Rassow, Peter. "Bach in den Zeiten." pp. 352-363.
B1133 Beyerlein, Franz Adam. "Karl Straubes Leben." pp. 364-385.

Kross, Siegfried, ed. Max Reger in seiner Zeit. Max-Reger-Tage Bonn 1973.
B1134 Kross, Siegfried. "Reger in seiner Zeit." pp. 7-22.
B1135 Jovari-Tholen, Reinhildnis. "Max Regers Aufsätze." pp. 23-29.
B1136 Reiners, Hanspeter & Wolfram Syrè. "Max Reger und die Orgel." pp. 31-43.
B1137 Wehmeyer, Grete. "Der Liederkomponist Reger in seiner Zeit." pp. 45-49. Wehmeyer sees Reger's song output as alternating between the styles of Brahms and Wagner, finally culminating around 1900 in an approach in which the voice freely declaims the text within the context of an independent

piano part, effecting, as it were, a "polyphonic" context.

B1138 Meurs, Norbert. "Reger als Dirigent." pp. 51-57.

B1139 Möller, Martin. "Max Reger und die alte Musik." pp. 59-67.

B1140 Bister, Herbert. "Max Regers Harmonik im Verhältnis zu Hugo Riemann." pp. 69-81.

B1141 Zienicke, Axel Hubertus. "Zur Kunstgeschichtlichen Entwicklung in Deutschland 1871 bis 1914." pp. 83-88.

Massenkeil, Günther & Susanne Popp. Reger-Studien 1: Festschrift für Ottmar Schreiber zum 70. Geburtstag am 16. Februar 1976. Wiesbaden: Breitkopf & Härtel, 1978. Volume I of Schriftenreihe des Max-Reger-Instituts

B1142 Sievers, Gerd. "Franz Liszts Legend Der Heilige Franziskus von Paula auf den Wogen schreitend für Klavier in Max Regers Bearbeitung für die Orgel." pp. 9-27.
In addition to the article's topic there are many insights given to Reger's attitude toward Liszt [Reger considered the Faust Symphony to be "Beethoven's 10th Symphony"] and about transcriptions and arrangements.

B1143 Walter, Rudolf. "Max Regers Kirchenkonzerte in Thüringen 1912-1916 und ihre Beziehung zu seinem Schaffen." pp. 29-46.
Lists the programs of Reger's church concerts 1912-16.

B1144 Wirth, Helmut. "Max Reger und seine Dichter." pp. 47-57.
Examines Reger's personal and musical relationship tothe poets whose texts he used for his lieder. Stefan Zweig is shown to have been fond of Reger's music ["...next to Richard Strauss, then Reger was the greatest living composer..."] and Reger's settings of his poems (Opp. 97/3 and 104/1).

B1145 Popp, Susanne. "Zur musikalischen Prosa bei Reger und Schönberg." pp. 59-77.
An excellent examination of the development of the concept of "musical prose" and its applicability to Reger's music. Opp. 72 and 84 are discussed in detail.

B1146 Barker, John Wesley. "The Recpetion of Max Reger in England." pp. 79-104.
Examines published reviews of Reger's music in performance in England. "Whereas earlier English critical opinion found much of Reger's music unacceptable because of its complexity and its apparent absence of emotion, influential post-war critics,...were only too ready to label it as 'aggresively German' and 'unfit for German export.'" [p. 104]

B1147 Manz, André. "Max Reger als Orgelkomponist--'Extremer Fortschrittsmann?'" pp. 105-117.
An attempt at determining the historical significance of Reger as an organ composer.

B1148 Troskie, Albert J.J. "Die Tonsymbolik in Regers

Chorwerken." pp. 119-125.
An examination of musico-rhetorical devices in Reger's choral works.
B1149 Fellerer, Karl Gustav. "Das Reger-Bild von Joseph Haas." pp. 127-133.
An overview of Haas' contribution to Reger scholarship.
B1150 Heldt, Gerhard. "Hermann Ungers Klavierlieder: Versuch einer Standortbestimmung des deutschen Liedes noch Max Reger." pp. 135-158.
Examines Reger's development as a song composer (in origins stemming from Schumann, Brahms, and Wolf) and his influence on Unger and later generations of song composers. Contains musical examples.
B1151 "Aufstellung der musikalischen Reger-Autobiographien in Besitz des Max-Reger-Institut." pp. 159-161.
Lists Reger autographs possessed by the Max-Reger-Institut in Bonn as of ca. 1976-1978.

Max Reger--Beiträge zur Reger-Forschung. Meiningen, 1966.
B1152 Laux, Karl. "Bekenntnis zu Max Reger." pp. 7-21.
B1153 Müller, Helmut. "Das Verhältnis Max Regers zu den gesellschaftlichen: Kräften seiner Zeit im Spiegel zeitgenössicher Quellen." pp. 22-81.
B1154 Klemm, Eberhard. "Über Reger und Szymanowski." pp. 82-89.
Examines Reger's influence on Szymanowski. "One may hear in the 5th number of [Szymanowski's] Piano Studies (Op. 33) an 'Hommage' a Reger, and also in the fugue of Szymanowski's 3rd Piano Sonata (Op. 36)...."
B1155 Otto, Eberhard. "Max Regers orchestraler Reifestil." pp. 90-97.
B1156 Köhler, Johannes-Ernst. "Max Regers Orgelschaffen in unserer Zeit." pp. 98-102.
B1157 Bongartz, Heinz. "Die Interpretationskunst Max Reger." pp. 99-104.
B1158 Roterberg, Max. "Regers Krankheiten und Tod." pp. 105-116.
B1159 Schmidt, Friedrich. "Gedanken zu einem Reger-Gemälde im Max-Reger-Archiv." pp. 117-120.
B1160 Krause, Peter. "Das Max-Reger-Schriftum 1945-1965. Bibliographie." pp. 121-158.

Max-Reger-Festschrift 1973. Meiningen: Südthüringer Forschungen 10/74: 1974.
B1161 Rackwitz, Werner. "Festansprache zum 100. Geburtstag von Max Reger am 19. März 1973 in Meiningen." pp. 9-16.
B1162 Schaltuper, Julia. "Reger in Russland." pp. 17-21.
Examines Reger's influence on Russian composers and musicians (mostly before the 1917 Revolution).
B1163 Lissa, Zofia. "Max Regers Metamorphosen der 'Berceuse' op. 57 von Frèdèric Chopin." pp. 22-27.
Examines Reger's use of Chopin's "Berceuse" as a model for Opp. 82/12 and 143/12.

B1164 Rienäcker, Gerd. "'Musik über Musik'--Bemerkungen zu einem kompositorischen Problem." pp. 28-37.
Discusses Reger's use of musical quotations in his compositions, earlier musical forms, and hidden symbolism such as the B-A-C-H motive.

B1165 Köhler, Johannes Ernst. "Gedanken zur Pflege des Regerschen Orgelschaffens in Weimar." pp. 38-39.

B1166 Köhler, Karl-Heinz. "Max Reger--Grösse und Vermächtnis als Problem." pp. 40-52.
An examination of Reger's artistic legacy. The discussion of dynamics in general and the musical displacement of poetic meter in Reger's songs is most valuable.

B1167 Müller, Helmut. "Probleme der gesellschaftlichen Bezogenheit in Regers Fortschrittsbegriff." pp. 55-65.
An examination of Reger's conception of progress and its social implications. Presents good background material on Reger's political, religious, and cultural thinking.

B1168 Oesterheld, Herta. "Beitrag zum Persönlichkeitsbild Max Regers--eine Skizze anhand un veröffentlichter Quellen." pp. 66-78.
Examines Reger as a businessman and entrepreneur from records of his dealings with the publishing company of Lauterbach & Kuhn.

B1169 Siegmund-Schultze, Walther. "Regers kammermusikalische Leistung--Tradition und Neuertum." pp. 79-86.
Examines different styles of performance of Reger's chamber music, especially Op. 139.

B1170 Hennenberg, Fritz. "'Volkston' bei Max Reger.'" pp. 87-91.
Hennenberg states that the seemingly simplistic melodic resources employed by Reger in "Volkston" are meant to parody the text, which results in a close musical rendering of the poetry.

B1171 Haupt, Hartmut. "Max Regers Orgelmusik--Ausdruck unserer Zeit." pp. 92-103.
Haupt says that Reger is a composer of the 20th century and that his organ music is an expression of our era. Also includes organ registrations and a discussion of the wide range of dynamics in Reger's organ music.

Neue Beiträge zur Regerforschung und Musikgeschichte Meiningens. Meiningen: Südthüringer Forschungen 6/70: 1970.

B1172 Michel, Paul. "Max Regers musikpädagogische Auffassungen." pp. 7-42.
A very thorough examination of Reger's teaching methods and the way they have been interpreted by later generations of scholars and writers. Reger's prose writings are quoted extensively.

B1173 Otto, Eberhard. "Max Reger und Richard Strauss." pp. 43-66.
An excellent comparison and contrast of the music of the

two composers. Especially useful is the examination given to the songs of both composers set to the same texts.

B1174 Oesterheld, Herta. "Max Reger und Stefan Zweig." pp. 67-82.
A discussion of the relationship between Reger and Zweig including letters between the two men (with facsimiles). Also includes an examination of Reger's settings of Zweig texts with the suggestion made that perhaps Reger was contemplating setting more of Zweig's lyrics than he actually did.

B1175 -----. "Dokumente zur Musikgeschichte Meiningens." pp. 83-105.

B1176 Mohr, Herbert. "Formübersicht mit Anmerkungen zu op. 82/I Nr. 5 von Max Reger." pp. 106-107.
Schematic formal outline of Op. 82/I/5.

B1177 Ramge, Heinze. "Einige Urteile Max Regers über Komponisten seiner Generation aus unveröffentlichten Briefen der Münchener Jahre 1902-1905." <u>Festschrift Hans Engel zum siebzigsten Geburtstag</u>. Kassel: Bärenreiter, 1964, pp. 290-297.
Reger's views on many of the major and minor composers of his day are revealed in these extracts from previously unpublished letters.

Röhring, Klaus. <u>Max Reger 1873-1973. Ein Symposion</u>. Wiesbaden: Published in cooperation with the Max-Reger-Institut (Elsa-Reger-Stiftung) and the Internationalen Orgelwoche Nürnberg, 1974.

B1178 Wirth, Helmut. "Der Einfluss von Johann Sebastian Bach auf Max Regers Schaffen." pp. 3-20.

B1179 Stockmeier, Wolfgang. "Karl Straube als Reger-Interpret." pp. 21-29.

B1180 Walcker-Mayer, Werner. "Die Orgel der Reger-Zeit." pp. 31-54.
Contains information on organ specifications and registrations.

B1181 Sievers, Gerd. "Die Harmonik im Werk Max Regers." pp. 55-82.
Siever views the linear aspect of Reger's music to be the hierarchical and generative force for his music which controls and shapes the harmonic aspect. Sievers disagrees with some of Hermann Grabner's findings concerning Reger's harmonic practices.

B1182 Brinkmann, Reinhold. "Max Reger und die neue Musik." pp. 83-111.

B1183 Blankenburg, Walter. "Max Reger und die evangelische Kirchenlied." pp. 113-122.

B1184 Walter, Rudolf. "Max Regers Beziehungen zur katholischen Kirchenmusik." pp. 123-148.

B1185 Lewinski, Wolf-Eberhard von. "Gedanken zum Reger-

Symposion in Nürnberg." pp. 149-153.

Schreiber, Ottmar & Gerd Sievers, eds. Gedenkschrift zum 50. Todestag Max Regers am 11. Mai 1966. Bonn: Dümmler, 1966. Volume 4 of Veröffentlichungen des Max-Reger-Institutes Elsa-Reger-Stiftung Bonn.

B1186 Bagier, Guido. "Max Reger--Leben und künstlerische Erscheinung." pp. 7-102.

B1187 Niemann, Helmut. "Max Reger in München." pp. 103-140.

B1188 Söhngen, Oskar. "Max Regers geistliche Musik." pp. 141-154.

B1189 Becker, Alfred. "Max Reger als Komponist katholischer Kirchenmusik." pp. 155-168.

B1190 Rösner, Helmut. "Max Regers Violinsonate op. 72--Entwurf und endgültige Gestalt." pp. 169-188.
Provides background and analytical data on Reger's controversial Op. 72, sometimes referred to as "Max Reger's Heldenleben."

B1191 Dorfmüller, Kurt. "Regers Klarinettenquintett op. 146." pp. 189-204.
Examines the genesis and compositional development of Op. 146.

B1192 Sievers, Gerd. "Reger-Gesamtausgabe--Entstehungsgeschichte." pp. 205-217.

Shigihara, Susanne, ed. Reger-Studien 2: Neue Aspekte der Regerforschung. Wiesbaden: Breitkopf & Härtel, 1986. Volume V of Schriftenreihe des Max-Reger-Instituts. The volume contains an index of works cited (listed by opus number).

B1193 Introduction

B1194 Popp Susanne. "Stand und Aufgaben der Regerforschung." pp. 11-26.
Popp describes the state of modern Reger research and suggests areas for further study, including Rezeptionsgeschichte, the development of Reger's style and compositonal technique, Reger's place between tradition and progress, the tonality-atonality controversy, etc.

B1195 Weiss, Günther. "Max Reger und Henri Marteau." pp. 27-37.
Discusses Reger's relationship with the violinist Marteau and examines concerts betweem 1904 and 1911 in which the two men collaborated.

B1196 Bauer, Hans-Joachim. "Max Reger und Richard Wagner." pp. 39-46.
Bauer examines the influence of Wagner on Reger's music and also looks at the works by Wagner performed by Reger in his concerts.

B1197 Mattner, Lothar. "Integration und Vereinzelung--Zur Konzeption des Variationszyklus im Streichquartett d-moll op. 74 von Max Reger." pp. 47-58.
Good examination of the third movement variations of Op. 74. Includes musical examples.

B1198 Mauser, Siegfried. "Chromatik und Klangfärbung: Satztechnische Überlegungen zum Beginn von Max Regers Violinsonate in c-moll op. 139." pp. 59-66.
An examination of linear chromaticism at the beginning of movement one of Op. 139. The author suggests that such techniques as used by Reger accounted for the high esteem in which the composer was regarded by the members of the Second Viennese School.

B1199 Brotbeck, Roman. "Überlegungen zu Regers Spätwerk am Beispiel der Serenade op. 141a." pp. 67-71.
Brotbeck comments on the stereotypical nature of Op. 141a and its dependency on classical models.

B1200 Cadenbach, Rainier. "'Das Werk will nur Musik sein'--Zitate in Max Regers Kompositionen." pp. 73-104.
Very thorough examination of Reger's use of cantus firmi and quotations (especially the B-A-C-H motive) in the composer's music.

B1201 Schmidt, Christian Martin. "Von Satztypen Regerscher Charakterstücke." pp. 105-113.
Schmidt defines 3 types of Reger characteristic piano pieces: (1) fast in 2/4; (2) moderate or slow in 4/4 or 4/8; and (3) slow in 6/8.

B1202 Berchem, Axel. "Max Regers Weidener Orgelstil und seine Grenzen in der heutigen Praxis." pp. 115-134.
An examination of Reger's organ music from his years in Weiden (includes Opp. 46, 52, 57, etc.). Music examples and organ registrations are included.

B1203 Shigihara, Susanne. "Max Reger und die bildende Kunst." pp. 135-174.
Examines Reger's relationship with painters and sculptors of his day and includes plates featuring some of the most important Reger portraits.

Monographs

B1204 Altmann, Wilhelm. Reger-Katalog. 2nd edition. Berlin: Simrock, 1926.

B1205 Dümling, Albrecht. Friedrich Hölderlin: Vertont von Hanns Eisler, Paul Hindemith, Max Reger. Munich: Kindler, 1981.
Contains a very fine discussion of Reger's setting of Hölderlin's "An die Hoffnung", Op. 124. Contains the complete music of this song.

B1206 Fischer, Walter. Über die Wiedergabe der Orgelkompositionen Max Regers. Cologne: Tischer & Jagenberg, 1910.
A brief discussion of the main compositional procedures employed in Reger's organ music. Very general in nature. No musical examples.

B1207 Fleischman, Benno. Max Reger: Der 100. Psalm. Berlin: Schlesinger, 1909.
A very brief thematic and formal overview of Op. 106 with musical examples.

B1208 Grabner, Hermann. Regers Harmonik. 2nd edition. Wiesbaden: Breitkopf & Härtel, 1961.
One of the most thorough examinations of Reger's harmonic ideas as they are utilized in his works. Grabner pays particularly close attention to the correlation between Reger's harmonic practices and his theoretical writings.

B1209 Gräner, Georg. Max Reger: Orchesterwerke. Berlin: Lienay [no date given].
Contains chapters on Opp. 90, 95, 100, 108, 120, 123, 125, 132, 86, and 106. Musical examples given.

B1210 Häfner, Roland. Max Reger Klarinettenquintett op. 146. Munich: Wilhelm Fink Verlag, 1982. Volume 30 of Meisterwerke der Musik.
Häfner provides a very finely detailed analysis of Op. 146 along with synopses of reviews and a list of pertinent reference materials.

B1211 Hehemann, Max. Max Reger: Eine Studie über moderne Musik mit einem Bildnis und vielen Notebeispielen. Munich: Piper, 1911.
Excellent and thorough analyses of Reger's oeuvre to 1911. Contains a work list and a complete reproduction of the song "Aeolsharfe," Op. 75/11. In the final chapter Hehemann challenges many of the common criticisms of Reger's music, such as the complaint that Reger wrote too much music.

B1212 Hitzig, Wilhelm. Katalog des Archivs von Breitkopf & Härtel, Leipzig. I: Musik-Autographe. Leipzig: Breitkopf & Härtel, 1925.
Reger items include Nos. 313-330.

B1213 Holle, Hugo. Regers Chorwerke. Munich: Otto Halbreiter, 1922. Volume III of Max Reger--Eine Sammlung von Studien aus dem Kreise seiner persönlichen Schüler.
An extended and detailed examination of Reger's choral music. Contains many musical examples.

B1214 Junk, Viktor. Max Reger als Orchesterkomponist und sein Symphonischer Prolog zu einer Tragödie. Leipzig Max Hesses Verlag, 1910.
Brief overview of thematic and formal structure with musical examples.

B1215 Kalkoff, Artur. Das Orgelschaffen Max Regers in Lichte der deutschen Orgelneuerungsbewegung. Kassel: Bärenreiter, 1950.
A consideration of the performance of Reger's organ works in view of the demands of the new performance movement of organ playing which gained considerable influence after Reger's death.

B1216 Keller, Hermann. Reger und die Orgel. Munich: Otto Halbreiter, 1923. Volume IV of Max Reger--Eine Sammlung von Studien aus dem Kreise seiner persönlichen Schüler.
Very thorough examination of Reger's organ music. Contains many musical examples along with discussion of harmonic and contrapuntal practices.

B1217 Leichtentritt, Hugo. Max Reger: Serenade G dur für Orchester. Leipzig: Breitkopf & Härtel, 1908.
A very brief overview of the major thematic and formal procedures found in Op. 95. Contains musical examples.

B1218 -----. Sinfonietta von Max Reger. Leipzig: Breitkopf & Härtel, 1908.
Very brief thematic and formal analysis of Op. 90. Contains musical examples.

B1219 -----. Variationen und Fuge über ein lustiges Thema von Joh. Ad. Hiller. Leipzig: Breitkopf & Härtel, 1908.
Very brief thematic and formal analysis of Op. 100 with musical examples.

B1220 Lorenzon, Johannes. Max Reger als Bearbeiter Bachs. Wiesbaden: Breitkopf & Härtel, 1982. Volume II of Schriftenreihe des Max-Reger-Instituts Bonn.
Extremely detailed examination of Reger's editions and arrangements of the music of J.S. Bach. Comparisons are made among the Bach editions of Reger, Busoni, and d'Albert. Also deals with Reger's performing interpretations of Bach's music. Indispensable work for this topic.

B1221 Mattner, Lothar. Substanz und Akzidens: Analytische Studien an Streichquartettsätzen Max Regers. Wiesbaden: Breitkopf & Härtel, 1985. Volume IV of Schriftenreihe des Max-Reger-Instituts Bonn.
An extremely detailed analysis of Opp. 121/movt. 3, 109/movt. 1, 74/movt. 1, and 121/movt. 1. Attention is given to compositional practices that became standard in Reger's string quartet writing.

B1222 Mendelssohn-Bartholdy, Albrecht. Das deutsche Wesen in Regers Werk. Würzberg: Banger, 1916.

B1223 Möller, Martin. Untersuchungen zur Satztechnik Max Regers. Wiesbaden: Breitkopf & Härtel, 1984. Volume III of Schriftenreihe des Max-Reger-Instituts Bonn. Excellent study on the formal, harmonic, and contrapuntal techniques employed by Reger. Works examined are chamber compositions, somelieder, and a few choral works. Very organized and useful work. Also contains some good discussion of the theoretical teachings of Hugo Riemann.

B1224 Otto, Eberhard. Max Reger und sein oberpfälzisches Fundament. Regensburg: 1969. Volume 10 of Blätter zur Geschichte und Landeskunde der Oberpfalz.

B1225 Poppen, Hermann. Eine vaterländische Ouverture von Max Reger. Berlin: Simrock, 1915.
A very brief thematic and formal overview of Op. 140 with musical examples. Also contains excerpts from reviews.

B1226 Rabich, Franz. Regerlieder. Beyer & Mann, 1914.
A brief study of Reger's lieder up to 1914. Contains a catalog of the lieder in opus order by publisher and musical examples. "Without Wagner and Liszt these lieder wereunimaginable."

B1227 Rahner, Hugo Ernst. Max Regers Choralfantasien für die Orgel: Eine Studie über Grundlagen und Werden des Regerschen Orgelstils. Kassel: Bärenreiter, 1936. Volume V of Heidelberger Studien zur Musikwissenschaft. Very fine analysis of Reger's chorale fantasies with many musical examples.

B1228 Robert-Tornow, Gustav. Max Reger und Karl Straube. Göttingen: Hapke, 1907 [2nd edition, 1929].
Very short monograph on the association and friendship of Reger and Straube. Includes some discussion of the organ works.

B1229 Roth, Hermann. Max Regers Symphonischer Prolog zu einer Tragödie. Leipzig: C.F. Peters, 1909.
Very brief thematic and formal analysis of Op. 108 with musical examples.

B1230 Salomon, Karl. Zwei Gesänge für gemischten Chor und Orchester. Berlin: Simrock [no date given].
Very brief thematic and formal overview of Op. 144 with musical examples.

B1231 Schmid-Lindner, August. Das Klavier in Max Regers Kunst. Danzig: 1942.

B1232 Schmitz, Eugen. Max Regers Sinfonietta. Munich: Georg Müller, 1905.
Brief overview of thematic and formal structure with musical examples.

B1233 Schreiber, Ingeborg. Max Reger in seinen Konzerten Teil 2. Programme der Konzerte Regers. Bonn: Dümmler, 1981. Volume 7 of Veröffentlichungen des Max-Reger-Institutes Bonn.
Contains a program listing of every concert in which Reger participated (as performer or conductor) or in which Reger's compositions were performed from 1890 to 1916. Source information for all concerts is given as well as indices by opus numbers, Reger's performances of works by other composers, interpretors of Reger's music (listed by performing media or musical organization), reviewers of concerts, cities in which concerts were performed, and corrected dates for premiere performances. This book (and its companion volumes) is a must is a must for serious Reger research.

B1234 Schreiber, Ottmar. Max Reger in seinen Konzerten Teil 1. Reger konzertiert. Bonn: Dümmler, 1981. Volume 7 of Veröffentlichungen des Max-Reger-Institutes Bonn.
Contains extremely fine scholarship. Detailed examination of Reger as performer and conductor of his own works and those of other composers. Proper names, Reger's compositions, and cities in which performances took place are indexed. Also includes fine bibliography.

B1235 Schreiber, Ottmar & Ingeborg. Max Reger in seinen Konzerten Teil 3. Rezensionen. Bonn: Dümmler, 1981. Volume 7 of Veröffentlichungen des Max-Reger-Institutes Bonn.
Contains reviews of performances of Reger compositions.

B1236 Sievers, Gerd. Die Grundlagen Hugo Riemanns bei Max Reger. Wiesbaden: Breitkopf & Härtel, 1967.
Examines the influence of the theoretical writings of Riemann (who was Reger's teacher) on Reger's oeuvre. Extremely detailed and thorough. Sievers argues against many of the findings of Hermann Grabner in his book Regers Harmonik. In the conclusion Sievers states: "...in the advances into new harmonic territories, the hypertrophy of harmony, the irrationality of meter, the irregularity of polyphonic structures in Max Reger's compositions--all of these were neither first made possible nor perhaps based upon nor even brought about by Hugo Riemann; these all were much more in the personality of the composer from birth...."

B1237 Stein, Fritz. Thematisches Verzeichnis der im Druck

erscheinenen Werke von Max Reger. Leipzig: Breitkopf & Härtel, 1953.
Complete thematic catalog of all of Reger's compositions (with and without opus numbers). Contains data on publishers, dates of composition, and dates of premieres. Corrections to the dates of premieres may be found in B1233.

B1238 Wehmeyer, Grete. _Max Reger als Liederkomponist: Ein Beitrag zum Problem der Wort-Ton-Beziehung_. Regensburg: Gustav Bosse, 1955. Volume 8 of Kölner Beiträge zur Musikforschung.
Excellent study which examines Reger's lieder in a wide variety of aspects, particularly musico-poetic rhythmic relationships. Reger's method of lieder composition is compared and contrasted to that of Brahms, Wolf, and other composers. Also included are indices of lieder (arranged chronologically) and poets (listed alphabetically with poems listed below each name). Very important study.

B1239 Wilke, Rainer. _Brahms. Reger. Schönberg. Streichquartette: Motivisch-thematische Prozesse und formale Gestalt_. Hamburg: Verlag der Musikalienhandlung, 1980. Volume 18 of Schriftenreihe zur Musik.
Contains an extensive analysis of Op. 74 along with some comparative remarks about Opp. 54/1 and 121. Wilke omits discussion of Opp. 54/2 and 109 as he sees very little relationship between these two works and the governing formal principles behind the quartets of Brahms and Schönberg.

B1240 Wirth, Helmut. _Max Reger: Variationen and Fuge über ein Thema von Mozart op. 132_. Munich: Institut für Film und Bild in Wissenschaft und Unterricht, 1962.
Very short thematic and formal overview of Op. 132. Designed as an introductory essay.

B1241 -----. _Max Reger: Werkauswahl für junge Hörer_. Munich: Institut für Film und Bild in Wissenschaft und Unterricht, 1968.
Contains a discussion of Opp. 82, 103b/1, 77b 89/1, 79e/1, 79/2, 76, and 130 for young people.

B1242 Würz, Richard. _Regers Persönlichkeit_. Munich: Otto Halbreiter, 1920. Volume II of Max Reger-- Eine Sammlung von Studien aus dem Kreise seiner persönlichen Schüler.
Contains three essays: Richard Würz, "Der Lebensgang"; Josef Haas, "Reger als Lehrer"; and Hermann Unger, "Reger als Mensch." Very good insights into Reger's personality and working habits by three of his students.

Reger's Writings and Letters

B1243 Berner, Alfred. "Max-Reger-Briefe." Musikblätter 10 (1956/57): 225-227.

B1244 Griesbacher, Peter. "Reger-Brief über meine Choral-Credo." Monatshefte für katholische Kirchenmusik (1928): 71-74.

B1245 Gurlitt, Willibald, ed. "Aus den Briefen Max Regers an Hugo Riemann." Jahrbuch der Musikbibliothek Peters 43 (1937): 67-83.
An annotated edition of Reger's letters to his teacher Hugo Riemann.

B1246 Hase-Köhler, Else von, ed. Max Reger: Briefe eines deutschen Meisters. Leipzig: Koehler & Amelang, 1928.
Excellent assortment of letters arranged in chronological order. Contains indices of persons and works.

B1247 Heger, Erich. "Die Infamie meines op. 72." MU (1953): 169-170.
Heger presents a previously unpublished letter by Reger to the distinguished pianist Pauline von Erdmannsdörfer-Fichtner (Nov. 1, 1903) in which the composer predicts a poor critical reception for his Op. 72.

B1248 Helm, Theodor. "Ein Jugendbrief Max Regers." ME 7:15/16 (1916).

B1249 Kühner, Hans. "Zu einem unbekannten Briefe Regers an Fritz Steinbach." K 3 (1941): 175.

B1250 -----. Neues Max-Reger-Brevier. Basel: Amerbach, 1948.

B1251 Mueller von Asow, Erich H., ed. Liebesbriefe berühmter Musiker. Frankfurt: Athenäum Verlag, 1962.
Contains Reger's love letters to his wife Elsa. [pp. 147-171]

B1252 Mueller von Asow, Hedwig & E.H., eds. Max Reger: Briefwechsel mit Herzog Georg II. von Sachsen-Meiningen. Weimar: Verlag Hermann Böhlaus, 1949.
Contains the collected exchange of letters between Reger and Duke Georg from 1911-1914 along with facsimiles of some of the letters, and programs of the Meiningen Hofkapelle Orchestra during Reger's tenure. Contains name and composition indices.

B1253 Ramge, Heinz. "Aus den Briefen von Max Reger an Felix Mendelssohns Schwiegersohn Adolf Wach." Mendelssohn Studien 1 (1972): 159-168.

Contains excerpts from the Reger-Wach correspondence, mostly from the years 1907-1909.

B1254 Reger, Elsa, ed. "Reger-Worte." M 23 (1931): 276. Short aphorisms from Reger's letters and prose works.

B1255 Reger, Max. "No Title." AMZ 21:41 (1894): 534. Concert review.

B1256 [Reger, Max]. "Unbekannte Briefe von Reger, Pfitzner und Alban Berg." MG 7 (1957): 340-343.

B1257 Reger, Max. "No Title." M 9 (1910): 225ff. Satirical analyses of Opp. 106 and 113.

B1258 -----. "No Title." NZFM 71:22/23 (1907): 448.

B1259 -----. "Begrüssungschor. Für Männerchor und Orchester." AMZ 21 (1894): 454.

B1260 -----. Beiträge zur Modulationslehre. Leipzig: C.F. Kahnt, 1903. This is Reger's book explaining the method by which he effected very remote modulations. Contains many cadential formulae with explanations.

B1261 -----. "Berichte und kleine Mitteilungen." AMZ 21:14 (1894): 200-201.

B1262 -----. "Brüll, Ignaz: 3. Serenade für Orchester. Op. 67." AMZ 21 (1894): 401.

B1263 -----. "Busoni, Ferruccio Benvenuto: Konzertstück für Pianoforte und Orchester. Op. 31a." AMZ 21 (1894): 401. See B899.

B1264 -----. "Degeneration und Regeneration in der Musik." NMZ 29 (1907): 49-51.

B1265 -----. "Drei Briefe an den Regensburger Domorganisten Prof. Josef Renner." [N]ZFM 99 (1932): 222.

B1266 -----. "Durham, Henry M.: 2. Sonate für Orgel. Paine, John Knowles: 2 Preludes für Orgel. Foote, Arthur: 3 Kompositionen für Orgel. Dubois, Théodore: 3 Stücke für grosse Orgel. Salomé, Th.: 10 Stücke für Orgel." AMZ 20 (1893): 646.

B1267 -----. "Faksimile einer 1. Briefseite an Chrzescinski." Jahrbuch Simrock 2 (1929).

B1268 -----. "Faksimile eines Briefes vom 15. III. 1903." Melos

1:1 (1920).

B1269 -----. "Felix Mendelssohn-Bartholdy's 'Lieder ohne Worte' --Zum 100. Geburtstag am 3. Febr. 1909." Leipziger Illustrirte Zeitung (January 28, 1909).

B1270 -----. "Four Hitherto Unpublished Letters to Professor Issay Barmas." Translated by C.H. Stepan. Music Survey 1 (1948): 85-88.
Four letters from 1910-1911 to the violinist Barmas with annotations.

B1271 -----. "Frank, Richard: Suite, vierhändig, op. 9. Menuett op. 13. 4 Klavierstücke op. 15." AMZ 21 (1894): 454.

B1272 -----. "Frenzel, Robert: Choralvorspiele op. 4. Choralbearbeitungen op. 5." MGKK 6:2 (1901).

B1273 -----. "Gotthelf, Felix: Frühlingsfest. Sinfon. Fantasie für Orchester op. 7." AMZ 20 (1893): 674ff.

B1274 -----. "Gotthelf, Felix: Tragödie. Op. 8. Lieder. Der Schmid op. 9 Lied. Streichquartett op. 10." AMZ 20 (1893): 674ff.

B1275 -----. "Hess, Emil: 6 Gesänge op. 9. 7 Gesänge op. 10." AMZ 21 (1894): 454.

B1276 -----. "Hildebrand, Ulrich: 2 Lieder. Heergewaldt, G.L.: Lied. Fried, Oskar: 3 Lieder op. 1. Mühlmann, Rudolf: 3 Lieder op. 1. Dannehl, Franz: 3 Lieder. 5 Lieder op. 8." AMZ 21 (1894): 494.

B1277 -----. "Hornstein, Robert von: Letzte Lieder." AMZ 21 (1894): 424.

B1278 -----. "Hor, W. Nicholl: 12 symphonische Präludien und Fugen für Orgel op. 30." Die Redenden Künste 6:27/30 (1900).

B1279 -----. "Hugo Wolfs künstlerischer Nachlass." Süddeutsche Monatshefte (1904): 157-164.

B1280 -----. "Ich bitte ums Wort." NZFM 71:2 (1904).

B1281 -----. "Kauffmann, Fritz: Konzert c-moll für Pianoforte und Orchester op. 25." AMZ 21 (1894): 454.

B1282 -----. "Kretzschmer, Hans: 2 Lieder. Warnke, Ferdinand: 3 Lieder op. 23, 24, 25. Weiss, Berthold: Lieder und Gesänge." AMZ 21 (1894): 469.

B1283 -----. "Lamond, Frederic: Sinfonie A-dur für grosses Orchester op. 3." AMZ 21 (1894): 56.

B1284 -----. "Max Reger an Joseph Haas." Mitteilungsblatt der Joseph-Haas-Gesellschaft 15 (1955): 7-11.

B1285 -----. Max Reger: Brief an Fritz Stein. Edited by Susanne Popp. Bonn: Dümmler, 1982. Volume 8 of Veröffentlichungen des Max-Reger-Institutes Bonn. Contains all of Reger's letters to his biographer Fritz Stein from the years 1907 to 1916. References to compositions and persons are indexed.

B1286 -----. "Max Reger im eigenen Wort." Monatsschrift der vereinigten rheinisch-westfälischen Lehrer- und Lehrerinnen-Gesangvereine 2:3/4 (1926).

B1287 -----. "Max Reger über seine Bearbeitungen Brahms'scher Werke." Edited by E.H. Müller. Jahrbuch Simrock 1 (1928): 64-71.
Contains Reger's letters to Simrock Publishers from 1913 to 1916 concerning his arrangements of compositions by Brahms.

B1288 -----. "Mehr Licht." NZFM 71:11 (1904).

B1289 -----. "Musik und Fortschritt." Leipziger Tageblatt No. 165 (June 24, 1907).

B1290 -----. "Naubert, August: 2 Duette op. 41. 4 Lieder op. 59." AMZ 21 (1894): 454.

B1291 -----. "Neal, Heinrich: 5 Lieder op. 21. 4 Lieder op. 27. 2 Stücke op. 28. Sonate für Klavier op. 30." AMZ 21 (1894): 454.

B1292 -----. "Neal, Heinrich: Harald. Für Männerchor, Tenor solo und grosses Orchester op. 18." AMZ 21 (1894): 454.

B1293 -----. "Offener Brief." M 7 (1907/08): 10-14.
Reger defends the breaking of "sacred" rules of harmony and hopes that these rules will continue to be broken. "All music, whether absolute or symphonic poem, is most welcome when it is just music."

B1294 -----. "Pottgiesser, Karl: 'Das 13. Kapitel der 1. Epistel St. Pauli an die Korinther.' Für Bariton-Solo, gem. Chor, Orchester und Orgel." MGKK 6:3 (1901).

B1295 -----. "Renner, Josef: 2. Sonate (c-moll) für Orgel op. 45." MGKK 6:3 (1901).

B1296 -----. "Robert Schwalm: Orgelschule." Die Redenden Künste 6:19/22 (1900).

B1297 -----. "Streichquartett op. 74 in d-moll." M 3 (1903/04): 244-247.
An analysis of Op. 74 by the composer.

B1298 -----. "Themenangabe zu op. 81 und op. 86." M 4:17 (1905).

B1299 -----. "Urspruch, Anton: Menschenlos. Für Männerchor mit willkürlicher Begleitung des Streichorchesters op. 30." AMZ 21 (1894): 424.

B1300 -----. "Urspruch: Violincell-Sonate op. 29." AMZ 20 (1893): 630.

B1301 -----. "Winkelmann, Theodor: Waldvöglein. Ballade mit Begleitung des Orchesters oder des Pianoforte op. 15." AMZ 21 (1894): 494.

B1302 -----. "Zum 1. April Burleske." NZFM 71:14 (1904).

B1303 Rothe, Hans-Joachim. "Fünf unveröffentlichte Briefe Max Regers und seine Leipziger Zeit." Die Musikstadt Leipzig. Volume 5. [See Beiträge zur Musikwissenschaft 8 (1966): 289-301.]
Contains five previously unpublished Reger letters from the 1907-1910 period.

B1304 Rufer, Josef, ed. Musiker über Musik: Aus Briefen, Tagebüchern und Aufzeichnungen. Darmstadt: Stichnote, 1956.
Pages 95-107 concerning Reger.

B1305 Schreiber, Ottmar, ed. Max Reger: Briefe zwischen der Arbeit. Bonn: Dümmler, 1956. Volume 3 of Veröffentlichungen des Max-Reger-Institutes Bonn.
Contains Reger's letters to Ferruccio Busoni, Cäsar Hochstetter, Ernst Guder, Otto Seelig, Hans Koessler, Carl Hartenstein, Beyer & Söhne, Wilhelm Weber, Walter Fischer, the Hugo-Wolf-Verein in Vienna, the Genossenschaft Deutscher Tonsetzer, the Ruben family, the Gesellschaft der Musikfreunde in Vienna, Eberhard Schwickerath, and Carl Holtschneider.

B1306 -----. Max Reger: Briefe zwischen der Arbeit, Neue Folge. Bonn: Dümmler, 1973. Volume 6 of Veröffentlichungen des Max-Reger-Institutes Bonn.
Contains letters to C.F. Peters Pub. Co., Emil Krause, Eugen Segnitz, Paul Zshorlich, Lauterbach & Kuhn Pub. Co., Fritz Cortolezis, Philipp Wolfrum, Karl Hasse, Anna

Erler-Schnaudt, Universal Edition, Hans vom Ohlendorff, and N. Simrock Pub. Co. Composition and proper name indices included.

B1307 Spemann, Adolf, ed. Max-Reger-Brevier. Stuttgart: Engelhorn, 1923.
Contains Reger's commentaries on various subjects by using short sections taken from his letters.

B1308 Stollberg, Oskar. "Ein unbekannter Brief Max Regers." Gottesdienst und Kirchenmusik 3 (1970): 91-93.

B1309 Weiss, Günther. "Sechs unbekannte Briefe von Max Reger an den Dirigenten Karl Panzner. Zur Widmung der Regerschen op. 86." Die Musikforschung 34 (1981): 456-461.
First publication of six letters between Reger and Panzner, the latter for whom Op. 86 was dedicated.

Reviews (Compositions, Performances, Books)

B1310 No Author. "No Title." MW 37:5 (1906).
Review of a performance of Op. 90 in Vienna.

B1311 -----. "No Title." MW 37:21 (1906).
Review of a performance of Op. 90 in Munich.

B1312 -----. "Allerlei Kritisches und Unkritisches.' NMZ 27:11 (1906): 25.

B1313 -----. "Aufführung des gesamten Orgelwerks von Reger in Basel." MG 27 (1973): 21.

B1314 -----. "Bach-Reger-Fest in Heidelberg." Zeitschrift für Musikwissenschaft 5 (1922): 100ff.

B1315 -----. "Bremen: Unbekannte Reger-Werke." K 24 (1973): 118-120.
Review of a performance of Op. 145.

B1316 -----. "A Glimpse of Reger." Musical Courier (1910): 46.
Enthusiastic review of a concert of the Stuttgart Orchestra in which Reger appeared as composer, conductor, and soloist. [Probably the concert of Nov. 11, 1909; see p. 344 of B1233.] The controversy between the partisans of Reger and Strauss is noted: "In Germany Strauss' and Reger's respective followers are so violently opposed to each other's gods that it is wise when admiring the one writer in the presence of the other's followers, to 'speak softly and carry a big stick...."

B1317 -----. "Kunst und Künstler." NMZ 28:14 (1907): 313.

B1318 -----. "Ein kurzes Geplauder." MS 17:10 (1905).
Review of Op. 46.

B1319 -----. "Max Reger: Drei sechsstimmige Chöre op. 39; Phantasie und Fuge für Orgal op. 46; Drei Trios für Orgel op. 47." RMI 8 (1901): 760.

B1320 -----. "Max Reger: Dritte Sonate für Violine und Pianoforte; Vier Sonaten für Violine allein." RMI 7 (1900): 85.

B1321 -----. "Max-Reger-Fest in Weimar." SMW (1926): 631.

B1322 -----. "Max Reger: Monologe op. 63." MS 14:10 (1902).

B1323 -----. "Max Reger: Schlichte Weisen Bd. III; Vier Lieder op. 97; Sechs Präludien und Fugen op. 99; Introduktion und Passacaglia für Orgel." RMI 15 (1908): 231.

B1324 -----. "Max Reger: Zweiundfünfzig Choral vorspiele op. 67." RMI 11 (1904): 189.

B1325 -----. "Max Regers 100. Psalm." SMW 68: 27/29 (1910).

B1326 -----. "Neue Musikalien." NMZ 20:33 (1899): 313.
Reviews of Opp. 27 and 29.

B1327 -----. "Neue Musikalien: Kompositionen von Max Reger." NMZ 21:14 (1900): 173-174.
Reviews of Opp. 39-44.

B1328 -----. "Neue Musikalien. Max Reger: Cinq Pièces pittoresques op. 34; Sieben Männerchöre op. 38; Acht ausgew. Volkslieder für gem. Chor." NMZ 21:4 (1900).

B1329 -----. "Neue Musikalien. Max Reger: Fünf Humoresken op. 20; Sechs Walzer op. 22; Vier Lieder op. 23; Cellosonate op. 28; Sechs Gedichte op. 31; Sieben Charakterstücke op. 32." NMZ 20:23 (1899).

B1330 -----. "Neue Musikalien. Max Reger: Phantasie 'Freu dich sehr' op. 30; Orgelsonate op. 33; Sechs Lieder op. 35; Fünf Gesänge op. 37." NMZ 21:3 (1900).

B1331 -----. "Orgelmusik von Reger und Genzmer." MS 101 (1981): 215.

B1332 -----. "Prag." M 16 (1924): 452.
Contains an account of a concert of Reger's works sponsored by the new Reger-Gesellschaft.

B1333 -----. "Reger-Fest in Bonn." Der Musikhandel 24:2 (1973): 57.

B1334 -----. "Das Reger-Fest in Bückeburg 24/25 III. 1911." M 10:14 (1911).

B1335 -----. "Reger-Jahr 1973." MK 43 (1973): 56.
Brief mention of several Reger recordings on cassette tapes.

B1336 -----. "Reger-Komposition aus den USA." Schwäbische Landeszeitung [Augsburg] (September 9, 1957).

B1337 -----. "Reger, Max. Op. 24. Six Morceaux pour le Piano." NZFM 68 (1901): 234.
"These works arise from an unusual talent."

B1338 -----. "Reger, Max.--Op. 116. Sonate (A-moll) für Violoncello und Pianoforte." RMI 18:2 (1911): 495.

B1339 -----. "Reger-Tage in Linz." Sigende Kirche 21 (1973/74): 27.

B1340 -----. "Reviews." Musical News 27:696 (1904): 15.
Review of Op. 76.

B1341 -----. "Tageschronik." M 15 (1923): 555-556.
Details a Sonata for Horn and Piano by one Helmut Gropp that was plagiarized by collating different works of Max Reger.

B1342 -----. "Umschau: Max-Reger-Musik in der Stadtkirche Meiningen anlässlich seines 80. Geburtstags." MK 23 (1953): 218.
Brief account of performances of Opp. 27, 46, 145/1, and other works.

B1343 -----. "Zu Regers unvollendetem Klavierkonzert von 1897." M 15 (1923): 657.

B1344 Adorno, Theodor W. "No Title." M 23 (1930): 213.
Review of Op. 100.

B1345 Altmann, Gustav. "No Title." M 5 (1906): 279.
Review of 'O Haupt voll Blut und Wunden.'

B1346 -----. "No Title." M (1909): 258.
Review of Op. 101.

B1347 -----. "No Title." M 12 (1913): 63.
Review of Op. 100.

B1348 -----. "Strassburg." M 4 (1904/05): 77-78.

Altmann praises Karl Straube and says that his enthusiasm for Reger is not to [his] detriment. "The Reger problem is, in my opinion, psycho-physiological rather than musica....[T]his question may be decided in the future!..."

B1349 Altmann, Wilhelm. "No Title." M 2 (1902/03): 42-43.
Reviews of Opp. 41, 42, 50, and 54. Op. 42, "in my opinion is no substitute for the great works of Bach" in this genre.

B1350 -----. "No Title." M 4 (1904/05): 57.
Brief mention of a performance of Op. 84 by Henri Marteau and Max Reger.

B1351 -----. "No Title." M 4 (1904/05): 447.
Reviews of Opp. 74 and 77b. "In reality, the Quartet [Op. 74] offers the listener only difficulties in the very long first movement." The Op. 77b Trio "is an important enrichment of the scanty literature for violin, viola, and cello for amateurs...."

B1352 -----. "No Title." M 8 (1909): 44.
Review of Op. 103a.

B1353 -----. "No Title." M 8 (1908): 185.
Review of Op. 102.

B1354 -----. "No Title." M 8 (1909): 305.
Review of Op. 101.

B1355 -----. "No Title." M 9 (1909): 188ff.
Reviews of Opp. 28 and 109.

B1356 -----. "No Title." M 9 (1909): 246-248.
Favorable review of Op. 107. Altmann reports that Op. 74 was not well received by its Berlin audience.

B1357 -----. "No Title." M 9 (1910): 119.
Review of Op. 101.

B1358 -----. "No Title." M 10 (1910): 185.
Review of a performance of Op. 113. "It is, in my opinion, a grandiose work, the first movement of which displays a symphonic character."

B1359 -----. "No Title." M 11 (1911): 242.
Review of Opp. 118 and 121.

B1360 -----. "No Title." M 12 (1912): 244.
Reviews of Opp. 72, 93, and 102.

B1361 -----. "No Title." M 12 (1913): 116.

Reviews of Opp. 124 and 125.

B1362 -----. "Berlin." M 10 (1911): 302.
Brief mention of Op. 78: "ghostly scherzo."

B1363 -----. "J.S. Bach: Sonate A-dur für Violine und Klavier. Neue Bearbeitung von Max Reger." M 15 (1915): 533.
"It is to be hoped that the other Bach sonatas will be published."

B1364 -----. "J.S. Bach: Sonate f-moll für Violine und Pianoforte. Bearbeitet von Max Reger." M 14 (1915): 36.
"Max Reger has added expressive markings in a sensitive way...."

B1365 -----. "Max Reger: Erstes Quintett für Klavier, zwei Violinen, Viola und Violincell." M 15 (1923): 824.
Favorable review . The composer's use of sonata forms is compared to that of Beethoven's third period and Brahms.

B1366 ------. "Max Reger: Klarinettensonate op. 107; Streichquartette op. 109." M 9 (1910): 250.
Altmann says of Op. 107: "...I especially desire for the sonata the widest possible dissemination, even though this means a very difficult work for amateurs."

B1367 -----. "Max Reger: Klavierquintett op. 64." M 3 (1903/04): 279.

B1368 -----. "Max Reger: Romanze (G-dur) für Klavier und Violine." M 10:4 (1911): 189.
"...very pleasing piece...."

B1369 -----. "Max Reger: Sonate für Violine und Klavier op. 122." M 11 (1912): 168.
Altmann praises the sixth sonata of this opus, especially the final movement which he feels is, for the most part, "clear and light."

B1370 -----. "Max Reger: Suite im alten Stil für Violine und Klavier op. 93." M 7:1 (1907): 51.
Altmann singles out the Largo movement of this work for praise.

B1371 -----. "Max Reger: Violinsonate op. 72." M 4 (1904/05): 463.
Altmann says that after playing this work in front of many people who were kindly disposed to Reger's music it was "unanimously rejected" due mainly to the sharp dissonances, particularly those beginning the final

movement.

B1372 -----. "Max Reger: Zwei kleine Sonaten für Violine und Klavier; Quintett für Violine, Bratsche, Violincell und Klavier." M 10 (1911): 313.
Brief descriptive reviews of Opp. 103b and 113. Op. 103b is mentioned as being one of Reger's works that he designated as Hausmusik.

B1373 -----. "Max Reger: Zwei Trios: (a) Serenade für Flöte, Violine und Viola; (b) Trio für Violine, Viola und Violincell op. 77." M 5 (1905/06): 343.
Altmann praises Op. 77 ("deserves the widest possible dissemination") and notices similarities between Op. 77 and "Aus meinem Tagebuch."

B1374 -----. "Max Regers 'An der schönen blauen Donau.'" M 23 (1931): 281.

B1375 -----. "Max Regers 'Blätter und Blüten.' 12 Klavierstücke für Violine und Klavier, bear. von Ad. Lindner." M 23 (1931): 280.

B1376 -----. "Präludium und Fuge für Violine allein op. 131a; Drei Duos für zwei Violinen op. 131b." M 14 (1914): 184.

B1377 Arend, Max. "Reger in Leipzig." Blätter für Haus- und Kirchenmusik 10 (1905/06): 60ff.
See B1235, pp. 101-102.

B1378 Bartels, Wolfgang von. "Max Reger-Gedächtnisfeier in München." Das Orchester 7:11 (1930): 126.

B1379 Baselt, Fritz. "Max Reger: Zwölf Madrigale für Männerchor bearbeitet--Sechs Madrigale für gemischten Choe bearbeitet." M 3 (1903/04): 119.
"As a composer Max Reger has been praised to Heaven and damned to Hell...."

B1380 Batka, Richard. "No Title." M 5 (1906): 442ff.
See B1235, p. 130. {Reviews of Opp. 72, 74, and 86.]

B1381 -----. "Max Reger: Siebzehn Gesänge op. 70." M 5 (1906): 260.

B1382 Bauer, Elsa. "8. deutsches Reger-Fest." SMW 90 (1932): 815-816.

B1383 Bekker, Paul. "No Title." AMZ 37:3 (1910).
Review of a performance of Op. 107.

B1384 -----. "Das 46. Tonkünstler-Fest des Allgemeinen

Deutschen Musikvereins in Zürich (27.-31.Mai 1910)." M 9 (1910): 372-377.
Bekker reviews performances of Opp. 113 and 106. Of the former work, the reviewer praises the lyricalism of the Larghetto movement, but regrets the excessive elements in the work as a whole, discerning an incongruity between the will and attainment of the composer's efforts. Op. 106 on the other hand is praised for the clear conception of its musical construction.

B1385 -----. "Max Reger: Sinfonietta." AMZ 32:45 (1905).

B1386 Bischoff, Hermann. "No Title." AMZ 22 (1895): 373.

B1387 Blum, Carl Robert. "No Title." M 13 (1913): 125.
Reviews of Opp. 46 and 73.

B1388 Blume, [Friedrich]. "No Title." AMZ 32:51/52 (1905).
Review of a performance of Op. 90.

B1389 Brandes, Friedrich. "No Title." SMW 65 (1907): 1282.
Review of a performance of Op. 100 in Dresden.

B1390 Breithaupt [Rudolf M. ?]. "No Title." M 6 (1906/07): 261.
Review of Op. 96.

B1391 Breithaupt, Rudolf M. "No Title." M 3 (1903/04): 462.
Review of Op. 42/1.

B1392 -----. "No Title." M 4 (1904/05): 58.
Brief reviews of Opp. 81 and 86. "These two works are of decisive importance in the development of absolute music."

B1393 -----. "Berlin." M 2 (1902/03): 471-472.
Details of a concert of Reger lieder with Ludwig Hess, tenor, and the composer accompanying. "The shapes [of the works] are bold, of an original spirit, but architecturally as well as melodically vulnerable, while at the same time without profound structure and foundation."

B1394 -----. "Max Reger: 'Sechs Burlesken' für Klavier zu vier Händen op. 58." M 4 (1904/05): 175-176.
"True Reger, full of technical virtuosity, spirit, and humor."

B1395 Brennecke, Wilfred. "Reger-Gedenktage." MU 10 (1956): 692-693.
Review of 1956 Reger Festival in Kassel. Works performed include "O Haupt voll Blut und Wunden," Opp.

109, 146, 144, and 100.

B1396 Brüch, H. "Reger, Max. Sechs Intermezzi op. 45; Fünf Spezialstudien, Bearbeitung Chopin'scher Werke." NZFM 68:22 (1901): 299-300.

B1397 Brust, Fritz. "Deutsches Reger-Fest Berlin." SMZ 78 (1938): 360-361.

B1398 Buchner, Otto. "No Title." Zeitschrift der Internationalen Musikgesellschaft 6 (1905): 257.
Review of a performance of Op. 72 and some lieder in Stuttgart.

B1399 Buck, Rudolf. "No Title." AMZ 32 (1905): 107ff.
See B1235, pp. 73-74. [Reviews of Op. 86 and other works.]

B1400 -----. "Vom Musikalienmarkt: Kompositionen von Max Reger." AMZ 26 (1899): 610.
A brief overview of a large number of Reger's works. The organ works are compared to those of Bach in architectural structure, while the piano works are said to reflect the individuality of Brahms.

B1401 Bülle, Heinrich. "Das Dortmunder Reger-Fest." M 9 (1910): 395.
Describes the events of this Reger festival which featured six concerts: two of church music; two of chamber music; and two of orchestral music. An important featured performer at the festival was the violinist Henri Marteau.

B1402 Cherbuliez, A.-E. "Max Reger und die Meininger Hofkapelle." SMZ 56: 29 (1916): 321-322, 30 (1916): 333-335.

B1403 -----. "Max Reger und die Meininger Hofkapelle." SMZ 57: 24 (1917): 274-275, 25 (1917): 283-284, and 26/27 (1917): 294.

B1404 Chevally, Heinrich. "No Title." M 5 (1905): 129ff.
Review of Op. 90.

B1405 -----. "No Title." M 7 (1908): 382ff.
Review of Op. 100.

B1406 -----. "No Title." M 12 (1912): 251.
Review of Op. 123.

B1407 -----. "No Title." M 13 (1913): 252.
Review of Op. 128.

B1408 -----. "Hamburg." M 8 (1909): 311-312.
In discussing Op. 101 Chevally says that the work is too complicated to be fully appreciated by non-musicians and many musicians as well.

B1409 -----. "Hamburg." M 10 (1911): 310.
Favorable reviews of performances of Opp. 100 and 114 by the Philharmonische Gesellschaft. Frau Kwast-Hodapp's interpretation of Op. 114 was singled out for praise.

B1410 Confluens. "Koblenz." M 10 (1911): 325.
Review of Op.106. "...[I]n spite of the colossal polyphonic structure...[the work] leaves behind an incomplete impression."

B1411 Crichton, Ronald. "Bonn." MT 114 (1973): 518-519.
Brief review of the 1973 Reger Centenary Festival in Bonn.

B1412 C.R.M. [Munschler]. "Amsterdamer Musikbrief." NMZ 37:20 (1916).
Contains reviews of Op. 101, 130, and 132.

B1413 Cunz, Rolf. "No Title." Deutsches Musikjahrbuch 3 (1925): 337ff.
Review of a performance of Opp. 96 and 106 in Essen.

B1414 -----. "Das Essener Reger-Fest 1926." Deutsches Musikjahrbuch 4 (1926): 120-124.

B1415 -----. "Rheinisch-westfälische Musikkultur: Bochumer Reger-Tage." Deutsches Musikjahrbuch 1 (1923): 85ff.

B1416 C.W. "Music Reviews. Foreign Music: Max Reger's Organ and Piano Music." The Musical Standard 6 (1899): 427.

B1417 Dahlhaus, Carl. "Hermann Grabner: Regers Harmonik. Zweite Auflage." Die Musikforschung 17 (1964): 212-213.
Dahlhaus disagrees with Grabner's thesis that Reger's harmonic practices were conducted "strictly in accordance with Riemann's practices," which Dahlhaus feels severely limits a proper understanding of the composer's music. Dahlhaus mentions Gerd Siever's assertion that Reger never "disproved" Riemann's theories, but always ignored them.

B1418 -----. "Max Reger: Briefe zwischen der Arbeit. Neue Folge, hrsg. v. Ottmar Schreiber. Verüffentlichungen des Max-Reger-Instituts, Heft 6." NZFM 134 (1973): 753.
Brief, explanatory review. Reger's letters were written "from immediate interest" and are in "the form of colloquial speech."

B1419 Dahms, Walter. "No Title." *M* 12 (1912): 247.
Dahms says that Op. 107 possesses a "wonderfully delicate lyric."

B1420 Dallmann, Wolfgang. "Max Regers Orgelwerk in Heidelberg." *MK* 37 (1967): 39-40.
Account of a highly acclaimed series of concerts of Reger's organ music in Heidelberg. Works performed included Opp. 27, 30, 40, 46, 52/1-3, 47, 57, 60, 59, 63, 67, 73, 80. 85, 127, and 135b.

B1421 Decsey, Ernst. "Das 41. Tonkünstlerfest des Allgemeinen deutschen Musikvereins--Graz 31. Mai bis 4. Juni." *M* (1904/05): 139-140.
Mention is made of performances of Opp. 81 and 86, the former performed by Schmid-Lindner [August] and the latter performed by Reger and Schmid-Lindner. Decsey compares Reger to Carl Loewe concerning the seriousness of their use of chorales. Reger is also described as a composer looking to the past in his choice of thematic material while at the same time looking to the future in his "organic expansion of tonality."

B1422 Deinhardt, Hans. "Heidelberg." *M* 4 (1904/05): 139.
Review of a Reger evening in Heidelberg, featuring Opp. 72 and 86. Reger and [Karl] Wolfrum performed Op. 86.

B1423 D.M. [Donald Mitchell]. "First Performances." *Music Review* 14 (1953): 296-298.
Mention is made of the first English performance of Op. 100. Some interesting details of the dating of this composition are given.

B1424 Doflein, Erich. "Das 3. Reger-Fest in Jena." *SMW* (1920): 711ff.

B1425 Dominik, Ruth. "Festliche Reger-Orgeltage in Hamburg." *MK* 43 (1973): 249-250.
A review of the three concerts of the Reger Festival which attempted to give an overview of the composer's significant organ works.

B1426 -----. "Nordelbische Kirche. Festliche Reger-Orgeltage in Hamburg." *K* 24 (1973): 147-148.

B1427 Dorn, Otto. "No Title." *M* 7 (1908): 383.
Review of Op. 100.

B1428 -----. "No Title." *M* 14 (1915): 288.
Reviews of Opp. 124, 132, and 140.

B1429 -----. "Wiesbaden." *M* 11 (1912): 63.

Review of a performance of Op. 106.

B1430 Draber, Hermann W. "No Title." NMZ 32:11 (1910).
Contains a review of performances of Opp. 106 and 114.

B1431 -----. "Die Berliner Reger-Woche." Deutsche Musikzeitung 1:1 (1919).

B1432 -----. "Das Max-Reger-Fest." SMW 68 (1910): 19ff.

B1433 Dubitzky, Franz. "Franz Schubert: Ausgewählte Lieder für eine Singstimme mit Orchester instrumentiert von Max Reger." M 13 (1914): 230.
After giving a brief overview of other orchestrations of Schubert's songs, Dubitzky states that "Schubert would be satisfied with his editor [Reger]."

B1434 -----. "Max Reger: Eine vaterländische Ouvertüre op. 140." M 14 (1915): 83.

B1435 E. "Das Max-Reger-Fest in Dortmund vom 7.-9. Mai 1910." Deutsche Musikzeitung 41:22 (1910): 335-336.

B1436 Ebel, Arnold. "No Title." AMZ 41:13 (1914).
Review of a performance of Op. 122.

B1437 Ecarius-Sieber, A. "No Title." M 6 (1907): 121.
Reviews of Opp. 77a, 93, and 96.

B1438 -----. "Die Bach- und Regerkonzerte der 'Musikalischen Gesellschaft' Essen, 7. und 8. Oktober." MW 36:48 (1905).

B1439 E.E. "Kompositionen von Max Reger." NMZ 21:6 (1900).
Contains reviews of Opp. 21 and 38.

B1440 Ehlers, Paul. "No Title." AMZ 37 (1910): 582.
See B1235, p. 278. [Review of Op. 113.]

B1441 -----. "No Title." M 9 (1909): 385.
Review of Op. 108.

B1442 -----. "No Title." M 9 (1910): 189.
Review of Op. 106.

B1443 -----. "No Title." M 9 (1910): 323.
Reviews of Opp. 86 and 96.

B1444 -----. "No Title." MW 27 (1906): 355ff.
Review of a performance of OpO. 90 in Königsberg.

B1445 -----. "Das Tonkünstlerfest in Graz." NMZ 26 (1905):

421-425.
A review of [August] Schmid-Lindner performing Reger's Bach Variations. Ehlers says of Reger that he "is a genius of polyphonic combination."

B1446 -----. "Die Versammlung des Allgemeinen Deutschen Musikvereins in Dresden." MW 35 (1904): 487ff.
See B1235, pp. 51-53.

B1447 Einstein, Alfred. "Lindner, Adalbert. Max Reger: Ein Bild seines Jugendlebens und künstlerischen Werdens." Zeitschrift für Musikwissenschaft 4:12 (1921/22): 630.
Book review.

B1448 Elson, L[ouis] C. "No Title." M 9 (1909): 315.
Review of Op. 106.

B1449 -----. "No Title." M 11 (1911): 380.
Review of Op. 120.

B1450 -----. "Boston." M 8 (1909): 182-183.
Elson reviews a performance of Op. 72 by Jacques Hoffmann and Charles Anthony. "The work seems ugly to me....The sonata was too long for our public...."

B1451 Elster, Alexander. "Jena." M 10 (1911): 323.
Favorable review of Op. 109. The performers were joined by Reger for a performance of the Eb Major Piano Quintet of Schumann.

B1452 Engelfred, Abele. "Eugen Segnizt [sic]: Max Reger." RMI 30 (1923): 300ff.

B1453 E.S. "No Title." NMZ 28:4 (1907): 80.
Reviews of Opp. 91 and 93.

B1454 Eschmann, K. "No Title." M 6 (1907): 133.
Review of Op. 95.

B1455 Eylau, W. "No Title." AMZ 37:5 (1910).
Review of a performance of Op. 74.

B1456 -----. "No Title." AMZ 37:7 (1910).
Review of a performance of Op. 93.

B1457 Farmer, A. "Organ Recital Notes." MT 95 (1954): 377.
Review of Op. 127.

B1458 Fischer, Walter. "No Title." AMZ 31:17 (1904): 309.
Review of Reger's arrangements of Bach's preludes and fugues.

B1459 -----. "Max Reger, 52 leicht ausführbare Vorspiele für die Orgel zu den gebräuchlichsten evangelischen Choralen op. 67." AMZ 30 (1903): 396-397.
These preludes are described as "paradise of tone" to which Reger "has contributed his individual musical craftsmanship."

B1460 -----. "Max Reger. Schlichte Weisen. Op. 76." AMZ 31 (1904): 576.
Short review of Op. 76. Generally favorable. Reviewer points out that not all of Reger's "folk songs" have folk texts.

B1461 -----. "Max Reger. Variationen und Fuge über ein Originalthema für die Orgel op. 73." AMZ 31 (1904): 166.
Brief review of Op. 73. "Reger has written these variations with his life's blood."

B1462 -----. "Max Reger. Zehn Stücke für die Orgel op. 69." AMZ 31 (1904): 51.
Short review of Op. 69. Mentions that the work contains only freely composed compositions (preludes, fantasias, improvisations, and such).

B1463 -----. "Neues von Max Reger." AMZ 32:1 (1905).
Reviews of performances of Opp. 76I, 81, 86, 82I, 77, 78, 75, and "O Haupt voll Blut und Wunden."

B1464 -----. "Schule des Triospiels. J.S. Bachs zweistimmige Inventionen für die Orgel bearbeitet von Max Reger und Karl Straube." AMZ 31 (1904): 165-166.
Explains the process by which Reger and Straube added a third part to Bach's 2-Part Inventions. Includes musical examples.

B1465 -----. "Vom Musikalienmarkt." AMZ 31 (1904): 309.
Reviews of Reger's arrangements of Bach's cantata "Wer nur den lieben Gott lässt walten" and the Prelude and Fugue in Eb Major (for piano duo). "Reger's arrangement [of the Prelude and Fugue] places itself within the Lisztian [tradition] of Bach transcription...."

B1466 -----. "Vom Musikalienmarkt: Max Reger, 17 Lieder op. 70." AMZ 30:42 (1903): 648.
Short review of Op. 70.

B1467 -----. "Vom Musikalienmarkt: Neue Kirchenmusik fürs Totenfest und die Weihnachtszeit." AMZ 31 (1904): 640.
A generally favorable review of "Vom Himmel hoch, da komm ich her" and "O wie selig seid ihr doch ihr Frommen." Fischer approves of Reger's settings of

Lutheran chorales and takes notice of the composer's indebtedness to Bach.

B1468 Flautau. "No Title." M 5 (1906): 440.
Review of Op. 90.

B1469 Frenzel, B. "Reger, Max. Op. 39. Drei sechsstimmige Gesänge für Sopran, 2 Alt, Tenor und 2 Bass." NZFM 68: 4 (1901): 54.

B1470 Friedland, Martin. "No Title." AMZ 49:13 (1914).
Review of a performance of Op. 130.

B1471 Funk, Heinrich. "Mozart-Reger-Fest in Jena." [N]ZFM 108 (1941): 402.
Short review of a 1941 festival given on the occasion of the 150th anniversary of Mozart's death and the 25th anniversary of Reger's death. Reger compositions performed included Opp. 77, 133, 146, 46, and "O Tod, wie bitter bist du."

B1472 Gauss, Kurt. "Max-Reger-Ehrung Meiningen." MU 20 (1966): 234-235.
Works performed included Opp. 130, 86, 146, and the Hiller Variations. Also included were a number of lectures and lecture-recitals.

B1473 G.B. "Max Reger: Komm, süsser Tod." Ars Organi 28 (1980): 132.
Brief descriptive review.

B1474 -----. "Max Reger: Zwölf Lieder für eine mittlere Singstimme op 66." SMZ 43 (1930): 194.

B1475 Geissler, F.A. "No Title." M 6 (1906/07): 131.
Review of Op. 95.

B1476 -----. "No Title." M 7 (1907): 382.
Review of Op. 100.

B1477 -----. "Max Reger: Zwei geistliche Lieder op. 105." M 8 (1909): 319.

B1478 -----. "No Title." M 10 (1911): 259.
See B1235, pp. 296-297. [Review of Op. 114.]

B1479 -----. "No Title." M 11 (1911): 190ff.
Review of Op. 121.

B1480 -----. "No Title." M 12 (1912): 187ff.
Review of Op. 125.

B1481 -----. "No Title." M 12 (1913): 119.

Review of Op. 123.

B1482 -----. "No Title." M 13 (1914): 181.
Review of Op. 130.

B1483 -----. "Dresden." M 4 (1904/05): 63.
Sanna von Rhyn organized a Reger concert with the composer and pianist Henriette Schelle and violinist Karl Wendling assisting. Works performed included a set of lieder, the Violin Sonata in C Major, and the Beethoven Variations. The String Quartet in D Minor was performed by the Petri Quartet on the following day. Very favorable review.

B1484 -----. "Dresden." M 8 (1909): 184-185.
The reviewer tells of the expectations surrounding the Symphonic Prologue to a Tragedy which he says were not completely fulfilled. Geissler sees a Brucknerian influence in this work.

B1485 -----. "Max Reger: 'Abendfrieden.'" M 8 (1909): 171.
Geissler rates that this work as below the standard set by Reger's other songs. "The melody is indeed plain..."

B1486 -----. "Max Reger: Vier Lieder op. 97." M 6 (1906/07): 300.
The need for an accomplished pianist to perform the accompaniments of these songs is stressed.

B1487 Gensel, Walter M. "Max Reger-Fest in Weimar." Das Orchester 3:10 (1926): 113.

B1488 Gerber, Rudolf. "Fritz Stein, Max Reger. (Die grossen Meister der Musik. Hrsg. v. E. Bücken). Potsdam, 1939." Deutsche Literaturzeitung 38 (1939): 1355-1358.

B1489 Gerbracht, Wolfgang. "Reger-Fest in Bonn." Das Musikleben 1:4 (1948).

B1490 Gerigk, Herbert. "No Title." M 36 (1937): 52.
Review of recordings of the Mozart Variations by the Sächsischen Staatskapelle Orchestra conducted by Karl Böhm. Electrola DB 4480/4483.

B1491 Gerstenberg, Walter. "Neue Bücher: Fritz Stein, Max Reger." Archiv für Musikforschung 6 (1941): 120-121.
Review of Stein's Reger biography. The reviewer notes that Stein's reminiscences will prove useful to future historians.

B1492 Gojowy, Detlef. "Max-Reger-Tage in Bonn." Musik und Bildung 5:7/8 (1973): 402-403.

B1493 Göttmann, Adolf. "Max Reger: op. 64--Quintett für Pianoforte, 2 Violinen, Viola und Violoncell." Zeitschrift der Internationalen Musikgesellschaft 4 (1903): 590.

B1494 -----. "Max Reger: Zwölf Lieder für ein mittlere Singstimme mit Begleitung des Pianoforte op. 66--Sechs Gesänge für eine mittlere Singstimme mit Begleitung des Pianoforte op. 68." M 4 (1904/05): 127-128.
A critical review of the composer and the works listed above. "And when a number of his musical raise up Reger as a second Messiah in the vanguard of compositional progress, I can only deplore this confused thinking...."

B1495 Götzinger, F. "24. Tonkünstler-Versammlung des Allgemeinen Deutschen Musikvereins." Zeitschrift der Internationalen Musikgesellschaft 4:10 (1903): 615.

B1496 Grabner, Hermann. Musikalische Betrachung. Stuttgart: Klett, 1950.
Contains sections on Op. 46, pp. 40-42; Op. 82/I/2, pp. 138-144; Op. 114, pp. 76-79; and Op. 132, pp. 97-99.

B1497 Greis, Siegfried. "Umschau: Reger-Tage in Schlüchtern." MK 26 (1956): 202-203.
Contains an account of lectures given on the 40th anniversary of Reger's death.

B1498 -----. "Zum Max-Reger-Jahr 1973." Gottesdienst und Kirchenmusik 2 (1973): 41-43.

B1499 Grunsky, Karl. "No Title. M 7 (1908): 255.
Review of Op. 100.

B1500 Günther, Ernst. "No Title." NZFM 70:21 (1903): 322.
Reviews of Opp. 61, 66, and 68.

B1501 Güntzel, Ottomar. "Max Reger-Fest in Meiningen am 10. und 11. April 1937." [N]ZFM 104 (1937): 543-544.
Elsa Reger and Adalbert Lindner were in attendance at this festival. Works performed included Opp. 128, 114, 132, 146, 109, 123, 144, 124, and 100.

B1502 Haberl, Franz X. "Die Bach-Reger-Feier in Heidelberg." NZFM 89:23 (1922).

B1503 Halbig, Hermann. "Die Bach-Reger-Feier in Heidelberg." NZFM 89:23 (1922).

B1504 Handschin, Jacques. "Max Reger, Briefwechsel mit Herzog Georg II. von Sachsen-Meiningen. Hrsg. v. Hedwig und E.H. Müller von Asow." SMZ 90 (1950): 38-39.

Book review.

B1505 Hansen, Bernhard. "Gerd Sievers: Die Grundlagen Hugo Riemanns bei Max Reger." Die Musikforschung 23 (1970): 485-486.
Thoughtful and detailed review. "The chapter 'Max Reger's Harmony as a Function of the Emancipated Line' ...is the core and the most significant writing of the book."

B1506 Hasse, Karl. "Bach-Reger-Fest in Heidelberg." Zeitschrift für Musikwissenschaft 5 (1922): 100-101.
Reger compositions performed included Opp. 73 and 106.

B1507 -----. "Drei Chorwerke von Max Reger." Die Orgel 10:3 (1910).
Reviews of Opp. 71, 106, and 110/1.

B1508 -----. "Max Reger: Lyrisches Andante für Streichen." NZFM 101:12 (1934).

B1509 -----. "Siegfried Kallenberg: Max Reger." NZFM 100:3 (1933).
Review of Kallenberg's 1930 biography of Reger published by Reclam of Leipzig.

B1510 Hehemann, Max. "No Title." M 5 (1905/06): 217-218.
Hehemann praises the premiere performance of Op. 90, especially the larghetto ("wunderherrliche Larghetto"). A performance by Karl Straube of Opp. 57 and 52/2 is mentioned as well as Reger's performance of the keyboard part in J.S. Bach's 5th Brandenburg Concerto.

B1511 -----. "No Title." M 6 (1906): 390.
Review of Op. 95.

B1512 -----. "Essen." M 4 (1904/05): 367.
Review of a Reger Evening which featured Opp. 72, 77b, 74, and 86. [Op. 86 is incorrectly identified as Op. 81.] The program "captivated over a thousand people" who "cheered stormily."

B1513 -----. "Max Reger: Achtzehn Lieder op. 75; Andante semplice con variazioni für Klavier zu zwei Händen; Aus meinem Tagebuche [sic]: Zwölf kleine Stücke für Klavier zu zwei Händen op. 82; Variationen und Fuge über ein Thema von Joh. Seb. Bach. Für Klavier zu zwei Händen op. 81; Variationen und Fuge über ein Thema von Beethoven. Für zwei Klaviere zu vier Händen op. 86." M 4 (1905): 430-431.
Short, generally favorable reviews of the compositions listed above.

B1514 -----. "Max Reger: Aus meinem Tagebuch, op. 82. Band II." M 6 (1906/07): 47.
"In general, modulatory devices are as important as melodic ones."

B1515 -----. "Max Reger: Introduktion, Passacaglia und Fuge, für zwei Klaviere zu vier Händen op. 96." M 7 (1907): 50-51.
Hehemann gives an extremely complimentary review of Op. 96, praising all aspects of the composition and stating that "a master's hand is displayed throughout the entire work."

B1516 Hellmers, Gerhard. "No Title." NMZ 38:10 (1917).
Contains a review of a performance of Op. 114.

B1517 Henseler, Theodor Anton. "Bonner Reger-Tage." Neue Musikzeitschrift 2:6 (1948).

B1518 Hermann, Joachim. "Süddeutsche Max Reger-Tage 1966." MU 20 (1966): 235-236.
Works performed at this Munich festival included Opp. 114 and 101.

B1519 Heuser, Ernst. "Reger in Köln." Blätter für Haus- und Kirchenmusik 10 (1905/06): 61.
See B1235, pp. 92-93.

B1520 Heuss, Alfred. "Über das 46. Tonkünstlerfest des Allgemeinen Deutschen Musikvereins in Zürich 25.-31. Mai 1910." Zeitschrift der Internationalen Musikgesellschaft 11 (1910): 331ff.
See B1235, pp. 275-276.

B1521 Heyer, Hermann. "Max-Reger-Gedächtnistage in Leipzig." AMZ 68 (1941): 296.

B1522 H.H. [Hugo Holle]. "Adalbert Lindner: Max Reger." NMZ 43:3 (1921).
Book review of Lindner's Reger biography.

B1523 -----. "Eugen Segnitz: Max Reger." NMZ 43:17 (1922).
Book review of Segnitz's Reger biography.

B1524 Hielscher, Paul. "Max Reger: Choralkantaten zu dem Hauptfesten des evangelischen Kirchenjahres. 1. Vom Himmel hoch da komm ich her. 2. O. wie selig seid ihr doch, ihr Frommen. 3. O Haupt voll Blut und Wunden." M 4 (1904/05): 49-50.
"The chorale cantatas of Reger show the Munich master in a completely new light....His chorale cantatas are not concertpieces...[they] take into account the prayers of

the congregation."

B1525 Hiemenz, Jack. "Philadelphia Orchestra (Ormandy)." HiFi/musical america 19 (1969): 32.
Review of Op. 144b.

B1526 Hiller, Paul. "No Title." M 5 (1905): 368ff.
Reviews of opp. 77a, 86, and 90.

B1527 -----. "No Title." M 6 (1906): 256.
Review of Op. 95.

B1528 -----. "No Title." M 7 (1907): 251.
Review of Op. 100.

B1529 -----. "No Title." M 8 (1909): 121.
Review of Op. 108.

B1530 -----. "No Title." M 10 (1911): 133.
Review of Op. 106.

B1531 -----. "No Title." M 11 (1912): 63.
Review of Op. 120.

B1532 -----. "No Title." M 12 (1912): 252.
Review of Op. 125.

B1533 -----. "No Title." MW 37:44 (1906).
Review of the premiere of Op. 96 in Cologne.

B1534 Hobbing, Heinrich. "No Title." AMZ 41:7 (1914).
Review of a performance of Op. 110/2.

B1535 H. Oe. "Meiningen. Reger-Kolloquium." MG 16 (1966): 858-859.

B1536 Hoedel, Otto. "No Title." M 12 (1913): 376.
Review of Op. 33.

B1537 Hoffmann, Rudolf Stephan. "No Title." NMZ 38:12 (1917).
Contains reviews of performances of Opp. 86a, 106, 123, 125, 132, and 144.

B1538 Hoffmeister, H. "Osnabrück." M 11 (1911): 383.
A brief account of a Reger festival in Osnabrück. Works performed included Op. 86, the Hiller Variations, several vocal works.

B1539 Holde, A. "Max-Reger-Fest zu Frankfurt am Main." AMZ 54 (1927): 524.

B1540 Holle, Hugo. "Bach-Reger-Feier in Heidelberg." NMZ 44

(1923): 74-75.
Account of the October 25-29, 1922 festival. Featured at the festival were performances of Reger compositions displaying the influence of Bach and historically accurate performances of Bach compositions.

B1541 -----. "Besprechungen." NMZ 44 (1923): 193.
Short explanatory reviews of musical compositions by Reger and prose works concerning the composer: Max Reger-Brevier, ed. by Adolf Spemann; Almanach der Deutschen Musikbücherei auf das Jahr 1923 (including an essay on Reger by Holle); Reger-Mappe, Vols. I & II; Max-Reger-Liederalbum, Zwei Lieder without opus no., and Op. 109.

B1542 -----. "Der Max Reger-Zyklus in Stuttgart." NMZ 44 (1923): 26-27.
Account of two chamber concerts and an organ concert in Stuttgart devoted to Reger's works. Compositions performed included Opp. 107, 139, 113, 131c, 118, 46, 52/2, and 73. Organist Arno Landman is described as a "preeminent Reger interpreter" who possesses "phenomenal technique."

B1543 Honold, Eugen. "No Title." AMZ 37:18 (1910).
Review of performances of Opp. 28, 93, and 102.

B1544 -----. "No Title." AMZ 37:42 (1910).
Review of performances of Opp. 82 and 96, and assorted songs.

B1545 Horn, Michael. "Ein kurzes Geplauder." MS 17 (1905): 123.
Contains a review of Op. 46.

B1546 Humbert, Georges. "Le Psaume C de Max Reger: Bref essai de mise au point, en manière de prélude a une discussion sur la cas Reger." La Vie Musicale 3 (1910): 20.

B1547 Ibe, Emil. "Max Reger-Fest in Sondershausen." [N]ZFM 107 (1940): 632-633.
Details given of a festival in honor of Reger who 50 years previously had gone to Sondershausen to study with Hugo Riemann. Works performed included the Telemann Variations, Opp. 131d/1-3, 109, 65, 80, 59, 100, 120, 130, 86, and 140, and four songs.

B1548 Isler, Ernst. "Neue Werke von Max Reger." SMZ 49:29 (1910).

B1549 Istel, Ernst. "Max-Reger-Abend in München." Zeitschrift der Internationalen Musikgesellschaft 5 (1904): 373ff.

B1550 Jaager, Werner. "Reger-Feierstunde in Plön." Musikblätter 13 (1948): 21.

B1551 Jacobi, Max. "No Title." M 11 (1912): 180. Reviews of Opp. 100, 116, and lieder.

B1552 Jensch, G. "Das Reger-Fest in Breslau April 1922." AMZ 49 (1922): 397.

B1553 Kahl, Willi. "Reger-Briefe." Die Musikforschung 2 (1949): 238-242.
Review.

B1554 Kahnt, Gustav. "No Title." M 10 (1910): 309.
Review of Op. 96.

B1555 Kaiser, Georg. "Der getanzte Reger." SMW 74:24/25 (1916).
Concerns Op. 130.

B1556 Kaiser, L. "Neuntes Deutsches Reger-Fest in Kassel." SMW (1933): 522.

B1557 Kalb, Friedrich. "Ottmar Schreiber und Gerd Sievers (Herausgeb.), Max Reger. Zum 50. Todestag am 11. Mai 1966. Eine Gedenkschrift." Gottesdienst und Kirchenmusik 2 (1973): 62.
Book review.

B1558 Kanth, Gustav. "No Title." M 10 (1910): 125.
Reviews of Opp. 33 and 60 performed by Alfred Sittard.

B1559 Kastner, Rudolf. "No Title." M 7 (1908): 127.
Reviews of Opp. 93 and 100.

B1560 Kaupert, Werner & Paul Poppe. "Max Reger-Festtage." MU 10 (1956): 513-514.
Extensive accounts of Reger festivals in Meiningen and Weiden. Many concerts and lectures are reported.

B1561 Kesser, Hermann. "No Title." M 8 (1909): 127.
Review of Op. 100.

B1562 Kieser, A. "Regers 'Vier Tondichtung nach A. Böcklin' op. 128." Die Harmonie 6:4 (1919).

B1563 Killer, H. "Reger-Feier der Berliner Hochschule für Musik." M 33 (1941): 430.

B1564 Killmayer, Wilhelm. "Tönendes Dasein auf schwankendem Boden: Zum 100. Geburtstag von Max Reger." Musik und Bildung 5:12 (1973): 663-665.

B1565 Kipke, Carl. "Besprechungen." Die Sängerhalle 42:21/21 (1902): 264.
Review of Op. 61.

B1566 -----. "Besprechungen: Zwölf Madrigale für Männerchor, bearb. v. Max Reger; Sechs Madrigale f. gem. Chor, bearb. v. Max Reger." Die Sängerhalle 42:14/15 (1902): 200.

B1567 Kissling, Gustav. "Bremen." M 5 (1905/06): 364.
Mention of a performance of Reger's Sinfonietta. "The musical event of the last week featured the presentation of Reger's 'Sinfonietta.'"

B1568 Klanert, Paul. "no Title." AMZ 37:14 (1910).
Review of a performance of Op. 107.

B1569 -----. "Max Reger-Gedächtnisfeiern. Meiningen. Halle a. Saale." NMZ 44 (1923): 211-212.
Accounts of Reger festivals commemorating the composer's 50th birthday. Works performed at Meiningen: Opp. 144b, 121, 131d/3, 115, 133, and 136; at Halle: Opp. 107 (incorrectly listed as Op. 110), 54, 109, 77b, and various organ, orchestral, and choral works.

B1570 Kohl, Bernhard A. "22. Internationale Orgelwoche Nürnberg." MK 43 (1973): 199-200.
Mention made of several concerts of Reger's music and a symposium entitled "The Contemporary View of Reger's Work."

B1571 König, A. "Meiningen." M 15 (1923): 551-552.
An account of the Reger Festival in Meiningen that was held from February 24-25, 1923. Three concerts were programmed, one each dealing with Reger's church, chamber, and orchestral music. The festival was directed by Peter Schmitz.

B1572 Korn, Peter Jona, "A Max Reger Festival." High Fidelity/musical america 16:8 (1966): 20-21.
Korn reviews the Süddeutsche Reger Tage 1966 held in Munich and suggests that "Reger was on the threshold of stylistic maturity at the time of his death."

B1573 Kotsmary, Anton. "No Title." M 5 (1906): 207.
See B1235, p. 113. [Review of Op. 90.]

B1574 Krause, Emil. "No Title." MW 39:19/20 (1908).
Review of a performance of Op. 84 in Hamburg.

B1575 Krause, Martin. "Max Reger." Die Musikwoche 1 (1901): 331-332.

See B1235, pp. 15-16.

B1576 Krauss, Karl August. "No Title." M 13 (1914): 314.
Reviews of Op. 128 and 130.

B1577 -----. "Heidelberg." M 15 (1922): 227-228.
An account of the Bach-Reger Festival held in Heidelberg from October 25-29, 1922. Reger works performed included Opp. 130, 73, 84,81, 117, 93, et al. Hermann Grabner presented a paper entitled "Max Reger as Man and Artist."

B1578 -----. "Heildelberg: Das Heidelberg Bach-Reger-Musikfest (22.-25. Juli)." M 12 (1913): 121-122.
The works of Reger performed included Opp. 122, 116, 125,124, 123, 100, 106, and 46.

B1579 -----. "Regerabend in Heidelberg." MW 37:37 (1906).
Reviews of Opp. 60 and 90, and lieder.

B1580 Krellmann, Hanspeter. "Die Reger-Tage 1973." MU 27 (1973): 264-265.
Gives details about the festivities in Bonn held during the 100th anniversary of Reger's birth. The author states that the problems of interpretation in Reger's music are not unlike those encountered in new music.

B1581 Krieger, E. "Regers Vermächtnis an das deutsche Heer." Die Musikwoche 8 (1940): 281.
Review of Op. 140.

B1582 Krienitz, Willy. "Münchner Reger-Gedenkfeier." AMZ 63: 25 (1936).

B1583 Kroyer, Theodore. "No Title." M 1 (1902): 1515-1516.
Review of a performance of Op. 49/1. Mentions the influence of Brahms' clarinet sonatas on those of Reger.

B1584 -----. "No Title." M 3 (1904): 229.
Review of Op. 72.

B1585 -----. "No Title." M 5 (1906): 260.
Reviews of Opp. 76 and 88, and lieder.

B1586 -----. "Max Reger, Briefe eines deutschen Meisters: Ein Lebensbild hrsg. v. Else von Hase-Koehler, Leipzig 1928." Deutsche Literaturzeitung 7 (1930): 309-317.
Book review.

B1587 Kühn, Oswald. "Betrachtungen zum Mannheimer Mahler-Fest." NMZ 33 (1912): 356-358.
Kühn states that the idea of the symphonic poem has

permeated chamber music, even that of Reger.

B1588 Kunze, Walther. "Beim Reger-Biographen Adalbert Lindner." [N]ZFM 100 (1933): 3.

B1589 Küsgen, Wolfgang. "II. Steglitzer Kirchenmusiktage 80." MK 50 (1980): 277.
Mention of performances in Berlin of Op. 63 and the six chorale fantasies.

B1590 Kwasnik, Walter. "Reger-Gedenken in Herborn." MK 43 (1973): 156.
Works performed included Opp. 67, 145, 59, 65, 105, and 137.

B1591 L. "No Title." NMZ 35:12 (1914).
Contains a review of a performance of Op. 130.

B1592 Lang, Heinrich. "Vom Musikalienmarkt." AMZ 28 (1901): 800-801.
Reviews of Opp. 53, 59, 49/1, 50, et al. "I have very little enthusiasm for the Sonata No. 1 [Ab Major, Op. 49/1] for Clarinet and Piano. For all of their good qualities, the compositions of Reger that have been praised up till now, too much compositional extravagence and purely technical artistry alone have prevailed."

B1593 -----. "Vom Musikalienmarkt." AMZ 29 (1902): 116.
Review of Op. 57. "It is a complete Witches' Sabbath of superimposed harmonies, a tone-orgy...."

B1594 Lange, Ernst. "10. Max-Reger-Fest in Freiburg." AMZ 63:23/24 (1936).

B1595 Laux, Karl. "Meininger Reger-Festtage 1973." MG 23 (1973): 420-421.

B1596 Lederer, Viktor. "Max Reger, op. 83: Acht Gesänge für Männerchor." SMW 63 (1905): 800.

B1597 Leib, Walter. "7. Reger-Fest in Heidelberg." M 22:11 (1930).

B1598 Leichtentritt, Hugo. "No Title." AMZ 32:2 (1905).
Reviews of performances of Opp. 50, 72, 77a, and songs.

B1599 -----. "Neue Werke von Max Reger." SMW 65 (1907): 9ff.

B1600 Leitzmann, Albert. "J.S. Bach: Orchestersuiten. Für Pianoforte zu vier Händen bearbeitet von Max Reger," M 7 (1908): 97.
The reviewer remarks that Reger's arrangements for piano of the orchestral suites are easier than his arrangements of Bach's organ music.

B1601 -----. "Max Reger: 'Blätter und Blüten.' Zwölf Klavierstücke." M 10 (1911): 296.
This work is described as "average...without making a profound impression."

B1602 -----. "Max Reger: Sechs Stücke für Pianoforte zu vier Händen op. 94." M 6 (1907): 307.
Leitzmann has some reservations but remarks that "a Reger composition is never worthless."

B1603 Lessmann, Otto. "No Title." AMZ 32 (1905): 206.
See B1235, pp. 80-81. [Reviews of Opp. 81, 84, and 86.]

B1604 -----. "No Title." AMZ 37:43 (1910).
Review of a performance of Op. 113.

B1605 -----. "No Title." AMZ 37:48 (1910).
Review of performances of Opp. 27 and 106.

B1606 -----. "No Title." AMZ 39 (1912): 317.
Review of a Meiningen Hofkapelle Orchestra Concert conducted by Reger [Berlin, March 19, 1912]. Works performed included Beethoven's 3rd Symphony and Reger's Opp. 100 and 120. "In the Eroica Reger presented an unusal but not uninteresting conception to the listener."

B1607 -----. "No Title." AMZ 41:7 (1914).
Review of a performance of Op. 116.

B1608 -----. "Aus den Berliner Konzertsälen." AMZ 39 (1912): 1146.
Mention of a Reger Evening at which Opp. 72, 102, and 93 were performed. Op. 72 is described as "brutal and nerve-wracking."

B1609 -----. "Aus dem Konzertsaal." AMZ 21 (1894): 113.
See B1235, pp. 3-4.

B1610 -----. "Tonkünstlerfest in Graz." AMZ 32:23 (1905).
Mentions Opp. 81 and 86.

B1611 Liebert, Volkand. "Der Münchner Motettchor feiert Max Reger." Gottesdienst und Kirchenmusik 5 (1973): 169

B1612 Liepe, Emil. "Max Reger: 'An Zeppelin' and Drei Duette für Sopran und Alt op. 111a." AMZ 37:10 (1910).

B1613 -----. "Max Reger: Blätter und Blüten, Romanze G-dur für Violine und Klavier." AMZ 37:48 (1910).

B1614 -----. "Vom Musikalienmarkt: Max Regers neue Gesangswerke." AMZ 30 (1903): 532.
Reviews of Opp. 62 and 68. "In his creations rhythm and melody take a back seat to a richly prolific harmonic elaboration."

B1615 Liese, Joseph. "No Title." M 5 (1906): 425ff.
Reviews of Opp. 71, 84, 86, 90, and lieder.

B1616 -----. "No Title." M 7 (1908): 122.
Review of Op. 100.

B1617 Lindlar, Heinrich. "Max Reger--Mensch und Künstler: Bonner Gedenkfeier zum 80. Geburtstag des Komponisten." Das Musikleben 6:6 (1953): 228.

B1618 Lindner, Adalbert. "Max Regers Hymne an den Gesang op. 21 in Weiden uraufgeführt." Die Sängerhalle 39 (1899): 26ff.
See B1235, p. 4.

B1619 -----. "Max Regers 'In der Nacht.'" M 22:9 (1930).

B1620 Louis, Rudolf. "No Title." M 13 (1914): 187.
Review of Reger conducting the Meiningen Hofkapelle Orchestra in performances of Opp. 124 and 128.

B1621 -----. "Die 40. Tonkünstler-Versammlung des Allgemeinen Deutschen Musikvereins zu Frankfurt a. M." NMZ 25 (1904): 407.
Review of Op. 72.

B1622 -----. "Die 48. Tonkünstler-Versammlung des Allgemeinen Deutschen Musikvereins in Jena (3.-7. Juni 1913)." M 12 (1913): 20-25.
In reviewing Op. 126, Louis says that this work holds a position in Reger's oeuvre similar to that of Taillefer for Richard Strauss.

B1623 -----. "J.S. Bach: Kantate 'Wer nur den lieben Gott lässt walten.' Bearbeitet von Max Reger." M 4 (1905): 182-3.
"Reger's edition extends to expressive markings and the performance of the continuo in the organ accompaniment. ...This edition will hopefully contribute to Kretzschmar's prediction coming true, namely, that this composition, when generally known, will probably become one of the most popular of Bach's church cantatas."

B1624 L.T. "Max-Reger-Brevier." RMI 30 (1923): 301.

B1625 L.Th. "No Title." RMI 10 (1903): 157-158.
Review of Op. 63.

B1626 Lüttwitz, Heinrich von. "Reger-Fest." MU 14 (1960): 727-728.
Review of a Reger festival in Dortmund which featured, among other works, the premiere of a 6-minute symphonic movement composed by Reger when he was 17 years old. The work was found in the estate of Hugo Riemann.

B1627 Mack, Friedrich. "Das Heidelberger Bach-Reger-Musikfest 22. bis 25. Juni." AMZ 40 (1913): 998-999.
Details given of the 1913 Heidelberg Bach-Reger Festival. Major works of Reger performed included the B-A-C-H Fantasy, the Romantic Suite, the Hiller Variations, and the 100th Psalm. Reger performed at the keyboard for a performance of Bach's 5th Brandenburg Concerto.

B1628 Marckwald, Ernst. "Im Zeichen Max Regers." MU 20 (1966): 235.
An account of a Reger festival in Weiden which featured an address by Eberhard Otto on "Max Regers Spiritual Relationship to J.S. Bach."

B1629 Margrini, Giuseppe. "Max Reger--op. 67. Zweiundfünfzig Choralvorspiele für Orgel." RMI 11 (1904): 189

B1630 Martin, Karl. "No Title." M 11 (1912): 183.
Review of Op. 122 and lieder.

B1631 Martinotti, Sergio. "Max Reger zum 50. Todestag am 11. Mai 1966: Eine Gedenkschrift, hrsg. v. Ottmar Schreiber u. Gerd Sievers, Bonn 1966." Rivista Italiana di Musicologia 3:1 (1968): 202-206.
Book review.

B1632 Mechtold, G. "Max-Reger-Fest in Meiningen." AMZ 64 (1937): 251.

B1633 Mehler, Eugen. "Bach-Reger-Abend in Heidelberg." MW 39: 17/18 (1908).

B1634 Merian, W. "No Title." AMZ 40:4 (1913).
Review of a performance of Op. 106.

B1635 Michel, Paul. "Buchbesprechung: Max Reger, Beiträge zur Regerforschung..." MG 20 (1970): 136-137.
Book review.

B1636 Mojsisovics, Roderich von. "No Title." NMZ 32:14 (1911).
Contains reviews of performances of Opp. 81 and 114.

B1637 -----. "Max Reger: Beiträge zur Modulationslehr." MW 35: 16 (1904).
Book review.

B1638 -----. "Regers Choralfantasien für die Orgel." NMZ 29:22 (1908).

B1639 Möllers, Christian. "Lohnender Denkansatz." MU 35 (1981): 276-277.
A review of Rainer Wilke's Brahms. Reger. Schönberg. Streichquartette....

B1640 Moos, Paul. "Max Reger: Op. 8, 5 Lieder für eine hohe Stimme. Op. 12, 5 Lieder für eine Stimme." AMZ 21 (1894): 253-254.
"Max Reger displays an exquisitely sensitive nature in his choice of the attractive texts of Uhland, Wildenbruch, Isolde Kury, and others."

B1641 Moser, Hans Joachim. "Halle." M 15 (1923): 548-549.
Details of the Halle Reger Memorial Festival held on the occasion of the composer's 50th birthday. The highpoint of the festival was a Sunday morning concert that featured the Hiller Variations and the 100th Psalm.

B1642 Motta, José Vianna da. "Bach: Präludium und Fuge Es-dur von der Orgel für Klavier übertragen von Max Reger." M 3 (1904): 454.
"It is inconceivable how an organist and Bach scholar of his [Reger's] reputation could be carried away in error phrasing the second theme of the fugue in so coquettish a manner."

B1643 -----. "Max Reger: op. 20, 36, 44 und 5 Spezialstudien o.O." Das Klavierspiel 23:19 (1901).

B1644 Müller, E. Jos. "Fritz Stein, Max Reger. Potsdam: Akademische Verlagsgesellschaft Athenaion." K 2:4 (1939): 96.
Book review.

B1645 Müller-Reuter, Theodor. "Max Reger als Orchester-komponist." NZFM 72 (1905): 828ff.
See B1235, pp. 89-90. [Review of Op. 90.]

B1646 Müllner, H. "Viertes Reger-Fest Essen, Juni 1926." SMW (1926): 1052.

B1647 N. "No Title." NMZ 35:12 (1914).

Contains a review of a performance of Op. 127.

B1648 Nagel, Willibald. "Das dritte Reger-Fest." NMZ 41 (1920): 333ff.

B1649 -----. "Reger-Feier in Heidelberg." NMZ 37 (1916): 337ff.

B1650 [Nef, Karl]. "Neue Männerchöre." SMZ 40 (1900): 77-78. Review of work without opus number, Stein Catalog, p. 468.

B1651 Neufeldt, Ernst. "G.F. Händel: Concerto grosso No.1, B-dur (op. 3, No. 1) für Orchester. Bearbeitet von Max Reger." M 11 (1912): 248-249.
"They [Reger's transcriptions of Handel and Bach works] give excellent musicians, especially those in smaller cities, plenty of opportunities to look inside the works of Handel and Bach."

B1652 -----. "Max Reger: 'An Zeppelin.'" M 9 (1910): 387.
"Reger's composition stands somewhat, but not much, superior to these verses of Friderike Kempner...."

B1653 Niemann, Walter. "No Title." M 12 (1913): 55.

B1654 -----. "No Title." NMZ 37:14 (1914).
Contains reviews of performances of Opp. 128 and 132.

B1655 -----. "Max Hehemann: Max Reger: Eine Studie über moderne Musik." M 11 (1912): 164.
"The value of the book lies with its collection of [musical] examples and its analyses."

B1656 -----. "Max Reger: Sechs Präludien und Fugen für Klavier op. 99." M 8 (1908): 241.

B1657 -----. "Max Reger: Zwei Sonatinen in F-dur und a-moll op. 89, No. 3 und 4." M 8 (1909): 104-105.
Niemann remarks about the romantic nature of the sonatinas, but also states that these works are too difficult to be considered as useful for piano instruction.

B1658 -----. "Max Regers Hausmusik für Klavier." [N]ZFM 90:6 (1923): 126-130.
Reviews of Opp. 77a and 89.

B1659 -----. "Neue Klaviermusik." SMW 66 (1908): 1419.
Review of Op. 89/3 & 4.

B1660 -----. "Novitäten." SMW 65:5/6 (1907): 2.
Review of Reger's arrangements of works by J.S. Bach.

B1661 -----. "Uber Regers 100. Psalm." SMW 68 (1910): 1089-1090.

B1662 Nothenius, Hugo. "Max Reger-Avond." Weekblad voor Muziek 14 (February 23, 1907): 59ff.
See B1235, pp. 176-177.

B1663 Nüssle, Hermann. "Münchnen." M 15 (1923): 632.
Gives an outline of the six concerts of a Reger festival in Munich on the occasion of the composer's 50th birthday.

B1664 Oehlerking, H. "No Title." AMZ 41:7 (1914).
Review of a performance of Op. 122; also on Reger as an interpreter of Bach.

B1665 Oehmichen, Richard. "No Title." M 9 (1910): 11.
Review of Op. 106.

B1666 Orthmann, Willy. "No Title." M 12 (1913): 314.
Reviews of Opp. 86 and 108.

B1667 Otto, Eberhard. "Hindemith bearbeitete Reger." MU 13 (1959): 735-736.
Brief review of Hindemith's edition of Op. 106. The reviewer prefers the original.

B1668 Owens, Barbara. "Douglas Butler, Reger Centenary Program in Boston--A Review." Diapason 64:6 (1973): 14.
Laudatory review of an all-Reger recital performed by Douglas Butler. Works performed included Opp. 67, 135a, 127, et al.

B1669 Paulke, Karl. "No Title." M 11 (1912): 185.
Review of Reger as conductor.

B1670 -----. "No Title." M 12 (1913): 123.
Review of Op. 124.

B1671 -----. "No Title." M 12 (1913): 189.
Reviews of Opp. 86, 100, 107, 109, 112, 123, and lieder.

B1672 Paumgartner, Bernhard. "Bachs Violinsonate f-moll, bearbeitet von Max Reger." ME 6:4 (1915).

B1673 -----. "Max Reger: Introduktion, Passacaglia und Fuge e-moll für Orgel op. 127." ME 6:11/12 (1915).

B1674 -----. "Neue Bach-Bearbeitungen der Edition Breitkopf." ME 6:5 (1915): 211-212.

B1675 Payne, Anthony. "Reger: Piano Concerto in F minor, Op.

114." Music and Musicians 14 (1966): 57.
Very favorable review of Rudolf Serkin's recording of this work with the Philadelphia Orchestra.

B1676 Petschau, Fritz. "Neubearbeitung Bachscher Werke." ME 7:15/16 (1916).

B1677 Petschnig, Emil. "Das zweite Max Reger-Fest in Wien vom 27. bis 30. April 1923." [N]ZFM 90 (1923): 258-259.
Works performed included Opp. 46, 59, 65, 33, 27, 74, 77a, 132, 108, 128, 123, and 119. Lectures were given concerning Reger's life and illnesses, compositional style, and historical relationship to other composers.

B1678 Petzoldt, Richard. "Die künstlerische Schallplatte." AMZ
Contains remarks on Op. 125.

B1679 Pfeilschmidt, Hans. "No Title." M 7 (1907): 315.
Review of Op. 100.

B1680 -----. "No Title." M 6 (1907): 383.
Review of Op. 95.

B1681 Piesling, Siegmund. "Aus dem Wiener Konzertleben." ME 7:22 (1916).
Contains a report on Reger memorial concerts.

B1682 Poppe, Paul. "Im Zeichen Max Regers." MU 12 (1958): 286-287.
Review of a Reger festival in Weiden. Works performed included "O wie selig seid ihr doch, ihr Frommen," Opp. 65, 63, 58, 61, 123, and 128. Kar; Foesel delivered a paper entitled "Reger as Man."

B1683 P.R. "Die neue Breslauer Riesenorgel und ihre Einweihung." NMZ 35:4 (1913).
Contains a review of Op. 127.

B1684 Prelinger, Fritz. "Das Regerfest in Breslau." NZFM 89:11 (1922).

B1685 Püschel, Eugen. "Das 55. Tonkünstlerfest in Kiel 1925, 5. und letzter Tag." Deutsches Musikjahrbuch 4 (1926): 114.
Review of Op. 81.

B1686 Quittard, Henri. "Variations et fugue sur un thème d'Adam Hiller de Max Reger." La Revue Musicale (1908): 102-104.

B1687 Raskin, A. "Max-Reger-Fest in Saarbrücken." SMW (1925): 980.

B1688 Redhardt, Willy. "No Title." M 12 (1913): 376.
Reviews of Opp. 109, 113, and lieder.

B1689 Reichwein, Leopold. "Regers Orchesterwerke." Musikblätter des Anbruch 5 (1923): 114.
See B1235, p. 90. [Review of Op. 90.]

B1690 Reifner, Vincenz. "Max Reger: Opus 100. Variationen und Fuge über ein lustiges Thema von Joh. Ad. Hiller." NMZ 29 (1908): 273-277.
A very complete review of Op. 100 with analyses of each variation given. Bachground information about the source and derivation of the "lustiges Thema" is given.

B1691 Renz, Willy. "No Title." M 13 (1914): 250.
Review of Op. 128.

B1692 Reuter, Otto. "Max-Reger-Fest in Weimar." SMW (1923).

B1693 -----. "Weimar." M 15 (1923): 772.
Details of the Weimar Reger Memorial Festival given on the occasion of the composer's 50th birthday. Various lectures were given and works performed included Opp. 107, 84, selected lieder, and the Böcklin Suite. Reger's widow and two adopted daughters were in attendance.

B1694 Richard, August. "Das 8. Deutsche Reger-Fest in Baden-Baden." AMZ 59 (1932): 505.

B1695 Riemann, Hugo. "Von Musikalienmarkt--Kompositionen von Max Reger." AMZ 20:27 (1893).
Reviews of Opp. 1, 2, 3, 4, and 6.

B1696 Riemann, Ludwig. "Max Regers Sinfonietta: Uraufführung in Essen am 8. Oktober 1905." NMZ 27 (1906): 51-53.
Laudatory review of the premiere performance of the Sinfonietta which was performed at a Reger festival in Essen. "A phenomenal manifestation appears out of the musical firmament which has been dimly lit for years: Max Reger." Copious musical examples and insightful comments.

B1697 Riemer, Otto. "Brahms-Reger-Tage in Heidelberg." MK 36 (1966): 284-285.
Works performed included Opp. 127, 106, and 138.

B1698 Riesenfeld, Paul. "Die Breslauer Musikfestwoche II." AMZ 40 (1913): 1417-1419.
Brief review of Karl Straube's performance of Op. 127 (Breslauer premiere).

B1699 -----. "Das Breslauer Reger-Fest." SMW (1922): 618.

B1700 Rochlich, Edmund. "No Title." NZFM 68:43 (1901): 526.
Review of Op. 53.

B1701 -----. "No Title." NZFM 69:5 (1902): 73.
Review of Op. 44.

B1702 Rorich, Carl. "Max Reger: Drei Duette für Sopran und Alt mit Klavierbegleitung op. 111a." M 9 (1910): 325.
"These lates [works] of Reger are certainly welcome additions to the genre of duet songs."

B1703 Rösner, Helmut et al. "Das Werk Max Regers auf Schallplatten: Eine Überblick zum Reger-Jahr 1973: Orchesterwerke." Buch und Bibliothek 25:7/8 (1973): 647-659.

B1704 Rothe, Hans-Joachim. "Max-Reger-Kolloquium in Meiningen." MG 19 (1969): 119-120.

B1705 Salomon, Karl. "Max Regers Chöre op. 144." NMZ 37 (1916): 315-318.

B1706 Sammetreuther, Hermine. "48. Bachfest dere Neuen Bachgesellschaft." MK 43 (1973): 197-198.
Mention of Reger concerts in and around Weiden. Works performed included the motet "Ach Herr, strafe mich nicht."

B1707 -----. "Nürnberg: Bach im Regerjahr, 48. Bachfest und 22. Internationalen Orgelwoche." NZFM 134 (1973): 515-516.
Mentions performances of Reger works including the Op. 141a Serenade, the F# Minor Variations & Fugue, the Fantasy on "Ein feste Burg," the Konzert im alten Stil, and a piano arrangement of the Mozart Variations. Also included was a performance by the organist Werner Jacob of the "Toccata Monumentum per Max Reger" of Bengt Hambraeus.

B1708 Schäfer, Theo. "No Title." M 10 (1910): 189.
Review of Op. 113.

B1709 -----. "No Title." M 11 (1911/12): 191.
Brief mention of a performance of Op. 118 in Frankfurt by the Hock-Quartett.

B1710 -----. "No Title." M 11 (1911): 312.
Review of Op. 121.

B1711 -----. "No Title." M 11 (1912): 122.

B1712 -----. "Frankfurt a. M." M 10 (1911): 196.
A review of a "meritorious first performance in Frankfurt" of Op. 106.

B1713 Schering, Arnold. "Reger, Max. Sonate für Klarinette und Pianoforte As-Dur, op. 49." NZFM 70:9 (1903): 140.
Review.

B1714 Schicha, Ulrich. "Uraufführungen neuer Kirchenmusik." MK 26 (1956): 204.
Mentions the premiere of three previously unknown orchestral pieces from Reger's early period.

B1715 Schink, J. "No Title." M 5 (1906): 349.
Reviews of Opp. 86 and 90.

B1716 -----. "No Title." 6 (1907): 380.
Reviews of Opp. 93, 95, and 96.

B1717 -----. "No Title." M 9 (1910): 381ff.
Review of Op. 106.

B1718 -----. "No Title." M 13 (1914): 116.
Review of Op. 128.

B1719 Schjelderup, Gerhard. "No Title." AMZ 32:14 (1905).
Review of performances of Opp. 74 and 86.

B1720 Schlemüller, Hugo. "Max Reger: Sonate." SMW (1905): 502.

B1721 -----. "Max Reger: Sonate für Violoncell und Klavier op. 78 (F-dur)." M 4 (1904): 287
"A work deserving admiration for the greatness of its ideas, the daring nature of its thought, and its masterly construction."

B1722 Schmid, Willy. "No Title." SMZ 68:1 (1928).
Review of a performance of Op. 146 in Munich.

B1723 Schmidt, Heinrich. "Raphael-Reger Sehlbach." MU 12 (1953): 577-578.
Brief account of a chamber music festival featuring the music of Reger. Of particular interest is a performance of Reger's 1899 Scherzino for string quintet and horn.

B1724 Schmitt, August. "Musica-Umschau: Eine Max-Reger-Erinnerung." MU 13 (1959): 670-671.
Recollections of Reger by his teacher and biographer Adalbert Lindner.

B1725 Schmitz, Eugen. "No Title." AMZ 41:8 (1914).
Review of performances of Opp. 124 and 128.

B1726 -----. "No Title." M 5 (1906): 349.
Review of Op. 90.

B1727 -----. "No Title." M 10 (1911): 255.
Review of Op. 114.

B1728 Schnackenberg, F.L. "No Title." NZFM 69 (1902): 393-394.
Review of Op. 60.

B1729 -----. "Kritischer Anzeiger." NZFM 67 (1900): 338.
Review of Op. 40.

B1730 -----. "Kritischer Anzeiger." NZFM 68:28 (1901): 378-379.
Reviews of Opp. 27 and 29.

B1731 -----. "Kritischer Anzeiger." NZFM 69:5 (1902): 73.
Reviews of several Reger works without opus numbers.

B1732 -----. "Max Reger: Übertragungen Seb. Bach'scher Klavierwerke für die Orgel." NZFM 69 (1902): 384-386.

B1733 -----. "Neue Orgelkompositionen von Max Reger." NZFM 69:1 (1902): 51-53.
Contains reviews of Opp. 52, 57, and 59.

B1734 -----. "Neue Orgelwerke und einiges andere von Max Reger." NZFM 68 (1901): 41ff.

B1735 Schnorr von Carolsfeld, Ernst. "Max Reger: op. 127 und 129." M 13 (1914): 163.

B1736 -----. "Orgel-Kompositionen zum Konzert- und gottesdienstlichen Gebrauche." M 7 (1907): 305.
Brief descriptive review. The collection contains "O Haupt voll Blut und Wunden."

B1737 Schoenaich, Gustav. "No Title." M 4 (1904): 79.
Review of Op. 72.

B1738 Schrader, Bruno. "Vom Musikalienmarkt." AMZ 27:36 (1900): 523.
"The Sturm und Drang in its extravagance now and then pleases him [Reger], and occasionally he does not shrink away from crass cacophony."

B1739 Schreiber, Ottmar. "Umschau: Max Regers Responsorien." MK 40 (1970): 341-342.
Brief review of Reger's Responsories, particularly on their adaptation by Harry Archer [one of Hugo Riemann's students] and Luther D. Reed for use in Lutheran churches in North America.

B1740 Schröter, Oscar. "No Title." M 9 (1909): 322.
Mention made of two Reger concerts in Stuttgart: one with the Hofkapelle Orchestra and the other a chamber recital. Works performed included Opp. 102, 107, 108, and 109. The Symphonic Prologue to a Tragedy is described as "interesting."

B1741 Schuhmacher, Gerhard. "Bach-Rezeption und Reger-Studien." MK 49 (1979): 301-302.
Contains short reviews of Bach-Stunden. Festschrift für Helmut Walcha zum 70. Geburtstag; Paul Mies, Gedanken zur Bearbeitung von Werken Joh. Seb. Bachs; Katalog der Sammlung Manfred Gorke; Hans-Jörg Nieden, Bachrezeption um die Jahrhundertwende: Philipp Wolfrum; and Reger-Studien 1. Festschrift für Ottmar Schreiber zum 70. Geburtstag.

B1742 -----. "Neuausgaben für Bach und Reger, Neues von Becker." MK 50 (1980): 89-90.
Contains review of Dies irae, piano reduction by Ulrich Haverkamp.

B1743 -----. "Friedrich Hölderlin, vertont von Hanns Eisler, Paul Hindemith, Max Reger." Die Musikforschung 37 (1984): 61-62.
Descriptive review.

B1744 Schünemann, Georg. "No Title." M 10 (1910): 384ff.
Reviews of Opp. 76/V, 103a, and 115.

B1745 -----. "No Title." M 11 (1912): 117.
Reviews of Opp. 100 and 120.

B1746 -----. "Berlin." AMZ 37 (1910): 217.
A favorable review of a concert of Reger's works including the Fantasy on "Wachet auf, ruft uns die Stimme," and Opp. 103a, 96, and 84. Schünemann says that since Richard Strauss has abandoned chamber music, Reger is the undisputed master of this field (along with organ composition).

B1747 -----. "Berlin." AMZ 39 (1912): 1350.
Favorable review of a Reger evening in Berlin. Singled out for favor were the songs "Wiegenlied Maria" and "Das Dorf."

B1748 Schuster, Bernhard. "No Title." M 1 (1902): 1025.
A review of Karl Straube's performance of Reger's Op. 52. "Certainly not an easily understood idiom...."

B1749 Schwarz, Monika. "Studien zu Max Reger." MU 33 (1979): 180-181.

Review of Reger-Studien 1. Mostly descriptive.

B1750 Schweizer, Gottfried. "Frankfurter Max-Reger-Tage 1966." MK 36 (1966): 194-195.
Brief account of four concerts.

B1751 -----. "Frankfurter Max-Reger-Tage als regelmässige Veranstaltung." MK 37:4 (1967): 180-181.

B1752 -----. "Frankfurter Reger-Tage 1971." MK 41 (1971): 319.
Works performed included Op. 133 and other works by Joseph Rheinberger, Joseph Haas, Arnold Schönberg, and Johannes Brahms. Also featured was a lecture by Ludwig Finscher.

B1753 -----. "Frankfurter Reger-Tage 1973." MK 43 (1973): 305.
Works performed included Opp. 57, 109, 146, and 117/5.

B1754 -----. "Orgelzyklus 'Reger konfrontiert' in Frankfurt/ Main." MK 43 (1973): 205-206.
Brief account of organ concerts that included works by Reger, Bach, Alain, and Franck.

B1755 Schwers, Paul. "No Title." AMZ 37:48 (1910).
Review of a performance of Op. 110/I.

B1756 -----. "Das Max Reger-Fest in Dortmund." AMZ 37 (1910): 469-470.
Detailed accounting of this festival. Major works performed included Opp. 74, 81, 108, 109, 110, 112, the Beethoven Variations (with Reger at the piano), and a number of lieder. [This festival took place from May7-9, 1910.]

B1757 -----. "Max Reger 'Romantische Suite.'" AMZ 40 (1913): 1455ff.

B1758 -----. "Tonkünstlerfest in Düsseldorf." AMZ 49:25 (1922).
Works performed included Op. 106 and the Piano Quintet, Op. post.

B1759 -----. "Das 46. Tonkünstlerfest des Allgemeinen Deutschen Musikvereins in Zürich." AMZ 37 (1910): 557-559.
Review of Op. 106. The reviewer commented on the large size of the work: "Who of the current generation could construct such a gigantic framework?"

B1760 Segnitz, Eugen. "No Title." AMZ 32:4 (1905).
Review of performances of Opp. 49/1, 72, 86, and assorted songs.

B1761 -----. "No Title." AMZ 32:14 (1905).
Review of performances of Opp. 74, 77b, and 86.

B1762 -----. "No Title." AMZ 37:52 (1910).
Review of a performance of Op. 114.

B1763 -----. "No Title." MW 32:42 (1901): 563.
Review of works without opus numbers.

B1764 -----. "Kritik: Compositionen von Max Reger." MW 31:27 (1900): 358-359, 31:28 (1900): 375-376.
Reviews of Opp. 27, 29, and 30.

B1765 -----. "Kritischer Anhang." MW 33:1 (1901): 12.
Reviews of Opp. 45-48.

B1766 -----. "Kritischer Anhang: Litterarische Umschau." MW 44:4 (1902): 574.
Review of Op. 63.

B1767 -----. "Leipzig." AMZ 37 (1910): 327-328.
Review of a performance of Op. 107 by Reger and a Mr. Bading in the sixth concert of the Gewandhaus chamber music series. The reviewer compares the opposing moods of the sonata to the Davidsbündler compositions of Robert Schumann.

B1768 -----. "Max Reger: Monologe op. 63. 'Heil dir im Siegerkranz' o.O." MW 33 (1902): 574.

B1769 -----. "Max Reger. Op. 82. 'Aus meinem Tagebuch' (III. Band." AMZ 39 (1912): 320-321.
"These new compositions contain various technical problems and, for that reason, place heavy demands on the player...."

B1770 -----. "Max Reger. Op. 117 No. 5. Präludium und Fuge (G-dur) für Violine allein." AMZ 39 (1912): 426.
Brief review.

B1771 -----. "Max Reger: Sechs Madrigale für Chor bearb. 12 Madrigale für Männerchor bearb." MW 33 (1902): 535.

B1772 -----. "Max Reger: 16 Gesänge op. 62." MW 34 (1903): 67.

B1773 -----. "Reger, Max, 'Gesang der Verklärten' (op. 71)." MW 37:3 (1906): 51, 37:4 (1906): 71-72, 37:5 (1906): 92-93, 37:6 (1906): 115-116.

B1774 -----. "Max Regers 'Gesang der Verklärten.'" NMZ 27:11 (1906): 250-251.
Review of Op. 71.

B1775 -----. "Streichquartett d-moll op. 74 von Max Reger." NZFM 71:22/23 (1904): 425.

B1776 -----. "Vom Musikalienmarkt." AMZ 27:11 (1900): 174. Review of Five Special Studies for the Piano. "Of greatest interest are Max Reger's 'Five Special Studies for the Piano.' Reger has edited in a frankly congenial way five Chopin piano works for study and concert use."

B1777 -----. "Werke von Max Reger." MW 36 (1905): 675-676. Contains reviews of Opp. 49/2, 64, 72, 77a, 77b, 78, 81, 82, 86, 69, 73, and the Romanze in A Minor for organ. Concerning Op. 74 Segnitz says: "The quartet shows Reger's close relationship with Bach, Beethoven, and Brahms."

B1778 Sievers, Gerd. "Regers 'Vater unser.'" MU 14 (1960): 512-513.
Review of aperformance of "Vater unser' conducted by Bernhard Scheidt. The non-liturgical nature of the work is remarked upon.

B1779 Simon, Fritz. "Max-Reger-Gedächtnisfeier in Heidelberg." ME (1916): 547.

B1780 Smolian, Arthur. "No Title." M 4 (1904): 455-457. Reviews of Opp. 49/1, 72, and 86. Reger is compared unfavorably to Eugen d'Albert [Reger--Tondenker; d'Albert--Tondichter]. Op. 72 is characterized as "unrefined," whereas Op. 49/1 is described as "very original."

B1781 -----. "No Title." M 5 (1906): 200ff.
Reviews of Opp. 78, 81, and 84.

B1782 -----. "No Title." M 7 (1907): 252.
Review of Op. 100.

B1783 -----. "No Title." M 8 (1908): 252ff.
Review of Op. 101.

B1784 -----. "No Title." M 8 (1909): 121.
Review of Opp. 100 and 103a.

B1785 -----. "No Title." M 9 (1909): 255.
Review of Opp. 93 and 109.

B1786 -----. "No Title." M 8 (1909): 314.
Review of Op. 96.

B1787 -----. "No Title." M 9 (1910): 61.
Review of Op. 71.

B1788 -----. "No Title." M 10 (1911): 134.
Review of Op. 108.

B1789 -----. "No Title." M 10 (1911): 199.
Review of Op. 114.

B1790 -----. "No Title." M 5 (1905): 441-442.
Review of a concert of Reger compositions including Opp. 43, 76, 83, 86, and 81. The lieder (Opp. 43, 76, and 83) were performed by soprano Adele Münz and pianist Henriette Schelle.

B1791 -----. "Leipzig." M 10 (1911): 60-61.
Contains reviews of Opp. 113 and 101. Alexander Schmuller's interpretation of Op. 101 is praised.

B1792 -----. "Max Reger--Hillervariationen op. 100." SMW 65 (1907): 1122.

B1793 -----. "Max Reger und seine Erstlingswerke." MW 25 (1894): 528ff, 546-549.

B1794 Söhngen, Oskar. "Kirchenmusik auf neuen Wegen." Melos 15:1 (1948): 6-10.

B1795 Sonne, H. "No Title." M 8:19 (1909): 60-61.
Review of a three-day chamber music festival at Darmstadt at which the premiere of Reger's Op. 107 Clarinet Sonata was performed by the composer and court musician Winkler. The work is described as "full of melancholy and dreamlike reflection," "possessing many moving poetic moments," and displaying "a mastery of technical construction."

B1796 -----. "No Title." M 9 (1910): 113.
Review of Op. 113.

B1797 Sonner, R. "Max-Reger-Fest in Weiden." M 31 (1940): 694.

B1798 Spannuth, Walter. "Regers Hiller-Variationen." SMW 65 (1907): 1271.

B1799 Specht, Richard. "No Title." ME 6:4 (1915).
Review of a performance of Op. 132 in Vienna.

B1800 -----. "No Title." ME 6:8 (1915).
Review of a performance of Op. 140 in Vienna.

B1801 -----. "No Title." M 7 (1908): 382ff.
Review of Op. 100.

B1802 -----. "No Title." M 8 (1909): 127.
See B1235, pp. 237-238. [Reviews of Opp. 102, 103a, and

108]

B1803 -----. "No Title." M 9 (1910): 200.
Review of Op. 106.

B1804 -----. "No Title." M 11 (1912): 127.
Review of Op. 112.

B1805 -----. "No Title." M 11 (1912): 191.
Review of Op. 120. The reviewer is more impressed with the work's dynamics than its formal construction.

B1806 -----. "No Title." M 14 (1915): 287ff.
Review of Op. 132.

B1807 Spencer, Vernon. "Reger's Piano Concerto." Music News (1911): 188ff.
Review of Op. 114.

B1808 Starke, Hermann. "No Title." AMZ 39 (1912): 1268.
Review of Op. 125.

B1809 Stege, F. "Le festival allemand Max Reger." Revue internationale de Musique (1938): 470ff.

B1810 Stein, Richard A. "Karl Hasse: Max Reger...." M 15 (1922): 58.
A Generally favorable review of Hasse's biography of Reger which is praised for its balanced approach.

B1811 Steinhardt, Erich. "No Title." M 13 (1914): 128.
Review of Op. 128.

B1812 -----. "Prager musikalische Nachrichten." NMZ 37:7 (1916).
Contains reviews of Opp. 121 and 132.

B1813 Steinitzer, Max. "Max Reger: Beiträge zur Modulationslehr." M 3 (1904): 49-50.
Steinitzer praises Reger's handling of bass movement.

B1814 Stephani, Hermann. "Max Reger: 'Meinem Jesum lass ich nicht', Choralkantate No. 4 für Solosopran, gemischten Chor, Solovioline, Solobratsche und Orgel." M 7:1 (1907): 50.
This work is described as "warm, tender, and sincere."

B1815 Stief, G. "Max Reger Days." Music(AGO) 8 (1974): 48-49.

B1816 Stolz, E.O. "Die Max-Reger-Feier in Heidelberg." AMZ 43:30 (1916).

B1817 Straube, Karl. "Hugo Wolf: Geistliche Lieder aus dem 'Spanischen Liederbuch', für eine Singstimme und Orgel bearbeitet von Max Regers--Geistliche Lieder aus dem Mörike-Buch für eine Singstimme und Orgel bearbeitet von Max Reger." M 3:13 (1903/04): 52.
Straube says that Reger has "solved a difficult problem admirably" in his Wolf transcriptions.

B1818 -----. "Max Reger: Leichtausführbare Kompositionen zum gottesdienstlichen Gebrauch op. 61." M 2 (1903): 39-41.
"Max Reger makes a deep bow before the Caecilians of the Roman Catholic composers with his Op. 61."

B1819 -----. "Max Reger: op. 63 Monologe. (Zwölf Stücke für Orgel.) Verlag: E.F.C. Leuckart; op. 65. Zwölf Stücke für Orgel. Verlag: C.F. Peters; op. 67. Zweiundfünfzig leicht ausführbare Vorspiele für die Orgel zu den gebräuchlichsten evangelischen Chorälen; op. 69. Zehn Stücke für Orgel. Verlag: Lauterbach & Kuhn, Leipzig." M 3 (1903): 131-132.
"...Max Reger is indisputedly the first of the modern organ composers."

B1820 -----. "Max Reger: Romanze (a-moll) für Harmonium oder Orgel." M 7:1 (1907): 50.
The reviewer says that this work does not rank with the great works of the masters, but is acceptable in its own small way.

B1821 Strunk, G. "9. Reger-Fest Kassel." AMZ 60 (1933): 368.

B1822 Taubert, E.E. "No Title." M 4 (1904): 201ff.
Reviews of Opp. 50, 72, and lieder.

B1823 -----. "No Title." M 9 (1909): 310ff.
Review of Op. 108.

B1824 -----. "No Title." M 10 (1911): 248.
Review of Op. 114.

B1825 -----. "No Title." M 12 (1913): 63ff.
Contains reviews of Opp. 96, 107, and 122.

B1826 -----. "No Title." M 13 (1913): 306ff.
Review of Op. 125.

B1827 -----. "No Title." M 14 (1915): 235.
See B1235, p. 374. [Reviews of Opp. 132 and 140.]

B1828 -----. "No Title." M 16 (1922): 304.
Review of Op. 120.

B1829 -----. "Berlin." M 5 (1905): 360-361.
Review of Reger's cantata "O Haupt voll Blut und Wunden" and Op. 45. "The Reger cantata is suitably sparse in its construction.

B1830 -----. "Berlin." M 10 (1910): 306-307.
A review of Op. 106. Taubert praises the work but not the venue in which it was performed.

B1831 Taubmann, Otto. "Reger, Max. Beiträge zur Modulationslehr." NZFM 70:50 (1903): 655.
Book review.

B1832 Teibler, Hermann. "Max Reger: Zwei Sonatinen für Klavier op. 89; Schlichte Weisen op. 76, Bd. 2." M 5 (1906): 107.

B1833 -----. "No Title." MW 34 (1903): 448.
Review of the premiere of Op. 64 in Munich.

B1834 Tessmer, Hans. "Eines neues Reger-Buch." AMZ 48 (1921): 49.
A review of Adalbert Lindner's Reger biography.

B1835 Therstappen, Hans Joachim. "Die Max-Reger-Feier der Staatlichen Akademischen Hochschule für Musik Berlin-Charlottenburg." AMZ 68 (1941): 200-201.

B1836 Thiessen, Heinz. "Zweites Orchesterkonzert." AMZ 40 (1913): 912.
Review of the premiere of Op. 126. "The success of the work was particularly strong, and as the composer appeared on the podium, he was presented with a laurel wreath and stormy applause."

B1837 Thiessen, Karl. "Max Reger in seinen neuen Liedern." SMW 61:10/11 (1903).

B1838 -----. "Max Reger: Op. 82, Band 3, Aus meinem Tagebuch. Sechs kleine Stücke für Klavier zu 2 Händen." SMW 70 (1912): 1272-1273.

B1839 -----. "Max Reger: Op. 117, Nr. 5. Präludium und Fuge (Themen von J.S. Bach) für die Violine allein." SMW 70 (1912): 990.

B1840 -----. "Max Reger: op. 122, Sonate in e-moll für Violine und Klavier." SMW 70 (1912): 1060-1061.

B1841 -----. "Max Reger und seine neuesten Kammermusikwerke." NMZ (1905).

B1842 -----. "Neue Lieder." SMW 62 (1904): 1153-1156.

Review of Op. 75.

B1843 -----. "Neuere Kammermusik." SMW 60 (1902): 765-766.
Reviews of Op. 49/1 and 54.

B1844 -----. "Neues von Max Reger." Musikalische Rundschau 1 (1905): 87-91.
Contains reviews of Opp. 76 and 89.

B1845 -----. "Orgelwerke von Max Reger. Op. 46. Phantasie und Fuge. Op. 52. Drei Choral-Phantasien. Op. 57. Symphonische Phantasie und Fuge." SMW 60 (1902): 741.

B1846 -----. "Sechs Burlesken für Clavier zu vier Händen von Max Reger, op. 58." SMW 60 (1902): 787-788.

B1847 -----. "'Silhouetten.' Sieben Stücke für Clavier zu zwei Händen componiert v. Max Reger." SMW 60 (1902): 887.
Review of Op. 53.

B1848 Thilo, Emil. "No Title." M 14 (1915): 43.
Review of Op. 134.

B1849 -----. "Max Reger: 'Aus meinem Tagebuch.' Sechs kleine Stücke für Klavier zu zwei Händen. op. 82. Band III." M 11 (1912): 234.
"These pieces sufficiently point out the renowned character of the composer....The main feature is always the harmony."

B1850 Thurn, Georg. "No Title." NMZ 38:12 (1917).
Contains reviews of performances of Opp. 103, 124, 132, and selected songs.

B1851 -----. Würzburger Musikbrief." NMZ 38:11 (1917).
Contains reviews of Opp. 137 and 139.

B1852 Tottmann, A. "No Title." NZFM 67 (1900): 384.
Reviews of Opp. 41 and 42.

B1853 -----. "No Title." NZFM 69:23/24 (1902): 342.
Review of Op. 54.

B1854 Unger, Hermann. "Elsa Reger: Mein Leben mit und für Max Reger." M 23:1 (1930).
Book review.

B1855 -----. "Max Reger und die Pathologie." [N[ZFM 98 (1931): 688-690.

B1856 Unger, Max. "No Title." M 14 (1915): 240.
Review of Op. 133.

B1857 Urban, Erich. "No Title." M 1 (1902): 1125-1126.
A brief mention is made of a recital in which the singer Susanne Dessoir (neė Triepel) performed six Reger songs. The specific songs are not indicated, but they are referred to as being "very original."

B1858 Varges, Kurt. "Das Frankfurter Reger-Fest." SMW (1927): 710-712.

B1859 Vogel, Max. "No Title." M 11 (1912): 309.
Review of Op. 122.

B1860 Vogt, Felix. "No Title." M 7 (1908): 126.
Review of Op. 100.

B1861 Voigt, Max. "Bochum." M 15 (1923): 701.
Details of the Bochum Reger Memorial Concerts given on the occasion of the composer's 50th birthday. Works performed included the Symphonic Prologue, the Mozart Variations, and "O Haupt vollBlut und Wunden."

B1862 -----. "Deutsche Reger-Tage in Bochum." AMZ 50:15 (1923).

B1863 Voigt, Max et al. "Max Reger-Gedächtnisfeiern: Bochum, München, Stuttgart, Tübingen." NMZ 44:14 (1923): 236-238.

B1864 Volbach, Fritz. "No Title." M 5 (1906): 133.
Review of Op. 77b.

B1865 -----. "Mainz." M 5 (1905): 205.
Reviews of performances of the Violin Sonata in F# Minor by Heermann and Reger, and the Sinfonietta conducted by E. Steinbach. The 2nd and 3rd movements of the violin sonata were praised.

B1866 Volkmann, Robert. "Das Reger-Fest in Jena." SMW (1920): 665-668.

B1867 Voss, Hermann. "No Title." M 5 (1906): 357.
See B1235, p. 126. [Review of Op. 90]

B1868 Wahl, Eduard. "No Title." M 7 (1907): 190.
Review of selected lieder.

B1869 -----. "No Title." M 8 (1909): 188.
Review of Op. 100.

B1870 -----. "München." D 10 (1910): 317-318.
A review of Reger conducting Op. 100: "powerful development as a conductor."

B1871 W.B. "Bonn: Max-Reger-Tage." Oper und Konzert 11:5 (1973): 31-32.

B1872 Weiss-Aigner, Günter. "Rainer Wilke: Brahms. Reger. Schönberg. Streichquartette. Motivisch-thematische Prozesse und formale Gestalt." Die Musikforschung 36 (1983): 164-165.
Book review.

B1873 Wellesz, Egon. "Max Reger: op. 117 und op. 122." ME 5: 11 (1914).

B1874 Werker, G. "Eerkerstel voor Max Reger?" Mens en Melodie 12 (1957): 2-4.
Review of Op. 100.

B1875 Werner, Karl. "No Title." M 13 (1914): 250.
Review of Reger conducting the Meiningen Hofkapelle Orchestra.

B1876 -----. "No Title." M 13 (1913): 313.
See B1235, p. 349. [Review of Op. 128.]

B1877 -----. "No Title." M 13 (1914): 312ff.
Reviews of Opp. 124 and 125.

B1878 Westermayer, Karl. "No Title." M 23:7 (1931).
Contains review of Op. 102.

B1879 Wirth, Helmut. "Max Reger: Briefe zwischen der Arbeit, hrsg. v. O. Schreiber, 1956." Die Musikforschung 10:2 (1957): 323-324.
Book review.

B1880 Wittmer, Eberhard Ludwig. "10. Deutsches Max-Reger-Fest in Freiburg i. B." M (1936): 689ff.

B1881 Wolf, J. "Max Reger: Sechs Burlesken." Zeitschrift der Internationalen Musikgesellschaft 4 (1903): 650.
Review of Op. 58.

B1882 Wolff, Karl. "Max Regers Serenade für Orchester op. 95." NMZ 28 (1907): 78ff.
See B1235, pp. 139-141.

B1883 Wolschke, Martin. "Iv. Max-Reger-Orgeltage Hamm 1978." MK 49 (1979): 43-44.
Works performed included those by Reger, Karg-Elert, Wolfgang Stockmeier, Janacek,Bach, and Haydn.

B1884 Worbs, Hans Christoph. "Material in Fülle." MU 36 (1982): 176.

Review of the first two volumes of Max Reger in seinen Konzerten by Ottmar and Ingeborg Schreiber.

B1885 -----. "Eine Renaissance ist denkbar: Chorwerke Regers in Hamburg." MU 34 (1980): 51-52.
A review of a Hamburg performance of the Requiem and Dies irae.

B1886 Wörner, Karl. "Max Reger: op. 130, Nr. 5, für Violine u. Klavier bearb. von G. Havemann." AMZ 60:48 (1933).

B1887 Wotruba, Albert. "Kritischer Anzeiger." NZFM 69:12 (1902): 181.
Review of Op. 50.

B1888 Wustmann, Rudolf. "Bachfest in Leipzig 1908." Zeitschrift der Internationalen Musikgesellschaft 9 (1907/07): 310.
See B1235, p. 207.

B1889 Zinne, Wilhelm. "Max Reger: Klavieralbum Bd. 1 und 2; Liederalbum Bd. 1 und 2; Fünf Duette, op. 14." M 15 (1923): 824.
Concerning the lieder Zinne says that although Reger accompaniments are often more interesting than his melodies, the songs of this collection are always singable; however, they are uneven in their inspiration and quality.

Miscellaneous: Reger in Literature

B1890 Bernhard, Thomas. Alte Meister. Frankfurt: Suhrkamp, 1985.
The protagonist of this novel is a music philosopher named Reger who rejects all art due to its lack of perfection or completeness. This may be seen as a reference to Max Reger's editions and arrangements of the works of earlier composers such as J.S. Bach and Franz Schubert.

B1891 -----. Concrete [Beton]. Translated by David McLintock. New York: Alfred A. Knopf, 1984.
Reger and his music are mentioned [pp. 33, 49ff] in this novel about a musicologist.

B1892 Hesse, Hermann. Musik. Edited by Volker Michels. Frankfurt: Suhrkamp, 1986.
In the 1906 short story "Eine Sonate" [pp. 39-44] two of the main characters discuss the enthusiasm for Reger of the young pianist Ludwig.

B1893 Stein-Czerny, Margarete. Stunden mit Max Reger. Wiesbaden: Bote & Bock, 1955.
Contains 15 poems based on Reger's life and music.

B1894 Steiner, George. The Portage to San Cristobal of A.H. New York: Washington Square [Simon & Schuster, Inc.], 1983.
One of the minor characters of the novel, Dr. Gervinus Röthling, who has knowledge about the existence of Hitler listens to one of Reger's works while contemplating the significance of [his] knowledge. "Reger. The Humoresque in B minor. She plays it well. Very well. But not brilliantly. Like everything she does a barrier at the edge where feeling should flow free. Music equals freedom in time, freedom from time." [p. 111]

Appendix I: Chronological Listing of Reger's Works

1888

Jugendquartett in D Minor for String Quartet

1890

Sonata in D Minor for Violin and Piano, Op. 1

1891

Trio in B Minor for Piano, Violin, and Viola, Op. 2
Sonata in D Major for Violin and Piano, Op. 3
Six Songs for Medium Voice and Piano, Op. 4

1892

Sonata in F Minor for Cello and Piano, Op. 5
Three Choruses for Soprano, Alto, Tenor, and Bass with Piano Accompaniment, Op. 6
Three Organ Pieces, Op. 7
Five Songs for High Voice and Piano, Op. 8
Waltz-Caprices for Piano, 4 Hands, Op. 9

1893

German Dances for Piano, 4 Hands, Op. 10
Seven Waltzes for Piano (2 Hands), Op. 11
Five Songs for One Voice (and Piano), Op. 12
"O Traurigkeit, o Herzelied" for Organ

1894

Lose Blätter for Piano, Op. 13
Five Duets for Soprano and Alto with Piano Accompaniment, Op. 14
Ich stehe hoch über'm See for Bass Voice and Piano, Op. 14b
Ten Songs for Medium Voice (and Piano), Op. 15
"Komm, süsser Tod" for Organ
"Es soll mein Gebet dich tragen" for Medium Voice and Piano
"Am Meer!" for Voice with Piano Accompaniment

1895

Suite for Organ in E Minor, Op. 16
Aus der Jugendzeit for Piano (2 Hands), Op. 17
Muzio Clementi Op. 36: Six Sonatinas for Piano with Additional Violin Part
Canons for Piano in All the Major and Minor Keys
Tantum ergo Sacramentum for Five-Voice Mixed Choir

1896

Improvisations for Piano (2 Hands), Op. 18

1898

Two Sacred Songs for Medium Voice with Organ Accompaniment, Op. 19
Five Humoresques for Piano (2 Hands), Op. 20
Hymne an den Gesang for Male Choir with Orchestral Accompaniment, Op. 21
Six Waltzes for Piano (4 Hands), Op. 22
Four Songs for Voice with Piano Accompaniment, Op. 23
Six Morceaux for Piano, Op. 24
Aquarellen for Piano (2 Hands), Op. 25
Seven Fantasy-Pieces for Piano, Op. 26
Fantasy for Organ on the Chorale "Ein' feste Burg ist unser Gott", Op. 27
Second Sonata in G Minor for Cello and Piano, Op. 28
Fantasy and Fugue in C Minor for Organ, Op. 29
Fantasy for Organ on the Chorale "Freu' dich sehr, o meine Seele!", Op. 30
Six Poems of Anna Ritter for Medium Voice with Piano Accompaniment, Op. 31
Liebestraum for String Orchestra (Lyrisches Andante)
Quartet (Posthumous) for String Quartet and Piano
Six Piano Pieces (Grüsse an die Jugend")
Miniature Gavotte for Piano
An die schönen blauen Donau: Improvisation for Piano (2 Hands) on a Waltz of Johann Strauss

Gloriabuntur for Four-Voice Choir a cappella
"In verschwiegener Nacht" for Voice with Piano Accompaniment
"Wiegenlied" for Medium Voice with Piano Accompaniment

1899

Seven Character Pieces for Piano (2 Hands), Op. 32
First Sonata in F# Minor for Organ, Op. 33
Five Picturesque Pieces for Piano (4 Hands), Op. 34
Six Songs for Medium Voice with Piano Accompaniment, Op. 35
Bunte Blätter for Piano (2 Hands), Op. 36
Five Songs for Medium Voice with Piano Accompaniment, Op. 37
Seven Male Choruses, Op. 38
Three Six-Voice Choruses for 1 Soprano, 2 Altos, 1 Tenor, and 2 Basses, Op. 39
Two Fantasies on the Chorales: "Wie schön leucht't uns der Morgenstern" and "Straf' mich nicht in deinem Zorn", Op. 40
Third Sonata in A Major for Violin and Piano, Op. 41
Scherzino for String Orchestra and Horn
Albumblatt for Piano
Five Special Studies for Piano (after Chopin)
Introduction and Passacaglia in D Minor for Organ
Two Songs for Voice with Piano Accompaniment

1900

Four Sonatas for Violin Alone, Op. 42
Eight Songs for Voice with Piano Accompaniment, Op. 43
Ten Small Recital Pieces for Piano in Use of Teaching, Op. 44
Six Intermezzi for Piano (2 Hands), Op. 45
Fantasy and Fugue for Organ on B-A-C-H, Op. 46
Six Trios for Organ, Op. 47
Seven Songs for Medium Voice with Piano Accompaniment, Op. 48
Two Sonatas (Ab Major and F# Minor) for Clarinet and Piano, Op. 49
Two Romances (G Major and D Major) for Violin and Small Orchestra, Op. 50
Twelve Songs for Voice with Piano Accompaniment, Op. 51
Organ Prelude in C Minor
"Wer weiss, wie nahe mir mein Ende" for Organ
Three Fantasies for Organ on the Chorales: "Alle Menschen müssen sterben"; "Wachet auf, ruft uns die Stimme"; "Halleluja! Gott zu loben, bleibe meine Seelenfreude", Op. 52
Silhouetten: Seven Pieces for Piano (2 Hands), Op. 53
Compositions, Op. 79g
"Maria Himmelsfreud!" for Four-Voice Choir a cappella
Two Sacred Songs for Medium Voice and Organ

1901

Two String Quartets (G Minor and A Major), Op. 54
Fifteen Songs for Voice with Piano Accompaniment, Op. 55
Symphonic Fantasy and Fugue for Organ, Op. 57
Six Burlesques for Piano (4 Hands), Op. 58
Twelve Pieces for Organ, Op. 59
Second Sonata (D Minor) for Organ, Op. 60
Easy Practical Compositions for Use in Church, Op. 61
Sixteen Songs for Voice with Piano Accompaniment, Op. 62
Quintet in C Minor for Piano, 2 Violins, Viola, and Cello, Op. 64
Compositions, Op. 79f
Caprice for Cello and Piano in A Minor
Four Special Studies for the Left Hand Alone for Piano
Variations and Fugue on the English National Anthem for Oragn
"Christ ist erstanden von dem Tod" for Organ
"Tragt, blaue Träume" for Medium Voice and Piano

1902

Monologe: Twelve Pieces for Organ, Op. 63
Twelve Pieces for Organ, Op. 65
Twelve Songs for Medium Voice and Piano, Op. 66
Fifty Two Preludes for Organ on Protestant Chorales, Op. 67
Six Songs for Medium Voice and Piano, Op. 68
Romanze in G Major for Piano and Violin
Petite Caprice in G Minor for Violin and Piano
Prelude and Fugue in A Minor for Violin Alone
Allegretto grazioso in A Major for Flute and Piano
Albumblatt in Eb Major and Tarantella in G Major for Clarinet and Piano
Blätter und Blüten: Twelve Piano Pieces
In der Nacht for Piano
Prelude and Fugue in D Minor for Organ
"Mit Fried und Freud ich fahr dahin" for Organ
O wie selig ihr doch, ihr Frommen" for Organ
"Jesus ist kommen, Grund ewiger Freude" for Organ
Palm Sunday Morning for Five-Voice Mixed Choir a cappella
"Befiehl dem Herrn deiner Wege" for Soprano and Alto with Organ Accompaniment
"Liebeslieder" for Voice and Piano
"Ostern" for Medium Voice and Piano

1903

Ten Pieces for Organ, Op. 69
Seventeen Songs for High Voice and Piano, Op. 70
Gesang der Verklärten for Five-Voice Choir and Large Orchestra Op. 71
Fourth Sonata in C Major for Violin and Piano, Op. 72

Variations and Fugue on an Original Theme for Organ, Op. 73
Eighteen Songs for High Voice and Piano, Op. 75
Compositions, Opp. 79a, 79b, 79c
Postlude in D Minor
Schule des Triospiels: J.S. Bach's Two-Part Inventions arranged for Organ by Max Reger and Karl Straube
"Wohl denen" for Medium Voice with Organ Accompaniment
"Nun kommt die Nacht gegangen" for Medium Voice and Piano

1904

Five Preludes and Fugues for Organ, Op. 56
Third String Quartet in D Minor, Op. 74
Schlichte Weisen for Voice and Piano, Op. 76
Serenade in D Major for Flute, Violin, and Viola, Op. 77a
Trio in A Major for Violin, Viola, and Cello, Op. 77b
Third Sonata in F Major for Cello and Piano, Op. 78
Compositions, Opp. 79d, 79e
Twelve Pieces for Organ, Op. 80
Variations and Fugue on a Theme of Johann Sebastian Bach for Piano (2 Hands), Op. 81
Aus meinem Tagebuch for Piano (2 Hands), Vol. I, Op. 82
Ten Songs for Male Choir, Op. 83
Four Preludes and Fugues for Organ, Op. 85
Variations and Fugue on a Theme of Beethoven for Piano (4 Hands), Op. 86
Romanze in A Minor for Harmonium
"O Haupt voll Blut und Wunden" for Organ

1905

Fifth Sonata in F# Minor for Violin and Piano, Op. 84
Two Compositions for Violin with Piano Accompaniment, Op. 87
Four Songs for Medium Voice with Piano Accompaniment, Op. 88
Sinfonietta in A Major for Orchestra, Op. 90
Seven Sonatas for Violin Alone, Op. 91
Suite for Organ in G Minor, Op. 92
Perpetuum mobile in C# Major for Piano (2 Hands)
"Es kommt ein Schiff gelader" for Organ
Chorale Cantatasa for the Major Festivals of the Protestant Church Year
"Ehre sei Gott der Höhe" for Voice with Piano, Harmonium or Organ Accompaniment

1906

Aus meinem Tagebuch for Piano (2 Hands), Vol. II, OP. 82
Suite im alten Stil in F Major for Violin and Piano, Op. 93
Six Pieces for Piano (4 Hands), Op. 94

Serenade in G Major for Orchestra, Op. 95
Introduction, Passacaglia and Fugue in B Minor for Two Pianos (4 Hands), Op. 96
Four Songs for Voice and Piano, Op. 97
Five Songs for Medium or Low Voice with Piano Accompaniment, Op. 98
Four Piano Pieces
Scherzo in F# Minor for Piano (2 Hands)
Caprice in F# Minor for Piano
Prelude and Fugue in G# Minor for Organ
"Der Maien ist gestorben" for Voice with Piano Accompaniment
"Abendfrieden" for Medium Voice and Piano
"Der Dieb" for Voice and Piano

1907

Six Preludes and Fugues for Piano (2 Hands), Op. 99
Variations and Fugue in E Major on a Theme of J.A. Hiller for Orchestra, Op. 100
Six Songs for Voice with Piano Accompaniment, Op. 104
Ewig Dein!: Salon Pieces for Piano

1908

Four Sonatinas for Piano (2 Hands), Op. 84
Concerto in A Major for Violin with Orchestral or Piano Accompaniment, Op. 101
Trio in E Minor for Violin, Cello and Piano, Op. 102
Six Recital Pieces for Violin and Piano, Op. 103a
Two Sacred Songs for Medium Voice with Organ, Harmonium, or Piano Accompaniment, Op. 105
Symphonic Prologue to a Tragedy in A Minor for Large Orchestra, Op. 108
Weihegesang for Alto Solo, Mixed Choir and Wind Orchestra
"In der Frühe" for Voice and Piano

1909

Two Small Sonatas (D Minor & A Major) for Violin and Piano Op. 103b
Twelve Small Pieces after Specific Songs (from Op. 76), Op. 103c
The 100th Psalm for Mixed Choir, Orchestra, and Organ, Op. 106
Third Sonata in Bb Major for Clarinet and Piano, Op. 107
Fourth String QWuartet in Eb Major, Op. 109
Three Duets for Soprano and Alto with Piano Accompaniment, Op. 111a
Three Songs for Four-Voice Female Choir a cappella, Op. 111b
Die Nonnen for Mixed Choir and Large Orchestra, Op. 112
"Wie schön leucht't uns der Morgenstern" for Organ

"An Zeppelin" for Voice and Piano
Wiegenlied for Voice with Piano Accompaniment

1910

Quartet in D Minor for Violin, Viola, Cello and Piano, Op. 113
Concerto in F Minor for Piano and Orchestra, Op. 114
Episoden: Piano Pieces for Adults and Children, Op. 115
Fourth Sonata in A Minor for Cello and Piano, Op. 116
Sextet in F Major for 2 Violins, 2 Violas & 2 Cellos, Op. 118

1911

Aus meinem Tagebuch for Piano (2 Hands), Vol. III, Op. 82
Die Weihe der Nacht for Alto Solo, Male Chorus and Orchestra, Op. 119
Eine Lustspielouvertüre for Orchestra, Op. 120
Fifth String Quartet in F# Minor, Op. 121
Eighth Sonata in E Minor for Violin and Piano, Op. 122
Easter Motet: "Lasset uns den Herren preisen" for Five-Voice Mixed Choir

1912

Aus meinem Tagebuch for Piano (2 Hands), Vol IV, Op. 82
Sacred Songs for Five-Voice Mixed Choir a cappella, Op. 110
Preludes and Fugues, Chaconnes, etc. for Violin Alone, Op. 117
Konzert im alten Stil for Orchestra, Op. 123
An die Hoffnung for Alto (or Mezzo Soprano) with Orchestral or Piano Accompaniment, Op. 124
Eine romantische Suite for Large Orchestra, Op. 125
Römischer Triumphgesang for Male Chorus and Orchestra, Op. 126
Prelude and Fugue in F# Minor
Three Songs after Poems of Elsa von Asenijeff for Voice and Piano

1913

Introduction, Passacaglia and Fugue in E Minor for Organ, Op. 127
Four Tone Poems for Large Orchestra after Arnold Böcklin, Op. 128
Nine Pieces for Organ, Op. 129
Eine Ballettsuite in D Major for Orchestra, Op. 130
Syl;vester-Canonen, Op. 1913

1914

Preludes and Fugues for Violin Alone, Op. 131a
Three Duos in the Old Style for two Violins, Op. 131b

<u>Variations and Fugue for Orchestra on a Theme of Mozart</u>, Op. 132
<u>Variations and Fugue for Two Pianos on a Theme of W.A. Mozart</u>, Op. 132a
<u>Quartet in A Minor for Violin, Viola, Cello & Piano</u>, Op. 133
<u>Variations and Fugue on a Theme of G.P. Telemann for Piano (2 Hands)</u>, Op. 134
<u>Thirty Small Chorale Preludes for Organ</u>, Op. 135a
<u>Hymnus der Liebe for Baritone (or Alto) with Orchestral Accompaniment</u>, Op. 136
<u>Twelve Sacred Songs for Voice with Piano, Harmonium or Organ Accompaniment</u>, Op. 137
<u>Eight Sacred Songs for Mixed Choir</u>, Op. 138
<u>Eine vaterländische Ouvertüre in F Major for Large Orchestra</u>, Op. 140
<u>Allegro in A Major for Two Violins</u>
<u>Totenfeier (unfinished Requiem) in D Minor for Four Solo Voices, Four-Voice Mixed Choir, Organ and Orchestra</u>
<u>Abschiedslied for Four-Voice Mixed Choir a cappella</u>

<u>1915</u>

<u>Three Suites for Cello Alone</u>, Op. 131c
<u>Three Suites for Viola Alone</u>, Op. 131d
<u>Ninth Sonata in C Minor for Violin and Piano</u>, Op. 139
<u>Serenade in G Major for Flute, Violin, and Viola</u>, Op. 141a
<u>String Trio in D Minor for Violin, Viola, and Cello</u>, Op. 141b
<u>Five New Children's Songs for High Voice and Piano</u>, Op. 142
<u>Träume am Kamin: Twelve Small Piano Pieces</u>, Op. 143
<u>Two Songs for Mixed Choir and Orchestra</u>, Op. 144
<u>Präludium in E Minor for violin Alone</u>

<u>1916</u>

<u>Fantasy and Fugue in D Minor for Organ</u>, Op. 135b
<u>Requiem (unfinished)</u>, Op. 145
<u>Seven Organ Pieces</u>, Op. 145
<u>Quintet in A Major for Clarinet and String Quartet</u>, Op. 146
<u>Andante and Rondo for Violin and Small Orchestra</u>, (Op. 147)
<u>Fughette on a German Song</u>

Appendix II: Listing of Reger's Works by Genre

Chamber Music

Jugendquartett in D Minor for String Quartet (1888)
Sonata in D Minor for Violin and Piano, Op. 1 (1890)
Trio in B Minor for Piano, Violin, and Viola, Op. 2 (1891)
Sonata in D Major for Violin and Piano, Op. 3 (1891)
Sonata in F Major for Cello and Piano, Op. 5 (1892)
Muzio Clementi Op. 36: Six Sonatinas for Piano with Additional Violin Part (1895)
Second Sonata in G Minor for Cello and Piano, Op. 28 (1898)
Quintet (Posthumous) for String Quartet and Piano (1898)
Third Sonata in A Minor for Violin and Piano, Op. 41 (1899)
Four Sonatas for Violin Alone, Op. 42 (1900)
Two Sonatas (Ab Major and F# Minor) for Clarinet and Piano, Op. 49 (1900)
Two String Quartets (G Minor and A Major), Op. 54 (1901)
Quintet in C Minor for Piano, 2 Violins, Viola, and Cello, Op. 64 (1901)
Caprice for Cello and Piano in A Minor (1901)
Romanze in G Major for Piano and Violin (1902)
Petite Caprice in G Minor for Violin and Piano (1902)
Prelude and Fugue in A Major for Violin Alone (1902)
Allegretto grazioso in A Major for Flute and Piano (1902)
Albumblatt in Eb Major and Tarantella in G Major for Clarinet and Piano (1902)
Fourth Sonata in C Major for Violin and Piano, Op. 72 (1903)
Third String Quartet in D Minor, Op. 74 (1904)
Serenade in D Major for Flute, Violin, and Viola, Op. 77a (1904)
Trio in A Major for Violin, Viola, and Cello, Op. 77b (1904)
Third Sonata in F Major for Cello and Piano, Op. 78 (1904)
Compositions for Violin with Piano Accompaniment, Op. 79d (1904)
Compositions for Cello with Piano Accompaniment, Op. 79e (1904)
Fifth Sonata in F# Minor for Violin and Piano, Op. 84 (1905)
Two Compositions for Violin with Piano, Op. 87 (1905)

Seven Sonatas for Violin Alone, Op. 91 (1905)
Suite im alten Stil in F Major for Violin and Piano, Op. 93 (1906)
Trio in E Minor for Violin, Cello and Piano, Op. 102 (1908)
Six Recital Pieces for Violin and Piano, Op. 103a (1908)
Two Small Sonatas (D Minor and A Major) for Violin and Piano, Op. 103b (1909)
Third Sonata in Bb Major for Clarinet and Piano, Op. 107 (1909)
Fourth String Quartet in Eb Major, Op. 109 (1909)
Quartet in D Minor for Violin, Viola, Cello and Piano, Op. 113 (1910)
Fourth Sonata in A Minor for Cello and Piano, Op. 116 (1910)
Sextet in F Major for 2 Violins, 2 Violas & 2 Cellos, Op. 118 (1910)
Fifth String Quartet in F# Minor, Op. 121 (1911)
Eighth Sonata in E Minor for Violin and Piano, Op. 122 (1911)
Preludes and Fugues, Chaconnes, etc. for Violin Alone, Op. 117 (1912)
Preludes and Fugues for Violin Alone, Op. 131a (1914)
Three Duos in the Old Style for Two Violins, Op. 131b (1914)
Quartet in A Minor for Violin, Viola, Cello & Piano, Op. 133 (1914)
Allegro in A Major for Two Violins (1914)
Three Suites for Cello Alone, Op. 131c (1915)
Three Suites for Viola Alone, Op. 131d (1915)
Ninth Sonata in c Minor for Violin and Piano, Op. 139 (1915)
Serenade in G Major for Flute, Violin and Viola, Op. 141a (1915)
String Trio in D Minor for Violin, Viola, and Cello, Op. 141b (1915)
Präludium in E Minor for Violin Alone (1915)
Quintet in A Major for Clarinet and String Quartet, Op. 146 (1916)

Choral Music

Three Choruses for Soprano, Alto, Tenor, and Bass with Piano Accompaniment (1892)
Tantum ergo Sacramentum for Five-Voice Mixed Choir (1895)
Hymne an den Gesang for Male Chorus with Orchestral Accompaniment (1898)
Gloriabuntur for Four-Voice Choir a cappella (1898)
Seven Male Choruses, Op. 38 (1899)
Three Six-Voice Choruses for 1 Soprano, 2 Altos, 1 Tenor, and 2 Basses, Op. 39 (1899)
Compositions for Three-Voice Female (or Boys) Choir, Op. 79a (1900)
"Maria Himmelsfreud!" for Four-Voice Choir a cappella (1900)
Compositions for Mixed Choir (Chorales), Op. 79f (1901)
Palm Sunday Morning for Five-Voice Choir a cappella (1902)
Gesang der Verklärten for Five-Voice Choir and Large Orchestra, Op. 71 (1903)

Ten Songs for Male Choir, Op. 83 (1904)
Weihegesang for Alto Solo, Mixed Choir and Wind Orchestra (1908)
Three Songs for Four-Voice Female Choir a cappella, Op. 111b (1909)
Die Nonnen for Mixed Choir and Large Orchestra, Op. 112 (1909)
Die Weihe der Nacht for Alto Solo, Male Chorus and Orchestra, Op. 119 (1911)
Sacred Songs for Five-Voice Mixed Choir a cappella, Op. 110 (1912)
Römischer Triumphgesang for Male Chorus and Orchestra, Op. 126 (1912)
Eight Sacred Songs for Mixed Choir, Op. 138 (1914)
Abschiedslied for Four-Voice Mixed Choir a cappella (1914)
Two Songs for Mixed Choir and Orchestra, Op. 144 (1915)

Church Compositions

Easy Practical Compositions for Use in Church, Op. 61 (1901)
Chorale Cantatas for the Major Festivals of the Protestant Church Year (1905)
The 100th Psalm for Mixed Choir, Orchestra, and Organ, Op. 106 (1909)
Easter Motet: "Lasset uns den Herren preisen" for Four-Voice Mixed Choir (1911)
Totenfeier (unfinished Requiem) in D Minor for Four Solo Voices, Four-Voice Mixed Choir, Organ and Orchestra (1914)
Requiem (unfinished), Op. 145 (1916)

Concertos

Scherzino for String Orchestra and Horn (1899)
Two Romances (G Major and D Major) for Violin and Small Orchestra, Op. 50 (1900)
Concerto in A Major for Violin with Orchestral or Piano Accompaniment, Op. 101 (1908)
Concerto in F Minor for Piano and Orchestra, Op. 114 (1910)
Andante and Rondo for Violin and Small Orchestra, Op. 147 (1916)

Orchestral Music

Liebestraum for String Orchestra (Lyrisches Andante) (1898)
Sinfonietta in A Major for Orchestra, Op. 90 (1905)
Serenade in G Major for Orchestra, Op. 95 (1906)
Variations and Fugue in E Major on a Theme of J.A. Hiller for Orchestra, Op. 100 (1907)
Symphonic Prologue to a Tragedy in A Minor for Large Orchestra, Op. 108 (1908)
Eine Lustspielouvertüre for Orchestra, Op. 120 (1911)
Konzert im alten Stil for Orchestra, Op. 123 (1912)

Eine romantische Suite for Large Orchestra, Op. 125 (1912)
Four Tone Poems for Large Orchestra after Arnold Böcklin, Op. 128 (1913)
Eine Ballettsuite in D Major for Orchestra, Op. 130 (1913)
Variations and Fugue for Orchestra on a Theme of Mozart, Op. 132 (1914)
Eine vaterländische Ouvertüre in F Major for Large Orchestra, Op. 140 (1914)

Organ Music

Three Organ Pieces, Op. 7 (1892)
"O Traurigkeit, o Herzelied" for Organ (1893)
"Komm, süsser Tod" for Organ (1894)
Suite for Organ in E Minor, Op. 16 (1895)
Fantasy for Organ on the Chorale "Ein' feste Burg ist unser Gott", Op. 27 (1898)
Fantasy and Fugue in C Minor for Organ, Op. 29 (1898)
Fantasy for Organ on the Chorale "Freu' dich sehr, o meine Seele!", Op. 30 (1898)
First Sonata in F# Minor for Organ, Op. 33 (1899)
Two Fantasias on the Chorales: "Wie schön leucht't uns der Morgenstern" and "Straf' mich nicht in deinem Zorn", Op. 40 (1899)
Introduction and Passacaglia in D Minor for Organ (1899)
Fantasy and Fugue for Organ on B-A-C-H, Op. 46 (1900)
Six Trios for Organ, Op. 47 (1900)
Organ Prelude in C Minor (1900)
"Wer weiss wie nahe mir mein Ende" for Organ (1900)
Three Fantasias for Organ on the Chorales: "Alle Menschen müssen sterben"; "Wachet auf, ruft uns die Stimme"; "Halleluja! Gott zu loben, bleibe meine Seelenfreud", Op. 52 (1900)
Symphonic Fantasy and Fugue for Organ, Op. 57 (1901)
Twelve Pieces for Organ, Op. 59 (1901)
Second Sonata (D Minor) for Organ, Op. 60 (1901)
Variations and Fugue on the English National Anthem for Organ (1901)
"Christ ist erstanden von dem Tod" for Organ (1901)
Monologe: Twelve Pieces for Organ, Op. 63 (1902)
Twelve Pieces for Organ, Op. 65 (1902)
Fifty Two Preludes for Organ on Protestant Chorales, Op. 67 (1902)
Prelude and Fugue in D Minor for Organ (1902)
"Mit Fried und Freud ich fahr dahin" for Organ (1902)
"O wie selig ihr doch, ihr Frommen" for Organ (1902)
"Jesus ist kommen, Grund ewiger Freude" for Organ (1902)
Ten Pieces for Organ, Op. 69 (1903)
Variations and Fugue on an Original Theme for Organ, Op. 73 (1903)
Compositions for Organ (Chorale Preludes), OP. 79b (1903)
Schule des Triospiels: J.S. Bach's Two-Part Inventions arranged

for Organ by Max Reger and Karl Straube (1903)
Five Preludes and Fugues for Organ, Op. 56 (1904)
Twelve Pieces for Organ, Op. 80 (1904)
Four Preludes and Fugues for Organ, Op. 85 (1904)
Romanze in A Minor for Harmonium (1904)
"O Haupt voll Blut und Wunden" for Organ (1904)
Suite for Organ in G Minor, Op. 92 (1905)
"Es kommt ein Schiff geladen" for Organ (1905)
Prelude and Fugue in G# Minor for Organ (1906)
"Wie schön leucht't uns der Morgenstern" for Organ (1909)
Introduction, Passacaglia and Fugue in E Minor for Organ, Op. 127 (1913)
Nine Pieces for Organ, Op. 129 (1913)
Thirty Small Chorale Preludes for Organ, Op. 135a (1914)
Fantasy and Fugue in D Minor for Organ, Op. 135b (1916)
Seven Organ Pieces, Op. 145 (1916)

Piano Music

Waltz-Caprices for Piano, 4 Hands, Op. 9 (1892)
German Dances for Piano, 4 Hands, Op. 10 (1893)
Seven Waltzes for Piano (2 Hands), Op. 11 (1893)
Lose Blätter for Piano, Op. 13 (1894)
Aus der Jugendzeit for Piano (2 Hands), Op. 17 (1895)
Canons for Piano in All the Major and Minor Keys (1895)
Improvisations for Piano (2 Hands), Op. 18 (1896)
Five Humoresques for Piano (2 Hands), Op. 20 (1898)
Six Waltzes for Piano (4 Hands), Op. 22 (1898)
Six Morceaux for Piano, Op. 24 (1898)
Aquarellen for Piano (2 Hands), Op. 25 (1898)
Seven Fantasy-Pieces for Piano, Op. 26 (1898)
Six Piano Pieces ("Grüsse an die Jugend") (1898)
Miniature Gavotte for Piano (1898)
An die schönen blauen Donau: Improvisation for Piano (2 Hands) on a Waltz of Johann Strauss (1898)
Seven Character Pieces for Piano (2 Hands), Op. 32 (1899)
Five Picturesque Pieces for Piano (4 Hands), Op. 34 (1899)
Bunte Blätter for Piano (2 Hands), Op. 36 (1899)
Albumblatt for Piano (1899)
Five Special Studies for Piano (after Chopin) (1899)
Ten Small Recital Pieces for Piano in Use in Teaching, Op. 44 (1900)
Six Intermezzi for Piano (2 Hands), Op. 45 (1900)
Seven Songs for Medium Voice with Piano Accompaniment, Op. 48 (1900)
Silhouetten: Seven Pieces for Piano (2 Hands), Op. 53 (1900)
Six Burlesques for Piano (4 Hands), Op. 58 (1901)
Four Special Studies for the Left Hand Alone for Piano (1901)
Blätter und Blüten: Twelve Piano Pieces (1902)
In der Nacht for Piano (1902)
Compositions for Piano, Op. 79a (1903)

Variations and Fugue on a Theme of Johann Sebastian Bach for Piano (2 Hands), Op. 81 (1904)
Aus meinem Tagebuch for Piano (2 Hands), Op. 82 (1904-1912)
Variations and Fugue on a Theme of Beethoven for Piano (4 Hands), Op. 86 (1904)
Perpetuum mobile in C# Major for Piano (2 Hands) (1905)
Six Pieces for Piano (4 Hands), Op. 94 (1906)
Introduction, Passacaglia and Fugue in B Minor for Two Pianos (4 Hands), Op. 96 (1906)
Four Piano Pieces (1906)
Caprice in F# Minor for Piano (1906)
Six Preludes and Fugues for Piano (2 Hands), Op. 99 (1907)
Ewig Dein!: Salon Pieces for Piano (1907)
Four Sonatinas for Piano (2 Hands), Op. 84 (1908)
Wiegenlied for Voice with Piano Accompaniment (1909)
Episoden: Piano Pieces for Adults and Children, Op. 115 (1910)
Variations and Fugue for Two Pianos on a Theme of W.A. Mozart, Op. 132a (1914)
Variations and Fugue on a Theme of G.P. Telemann for Piano (2 Hands), Op. 134 (1914)
Träume am Kamin: Twelve Small Piano Pieces, Op. 143 (1915)

Songs

Six Songs for Medium Voice and Piano, Op. 4 (1891)
Five Songs for High Voice and Piano, Op. 8 (1892)
Five Songs for One Voice (and Piano), Op. 12 (1893)
Five Duets for Soprano and Alto with Piano Accompaniment, Op. 14 (1894)
Ich stehe hoch über'm See for Bass Voice and Piano, Op. 14b (1894)
Ten Songs for Medium Voice and Piano, Op. 15 (1894)
"Es soll mein Gebet dich tragen" for Medium Voice and Piano (1894)
"Am Meer!" for Voice with Piano Accompaniment (1894)
Two Sacred Songs for Medium Voice with Organ Accompaniment, Op. 19 (1898)
Four Songs for Voice with Piano Accompaniment, Op. 23 (1898)
Six Songs of Anna Ritter for Medium Voice with Piano Accompaniment, Op. 31 (1898)
"In verschwiegener Nacht" for Voice with Piano Accompaniment (1898)
"Wiegenlied" for Medium Voice with Piano Accompaniment (1898)
Six Songs for Medium Voice with Piano Accompaniment, Op. 35 (1899)
Five Songs for Medium Voice with Piano Accompaniment, Op. 37 (1899)
Two Songs for Voice with Piano Accompaniment (1899)
Eight Songs for Voice with Piano Accompaniment, Op. 43 (1900)
Twelve Songs for Voice with Piano Accompaniment, Op. 51 (1900)
Two Sacred Songs for Medium Voice and Organ (1900)

Fifteen Songs for Voice with Piano Accompaniment, Op. 55 (1901)
Sixteen Songs for Voice with Piano Accompaniment, Op. 62 (1901)
"Tragt, blaue Träume" for Medium Voice and Piano (1901)
Twelve Songs for Medium Voice and Piano, Op. 66 (1902)
Six Songs for Medium Voice and Piano,Op. 68 (1902)
"Befiehl dem Herrn deine Wege" for Soprano and Alto with Organ Accompaniment (1902)
"Liebeslieder" for Voice and Piano (1902)
"Ostern" for Medium Voice and Piano (1902)
Seventeen Songs for High Voice and Piano, Op. 70 (1903)
Eighteen Songs for High Voice and Piano, Op. 75 (1903)
Compositions for Voice with Piano Accompaniment, Op. 79c (1903)
"Wohl denen" for Medium Voice with Organ Accompaniment (1903)
"Nun kommt die Nacht gegangen" for Medium Voice and Piano (1903)
Schlichte Weisen for Voice and Piano, Op. 76 (1904)
Four Songs for Medium Voice with Piano Accompaniment, Op. 88 (1905)
"Ehre sei Gott der Höhe" for Voice with Piano, Harmonium or Organ Accompaniment (1905)
Four Songs for Voice and Piano, Op. 97 (1906)
Five Songs for Medium or Low Voice with Piano Accompaniment, Op. 98 (1906)
"Der Maien ist gestorben" for Voice with Piano Accompaniment (1906)
"Abendfrieden" for Medium Voice and Piano (1906)
"Der Dieb" for Voice and Piano (1906)
Six Songs for Voice with Piano Accompaniment, Op. 104 (1907)
Two Sacred Songs for Medium Voice with Organ, Harmonium or Piano Accompaniment, Op. 105 (1908)
"In der Frühe" for Voice and Piano (1908)
Three Duets for Soprano and Alto with Piano Accompaniment, Op. 111a (1909)
"An Zeppelin" for Voice and Piano (1909)
An die Hoffnung for Alto (or Mezzo Soprano) with Orchestral or Piano Accompaniment, Op. 124 (1912)
Three Songs after Poems of Elsa von Asenijeff for Voice and Piano (1912)
Hymnus der Liebe for Baritone (or Alto) with Orchestral Accompaniment, Op. 136 (1914)
Twelve Sacred Songs for Voice with Piano, Harmonium or Organ Accompaniment, Op. 137 (1914)
Five New Children's Songs for High Voice and Piano, Op. 142 (1915)

Index

Page numbers, e.g., p. 4, refer to pages in the "Biography" and "Works and Performances" sections; numbers preceded by a "D" to the "Discography"; and numbers preceded by a "B" to the "Bibliography." Titles in quotation marks refer to individual songs or chorales that are part of an inclusive opus. The opus in which the individual number is contained will follow the title, e.g., "Ach bleib mit deiner Gnade" (Op. 135a), p. 34. Underlined titles of songs or chorales refer to those which comprise an entire opus in themselves, e.g., An die Hoffnung (Op. 124). Generic names in titles are translated into English, such as the English "chorale" instead of the German "choral." Titles of a more literary nature are left in the original German.

Recent Titles in
Bio-Bibliographies in Music
Series Advisers: *Donald L. Hixon and Adrienne Fried Block*

Thea Musgrave: A Bio-Bibliography
Donald L. Hixon

Aaron Copland: A Bio-Bibliography
JoAnn Skowronski

Samuel Barber: A Bio-Bibliography
Don A. Hennessee

Virgil Thomson: A Bio-Bibliography
Michael Meckna

Esther Williamson Ballou: A Bio-Bibliography
James R. Heintze

Gunther Schuller: A Bio-Bibliography
Norbert Carnovale

About the Author

WILLIAM E. GRIM is Visiting Professor of Music at Howard Payne University. He is the author of *The Faust Legend in Music and Literature*. His articles have appeared in a number of journals.

CPSIA information can be obtained
at www.ICGtesting.com
Printed in the USA
BVHW041857060620
580978BV00014B/294